HUMAN–COMPUTER INTERACTION
RESEARCH DIRECTIONS IN
COGNITIVE SCIENCE
EUROPEAN PERSPECTIVES
Vol. 3

Human-Computer Interaction

Research Directions in Cognitive Science

European Perspectives

Vol. 3

Edited by

Jens Rasmussen and Henning B. Andersen

Risø National Laboratory
DK 4000 Roskilde, Denmark

Niels Ole Bernsen

Cognitive Science Centre
Roskilde University
DK 4000 Roskilde, Denmark

LEA LAWRENCE ERLBAUM ASSOCIATES, PUBLISHERS LEA
Hove and London (UK)   Hillsdale (USA)

Published on behalf of the Commission of the European Communities by:
Lawrence Erlbaum Associates Ltd., Publishers
27 Palmeira Mansions
Church Road
Hove
East Sussex BN3 2FA
U.K.

Publication No. EUR 11768 Vol.3 of the
Commission of the European Communities,
Directorate-General Telecommunications, Information
Industries and Innovation,
Scientific and Technical Communication Service,
Luxembourg.

British Library Cataloguing in Publication Data

Research directions in cognitive science : European perspectives
    Vol.3, Human - computer interaction.
    1. Cognitive psychology
    I. Rasmussen, Jens, *1926* - II. Andersen, H.B. (Henning Boje)
    153

    ISBN: 0-86377-113-0
    ISSN: 0961-7493

The text in this book was produced direct from disks supplied by the authors, via a
desk-top publishing system. Printed and bound by BPCC Wheatons, Exeter, U.K.

Contents

General Introduction: A European Perspective on Cognitive Science

Niels Ole Bernsen
*Cognitive Science Research Centre, Roskilde
University, DK 4000 Roskilde, Denmark*

The present volume on human-computer interaction is one in a series of five presenting the findings of a joint European study in cognitive science 1987-88. The study was organised and funded as a collaborative network by the research unit FAST (Forecast and Assessment in Science and Technology) of the Commission of the European Communities and comprised about 35 scientists from the core disciplines of cognitive science. The research disciplines represented in the network were: cognitive psychology, logic and linguistics, cognitive neuroscience, human–computer interaction and artificial intelligence.

The aim of the network activity was to attempt a prospective mapping of research problems in cognitive science to be addressed over the next five to ten years. Prospective judgment of course has to be based on firm knowledge of the state of the art but a presentation of the state of the art of cognitive science as such was not our primary objective. This objective had already been addressed by a report presented to FAST in February 1986, *Cognitive Science in Europe* (ed. Michel Imbert et al.) and published by Springer-Verlag in October 1987.

As often happens in science nowadays, the dual aim of state-of-the-art presentation and prospective mapping realised through the FAST initiatives was linked to another, more practical, aim, namely that of making sure that cognitive science find its appropriate place in the European Community's long-term strategy for research and development in information technology. It is no doubt a pleasure to the contributors, and we hope to the European cognitive science community at large, that this has now happened to the extent that cognitive science has been included in the ESPRIT Basic Research Actions initiative which forms the upstream, basic research complement to the European Communities; ESPRIT programme in I.T.R. & D. In response to the first call for proposals for ESPRIT Basic Research Action (1988), some $65–70 million are currently being committed to basic research in cognitive science and artificial intelligence, computer science, and microelectronics. Moreover, now that European cognitive science is becoming increasingly visible partly through the FAST and ESPRIT initiatives, it seems reasonable to expect an increase in cognitive science funding at the national level.

As part of the more practical aim of funding procurement, the network agenda also included surveying and commenting upon the current institutional state and the state of collaboration in European cognitive science. Results and, we hope, some timely recommendations form part of a separate report of the network activity (Bernsen and the FAST Network, 1988).

The overall view of cognitive science taken in the papers published in the present volumes is fairly comprehensive though not exhaustive. Choice of topics for presentation and discussion has been made with a view to potential long-term relevance to information technology. Authors have been encouraged to take a personal view of their respective fields rather than a more comprehensive, and perhaps less exciting, encyclopaedic view. Each contribution has been written in order to make it comprehensible to cognitive scientists from other disciplines.

Since the general characteristics of current cognitive science are not, as such, addressed in the individual introductions or papers, a brief sketch may be in place here.

Sometimes a new theory can provide a unifying perspective to a number of hitherto disparate scientific endeavours and thus motivate a potentially drastic regrouping among the sciences. This is the case in cognitive science, where a new theory of the most general type which I shall call a *research programme* currently has this effect. The new research programme offering a unifying perspective to large parts of the sciences of logic, linguistics, psychology and neuroscience came from computer science and artificial intelligence and had been gaining ground steadily since the 1950s. It consists of the general idea that intelligent agents should be looked upon as information processing systems, that is, as systems receiving, manipulating, storing, retrieving, transmitting and executing information. Some of the general questions to ask concerning intelligent agents according to this research programme are: what information do such systems have? how is it represented? how is the information processed? and how are the processes implemented? The theoretical language of cognitive science is that of computation and information processing.

The objectives of cognitive science are to define, build and test information processing models of the various sub-systems (and of *their* sub-systems) making up intelligent agency, whether human (biological, natural) or artificial, and eventually to make them fit together into general cognitive theories and systems. The knowledge obtained can then be applied in various ways. Examples of cognitive sub-systems is vision, speech, natural language, sensory-motor control, memory, learning and reasoning. Each of these sub-systems are highly complex and may be further broken down into a number of functional components. Today's limited-capacity autonomous robots and knowledge based systems having a (written or spoken) natural language interface are examples of technologically implemented steps towards more general systems.

In somewhat more detail, the research programme of cognitive science may be characterised as follows:

1. Intelligence or cognition is physically implemented. However, a central level of analysis is the description of cognitive systems as systems for the manipulation of representations. Representations may consist of discrete symbols or may be of other types, such as distributed representations.

2. Widely different types of physical implementation are capable, in principle, of manipulating the same representations in the same ways: chips made of silicon or galliumarsenide, optical devices, mechanical or hydraulic devised, organic-biological systems.

3. Artificial, i.e. non-biological intelligence and hyperintelligence is therefore possible, at least in principle. Cognitive science is an investigation of both biological and artificial intelligence.

4. The level of description at which cognitive systems are described as manipulating representations cannot be reduced to: (a) The physical implementation of the system ; (b) the behaviour of the system ; (c) the conscious experiences of the system, if any.

5. Cognitive science is mechanistic. Intelligence or cognition, including semantics or meaning, and consciousness, is regarded as being produced by, in a wide sense, mechanical operations.

6. Acceptance of some version of functionalism. Functionalism states that cognition is constituted by the information processing functions which are physically implemented in the system.

7. Historically as well as in scientific substance and methodology, cognitive science is closely related to the computer and its information processing potential as studied by computer science and artificial

intelligence. The paradigms of cognitive science still derive from contemporary computer systems, whether serial or parallel, classical or connectionist. Use of computer simulations is essential to cognitive science except for the few areas, like problems involving social or organisational aspects, where specific computer modelling is not yet feasible.

8. Cognitive science is multidisciplinary. Methodologically, cognitive science aims at increased collaboration and cross-fertilisation between disciplines, the central assumption being that this is the most promising way of accelerating the achievement of the research programme, and hence also of realising the application potential of cognitive science. If anything has become apparent over the last twenty years, it is that cognition or intelligence are extremely complex phenomena whose investigation requires the full exploitation of a wide range of methodological tools. The basic idea behind the interdisciplinarity of cognitive science, then, is that each discipline employs its own *particular* methods in order to add *constraints* to the construction of *common* models and theories of the cognitive functions and their interrelationships. These models and theories are expressed in the common language of cognitive science, that is, in the language of the research programme and of one or other of the paradigms (discussed later). In addition, the basic idea behind interdisciplinarity assumes that each discipline could significantly contribute to the development of models and theories. So each discipline should, in order to belong to cognitive science, be concerned with both knowledge and processing (or competence and performance) in cognition, abstract programme and implementation, peripheral and central processes, sub-system integration, and the understanding of intelligent performance in complex, real-life tasks.

Present-day cognitive science is an interdisciplinary endeavour rather than a new science in its own right and speaking about core disciplines suggests that insights from other sciences like mathematics, physics, biology, computer science, anthropology, and the philosophy of science, mind and language actually do contribute to the advance of cognitive science. Furthermore, numerous sub-disciplines exist linking the core disciplines together, such as computational linguistics, computational logic, psycholinguistics, neuropsychology, and so on.

9. Cognitive science is closely related to application, in particular, though not exclusively, to the application of information technology. Applications of cognitive science are of, at least, three types.

(a) Specifying information processing models of the various sub-systems making up intelligent agency is essential to the building of increasingly intelligent artifacts such as the coming generations of vision systems, speech systems, natural language interfaces, robots, and knowledge-based systems. Interactions between the various disciplines of cognitive science have in the past produced such important AI knowledge representation and reasoning techniques as semantic networks, production systems, and logic programming, as well as significant results in areas like vision, speech and natural language processing. Future interaction will have to face still other areas of research where humans continue to perform far better than current artificial systems, as in casual reasoning, reasoning about time, plans and intentions, learning, or fluent, skill-based behaviour.

(b) It has become clear that the actual design of information processing systems should go hand in hand with research on their interactions with human agents in real-life task situations. Through the computerisation of work in all sectors of society, information technology has become an important tool at the interface between humans and their work. Successful system design, whether of large control systems, computer networks, manufacturing systems, office systems, tutoring systems, speech and language systems, or expert systems, not only depends on the training of users but also on the system's inherent adaptability to users. If a system's design is not successful, users are not likely to want to use it, and if they use it, serious accidents may occur, as in nuclear power plants or large chemical installations. In this situation, cognitive science research is strongly needed in the interaction between I.T. tools, task domain and work context, the cognitive resources of users, and the new patterns of social interaction arising from the use of computers. Thus, the rapidly evolving field of human–computer interaction research could be included among the core disciplines making up cognitive science as being sufficiently distinct from, and somewhat orthogonal to, the others to merit a disciplinary label of its own.

(c) Although these two points describing the application potential of cognitive science for information technology have been central to the present network activity, it should be noted that they do not exhaust the application potential of cognitive science. The human information processing system can be damaged or inoperative in various ways and from various causes, with neurological and psychological disorders or loss of certain mental abilities as a result. Studying the system and its behaviour in information processing terms promises better ways for diagnosing, repairing, and retraining the system as well as better ways of supplying the system with efficient prostheses.

The aforementioned points 1–9 are by no means uncontroversial among cognitive scientists. And needless to say, interdisciplinary collaboration among traditionally separate disciplines is not uncontroversial either. What is interesting, however, is that points 1–9 currently do seem to represent international convergence towards a common conception of cognitive science.

A research programme is in itself nothing very important. What matters are the research paradigm(s) demonstrating the practical viability of the programme. A research paradigm consists of one or more successful, specific applications of the research programme to particular problems falling within its scope. These applications, in casu models of specific cognitive functions, are seen by the scientific community as evidence that the principles on which they are based might be generalised to account for a much larger class of cognitive phenomena, and possibly to all of cognition. The central scientific task, then, is to implement and test this assumption. Cognitive science currently appears to have to consider two different research paradigms. The relationship between them is not clear at this point and is subject to strong, ongoing debate (e.g. Fodor and Pylyshyn, 1988; Smolensky, 1988).

According to the *Classical AI* paradigm, an intelligent system's input and output consist of physical signals and movements, whereas a large central part of the information processing linking input and output consists of automatic computation over language-like, discrete, and combinatorial symbolic codes, as in conventional serial or more recent parallel computers (Fodor, 1976; Newell, 1980; Pylyshyn, 1984). According to the *Neural Network Computation* paradigm or the *Connectionist* paradigm, which was been strongly revived in the 1980s, computation over discrete combinatorial symbols exists to a lesser extent, or does not exist at all, in intelligent biological systems. Instead, the complex cognitive abilities of higher organisms are based on the information processing abilities arising from the collective behaviour of large populations of highly interconnected and very simple processing elements, such as nerve cells or simple artificial processing elements. Consequently, it is maintained, cognitive scientists should develop and implement their theories of intelligent information processing in ways that resemble much more closely the way in which the brain actually operates (McClelland and Rumelhart, 1986).

Today, both paradigms can claim a number of successes in terms of concrete models jointly covering most areas of cognitive science.

This ongoing debate over research paradigms is a very real one because, at the present time at least, the two paradigms clearly do generate different systems providing different functional primitives (i.e. different elementary information processing capabilities) and possibly different behaviours.

Thus, the virtues of connectionist systems include their ability to rapidly acquire and apply large amounts of knowledge in noisy situations not governed by rigid laws but by context-sensitive regularities having many exceptions. And the paradigms generate importantly different directions for research and different technologies, and tend to attract different core disciplines of cognitive science. Thus, many researchers in classical AI tend to be sceptical about the potential of artificial neural network systems, despite the success of similar systems in nature; others do not doubt the importance for AI of "massive parallelism", but argue that connectionist systems do not really represent an alternative research paradigm, only a specific way of physically implementing classical cognitive architectures. Logicians and most linguists tend to disregard connectionist systems, whereas many cognitive psychologists and virtually all cognitive neuroscientists, who never really adopted the classical AI paradigm anyway, tend to embrace the neural network computation paradigm as the first firm basis for realistic models and general theories of cognition. The formal language of the classical AI paradigm is that of symbolic logic and algebra, whereas the formal language of the connectionist paradigm is that of dynamic systems theory belonging to mathematical physics. Also, researchers studying the peripherals of cognitive systems like speech, low-level vision, or movement, all of which involve considerable signal processing, appear to be more strongly attracted by neural network computation than those studying central processes. Not least, this latter point has led many cognitive scientists to believe that the two paradigms really are basically different cognitive architectures, but that they are compatible in the sense of being apt to model different types of cognitive function or different parts of cognitive functions, such as voluntary, introspectively accessible, attentive, and controlled processes versus skilled, automatic, pre-attentive, probably massively parallel processes. Research in the next five to ten years will no doubt result in important attempts to integrate these two approaches or paradigms of cognitive science.

Two interrelated themes dominate the network findings and cut across the distinction between scientific substance and methodology. These themes can be viewed as constituting some central tendencies of current research covering all the core disciplines of cognitive science. Since the themes or trends are based on prospective analyses of most areas of cognitive science, from research on vision and speech to research on natural language, logic, and reasoning, they appear to form a stable pattern. These trends should be encouraged by an appropriate research policy. The themes are integration in theory, computer models, and actual working implementations, and real-world validity of theories, models and applications.

The theme of integration covers the following aspects:

Integration of different cognitive functions;
Integration of cognitive sub-functions into cognitive functions;
Integration of models into more general theories;
Integration of partial models into full models;
Integration and convergence of approaches, methods and results from different disciplines;
A more theory-driven approach in traditionally experimental disciplines like cognitive psychology and neuroscience.

Integration clearly means a trend towards the construction and testing of general theories and towards increased interdisciplinarity. Moreover, as mentioned earlier, the possibility of integrating the two current research paradigms of cognitive science is currently the subject of lively debates.

The real-world theme covers the trend towards explaining, simulating and actually building larger-scale, more general-purpose, real-time, closer-to-real-life systems of speech and grammar, natural language and communication, vision, perception and movement or action, and problem-solving. This trend also receives strong support from human–computer interaction research, which from the outset has to face human information processing in complex, real-life situations. Real-world research in cognitive science contrasts with, e.g. research in cognitive psychology on the performance of abstract and ecologically meaningless tasks in the laboratory or AI research on system performance in "micro-worlds". The real-world trend marks an important step beyond these classical approaches in cognitive science and implies the disappearance from the field of the sharp, traditional distinction between basic and applied research.

The two themes of integration and real-world validity are closely related because, in a large number of cases, explanation and synthesis of performance in complex, real-life situations require an integration of different cognitive functions and systems, and of different approaches. The themes are also closely related to the technological applicability of models, systems, and theories because integration and real-world validity is what is needed, both in order to extend the range of applicability of systems and in order to adapt them to users. In many cases, computer simulations may function both as theoretical test-beds and as software prototypes of potential machines for technological applications.

Numerous examples of the above trends can be gathered from the network papers. I shall leave it to the reader to find these examples and to judge whether they are sufficient to justify the conclusions stated above. If they are, then it can confidently be stated that contemporary cognitive science in Europe demonstrates the viability of the research programme, the productivity of the research paradigms, the convergence of disciplines towards common models, theories and problems to the extent allowed by the existence of two different paradigms, and the potential applicability of results. Not everything is idyllic, however; nor could or should this be so within an emerging science. Most of the basic questions still remain unanswered, with the prospect that cognitive science may look very differently in ten years time from now.

I would like to thank all network participants for their friendly collaboration during the past two years. We all learned, I think, that even today, large-scale, multidisciplinary European collaboration in science is not a matter of course, but something that requires a substantial effort. I am especially grateful to the leaders of the four "network institutions" and Special Editors of the first four volumes in the series: Henning B. Andersen (Risø National Laboratory), Alan Baddeley (Cambridge APU), Guy A. Orban (Katholieke Universiteit te Leuven), Jens Rasmussen (Risø National Laboratory), Helmut Schnelle (Bochum University), and Wolf Singer (Max-Plank Insitute for Brain Research). Without their judgment, vigilance, patience and collaborative spirit the network would never have been set up, let alone have produced anything. Derek Sleeman (Aberdeen), Special Editor of Volume V, entered the collaboration at a later stage and has demonstrated impressive efficiency in catching up with the work that had already been done.

We are all deeply indebted to Dr Riccardo Petrella, Head of FAST, whose sensitivity to emerging trends in science and technology first brought cognitive science to the attention of EC scientific programmes and whose dynamism, non-hesitant support, and constant goodwill have made the network possible. I must personally thank Dr Petrella and the Danish Science and Engineering Research Council for making my one-year stay at FAST possible and the EC's ESPRIT programme for allowing me time to complete the work while assisting in setting up the ESPRIT Basic Research Actions.

REFERENCES

Bernsen, N.O. and the FAST Cognitive Science Network (1988). *Cognitive science: A European perspective.* (Report to the FAST Programme.) FAST, EC Commission, Brussels.

Fodor, J.A. and Pylyshyn, Z.W. (1988). Connectionism and cognitive architecture, *Cognition, 28,* (1-2), 3-71.

Fodor, J.A. (1976). *The Language of Thought.* Sussex: The Harvester Press.

Imbert, M., Bertelson, P., Kempson, R., Osherson, D., Schnelle, H., Streitz, N.A., Thomassen, A., Viviani, P. (Eds.) (1987). *Cognitive Science in Europe.* Springer-Verlag.

McClelland, J.L., Rumelhart, D.E. and the PDP Research Group (Eds.) (1986). *Parallel Distributed Processing* Vols. 1-2, Cambridge MA: Bradford Books, MIT Press.

Newell, A. (1980). Physical Symbol Systems, *Cognitive Science, 4,* 135-183.

Pylyshyn, Z.W. (1984). *Computation and Cognition. Toward a Foundation for Cognitive Science.* Bradford Books, Cambridge MA, MIT Press.

Smolensky, P. (1988). On the proper treatment of connectionism. *Behavioral and Brain Sciences Vol. 11,*(1), 1-74.

CHAPTER ONE

Human-Computer Interaction: An Introduction

Jens Rasmussen and Henning B. Andersen
Risø National Laboratory, 4000 Roskilde, Denmark

1. WHAT IS HUMAN-COMPUTER INTERACTION?

1.1 The Growth and Significance of the Discipline

It is difficult for outsiders and newcomers to the field of Human-Computer Interaction (HCI) to appreciate fully both the diversity and the rapid growth of the discipline in recent years —especially so if they conceive of it as a kind of "applied cognitive science". In fact, to depict HCI primarily as the application of a number of basic science principles is somewhat misleading, as we shall see.

The intense and constantly increasing research activity within HCI reflects the growing importance of the field for the introduction and use of information systems. It is generally agreed that the wider field of *information technology*—in which *information systems* would arguably form the most decisive part in the long run—will be the most significant production sector in the near future. Thus, in Europe today, information technology represents around 4.5% of GDP, and, based on common estimates, information technology will approach 7% GDP before the mid-nineties and will surpass any other industrial sector.

The widespread introduction and increasing use of information technology has immediate effects on people and organisations in industrialised countries, highlighting the need for even more extensive efforts in HCI. More and more people will use information systems in their work and daily life; and more and more information systems will be available to occasional users. This means that the usability of systems will become a crucial factor in the widespread introduction of information systems in production, administration, management and the home. Evidently, an information system which is opaque and unnecessarily difficult to employ will be tolerated only by users who are either computer professionals—who often seem willing to put up with perversely userhostile designs—or those who need not cope with more than a single system. However, neither of these conditions applies to the majority of current users, and future users will surely be even more demanding than those of today.

In section 1 of this introductory chapter to the present volume we want to characterise the objectives and methods of HCI; in section 2 we discuss briefly some major trends in the development of information systems and technology; in section 3 we outline some illustrative examples of current research issues; and finally, in section 4 we give an overview of the following chapters of the volume.

1.2 Characterising HCI

Considered as a discipline, HCI is concerned with providing knowledge about the use of information technological systems in work settings. Using this characterisation of HCI, let us note that its overall research goals are necessarily related to what may be called the essential triad: *Users—Information Systems—Work Settings*. But let us expand on this:

First, HCI is both a science and an engineering discipline. As a science, it is committed to discovering and establishing general, and not just *ad hoc*, principles and models governing human cognitive performance in man-made environments. At the same time, as an engineering enterprise, it aims at producing and exploiting principles for the design of systems which match the needs and capacities of human users. For both lines of research, the emergence of large-scale complex systems of production, administration and information management, creates an urgent need for predictive models of the performance of socio-technical systems, in contrast to the largely empirical evolution of HCI in the past.

Second, although the name "Human-Computer Interaction" may suggest otherwise, the overall goals of the discipline are certainly not focused on computer use *per se*, but they are inherently oriented towards the use of systems in work environments. Hence, the overall goals of HCI cannot be validly stated in terms of users and interfaces alone. That is to say, a great number of crucial issues surrounding HCI cannot be meaningfully formulated, let alone resolved, unless the intended work domain—the job that the users try to do with the aid of information tools—is explicitly included. However, while insisting that the essential HCI triad is "Users—Information Systems—Work Settings", we do not suggest that parts of this triad cannot be studied separately. In fact, much valuable research is being carried out solely within the confines of, for instance, the user-interface sphere. Similarly, it may often be possible and worthwhile to seek to optimise the functionality or usability of interfaces independently of the particular domain and work setting in which they will be put to use—just as one can optimise the ballpoint pen or the typewriter without considering the particular contents of the messages to be produced. Nevertheless, it is, almost without exception, quite pointless to discuss ways in which to reduce the cognitive complexity of interfaces in isolation; that is, independently of explicit consideration of the inherent complexity of the work and overall tasks, and of the particular social and organisational constraints that contribute to defining the work setting in question.

Third, since HCI is concerned with real users using real systems in real work settings, one has to be cautious when transferring results to the real world from laboratory experiments where, typically, a few parameters are compared and their differential effects measured. Again, this is not to belittle the value of narrow-focus parameter studies. But it would be a serious underestimation of the actual and potential strength of HCI to restrict its scope exclusively to empirically based accumulations of selective results. As briefly noted previously, the rapid growth in the use of information technology to create tightly coupled large-scale systems calls for a line of research that aims at establishing predictive models for design. Such models, which seek to describe the complex interaction of all three components of the essential triad of HCI (cf. earlier) will ideally be aimed at giving designers a basis for comparing concrete design proposals.

1.3 Sources of Design: The Cross-disciplinary Nature of HCI

A practical pursuit such as design is based on several types of information sources. A useful way to distinguish such sources is according to methodological and epistemological criteria—i.e. criteria that distinguish the information or knowledge behind design in terms of how it is acquired and justified. There are, in general terms, four main sources of the knowledge or assumptions underlying the design of information systems:

- systematic empirical evidence of user-interface relations;
- models and theories of human cognition and artificial systems;
- field studies of how humans cope with real tasks in real work settings;
- specific work domain knowledge derived from textbooks, interviews with experts, and analytical methods, including task analyses.

An additional pool of information sources is the designers' own intuition, their nonsystematic, anecdotal or episodic evidence which they and their colleagues have gathered. Indeed, these are perhaps the most powerful real influences behind the majority of designs that are not just repetitions of already existing implementations. Keeping these sources in a class of their own, let us note that each of the previously listed four subfields has a set of methodologies and is governed by one or more paradigms. Similarly, universities and engineering academies will typically offer courses that cover the spectrum contained in the list. However, to our knowledge, no university or school offers a single degree covering the entire spectrum. To put it differently, HCI is a massively cross-disciplinary enterprise. It necessarily involves subjects in natural science, engineering, and the humanities; and no person can be an all-round expert in HCI but will be acquainted only superficially with large parts of their discipline even after a lifetime's work.

However, even if it is granted that a broad spectrum of professional competence must be involved in modern HCI research, it might be said that individual pieces of research need not be broadly inter-disciplinary. This is a valid point, but it ought not obscure the fact that a multitude of research results have to be integrated in order to form a basis for practical design. This in turn presents certain problems for the discipline as such. Thus, on the one hand, in order to produce the highest quality of HCI research, those involved have to have a solid professional background—and such a background can be obtained only within a relatively narrow field (e.g. computer science, cognitive psychology, linguistics) or perhaps a combination of a couple of fields. On the other hand, institutions and research programmes doing HCI research cannot be so limited. Therefore, it is of great importance for the future of HCI research that there are institutions and long-term programmes (such as the European Esprit programme) that can accommodate and stimulate the cross-disciplinary integration of results and explanatory models stemming from different professional paradigms. Such paradigms are often incommensurable—which does not mean that they contradict each other but that they use concepts and models that share few common concepts or "measures"; i.e. they cannot be compared and evaluated against each other without common terms and concepts.

To improve this situation, it is sometimes suggested that HCI should be based squarely on a so-called "basic science" approach—namely that of cognitive science. However, with such a view the nature of both cognitive science and of HCI is portrayed in a way that is easily misleading. We will expand a little on this point in the following section.

1.4 HCI and Cognitive Science

It is not uncommon that outside observers of HCI and other members of the cognitive science community regard HCI as a kind of applied cognitive science—in fact, some distinguished HCI researchers do so as well. This view may be quite innocuous; and yet, in our opinion, it is liable to miss the point of HCI research and hence to misrepresent its results.

In one quite well-known and apparently fairly popular version of this view, HCI consists of the application of principles and knowledge derived from the basic science of cognition. Now, basic science is hard and quantifiable whereas applied science is typically approximate, qualitative and soft (cf. Newell & Card's influential position paper, 1985). This is, we would suggest, a somewhat misleading picture, both of cognitive science and of HCI.

The first point is that the classic distinction between basic science and applied science is hard to make good use of in characterising cognitive science. This is not specific to cognitive science—compare such diverse disciplines as, say, economics, microbiology, and medicine, each of which is bound up with both practical and theoretical aims. For one thing, the theoretical and practical aims of cognitive science are hopelessly intertwined. Cognitive science is bound up with practical concerns—though not exclusively, of course—and for many of its research fields there is no principled way of drawing the boundary between what the theoretical and the practical interests are. For instance, to study human learning involves, *inter alia*, consideration of a practical nature such as the design of tutoring material and the elaboration of training strategies; to study human problem solving is similarly bound up with the practical concern for differentiating among conditions that may predict or distinguish levels of performance.

Secondly, cognitive performance often involves phenomena of such complexity that they cannot be studied except by way of very complex models. It has often been pointed out, perhaps most clearly and eloquently by Simon (1981), that such complex models in turn have to be studied in part empirically (compare also the upsurge of interest in connectionist models which, again, are largely studied empirically). Since the partly empirical approach to such modelling is often the only one available, it will only in exceptional cases be realistic to proceed along an ideal basic science approach, i.e. one that rests on theoretical foundations and which in practice succeeds in yielding predictions about the behaviour of particular models. Information systems are artifacts. To study them in use is an empirical business—though not only so. Echoing Simon, we may note that to understand and predict the behaviour of artificial information systems involves a science of the artificial. Such a science, Simon observed, cannot be based on just deductive methods working out consequences from first principles; rather, for many kinds of very complex systems, the only way of studying them is either to study them *in situ* or, alternatively, to study simulations of them. This applies particularly to large-scale information systems run by cooperating human agents controlling and supervising some "real-world" processes.

Thirdly, and no doubt of greatest relevance for HCI, is the experience from cognitive science that one of the most fruitful methodologies is to focus a set of basic or theoretical research issues on some practical concerns (compare Anderson, 1987; Norman, 1987; Rasmussen, 1986). The advantages of such a methodology are several: it will often turn out that a practical concern—e.g. building an information technological tool that will support people in their learning, or perhaps joint decision making and group cooperation—will force researchers from diverse fields to establish common terms and try to add their results together; and that this in turn is apt to produce new ways of posing theoretical issues. It is often noted that a number of theoretically fruitful ideas within the so-called basic sciences have arisen out of research that aimed at solving practical problems; so, similarly, there is an important feedback to strictly theoretical concerns of cognitive science from engineering endeavours (witness, for instance, the significant import of ideas and concepts from practical AI concerns about devising knowledge representation formalisms to cognitive psychology). Put in general terms, it has been observed in many areas of research—starting during the Second World War—that when a group of researchers from various professional fields jointly undertake to work towards some practical goal, this tends to be a most effective way of focusing research efforts.

In conclusion, rather than regarding HCI as the application of cognitive science, a more adequate picture of the discipline depicts it as one of several approaches to increasing our knowledge about human cognition, namely the approach that studies human cognitive performance in complex, man-made environments. This conception of HCI reflects the increasingly influential view that cognitive performance and cognitive capacities cannot in general be studied and modelled independently of the particular kinds of task environment in which they manifest themselves.

1.5 Predictive and Qualitative Modelling

We have already stressed that HCI should strive towards developing predictive models of how different types of information system designs affect users, organisations and work environments; at the same time, we hold that the methodology of HCI must necessarily go beyond the quantitative approaches typical of the physical sciences. Some readers will no doubt think that there is some tension here, indeed, that the combination of such views is incoherent—for how can predictive models be developed unless based on quantitative methods?

Now, results about human performance in complex work settings are often restricted to mere descriptions of past behaviour, i.e. accumulations of empirical correlations of observable performance variables. Such results do have their uses, for instance, in optimising ergonomically particular items of the user interface. However, there is also a danger that such exclusively observation-based studies of how users' overt behaviour and interaction with their environment become substitutes for something they cannot provide, namely, broadly generalisable models of human cognitive performance in complex work settings. Therefore, we need predictive models of human purposive activity; and this, in turn, implies two significant differences from efforts at establishing predictive models within the natural sciences.

First, the performance of a complex socio-technical system is shaped by the high level goals and plans of the agents involved; and useful models cannot be developed by merely adding together local, predictive models. Indeed, it would be like trying to build a house with perfect knowledge of the different ways in which bricks may be put together but without any plan or design for the house. Secondly, the reason why the notion of predictive models seems tied up with quantitative approaches is, on the one hand, that qualitative modelling is a fairly young endeavour and there are not yet many successful examples of non-quantitative predictive models; and, on the other hand, that the predictive models in the natural sciences are typically models of what may be called "practically isolated" relationships, i.e. they are models which are expressed in terms of mathematical relations among quantitative variables and the systems may typically be regarded, either for practical purposes or for the purpose of useful idealisations, as causally isolated from their environment.

Yet, as soon as we turn to modelling human cognitive performance in semantically rich domains, we are forced to consider human knowledge, decision-making and planning, and we have to take into account the fact that agents' behaviour is shaped by how they make sense of their environment, by their mental representation of current exigencies and possibilities, typically in qualitative terms relating to causal and intentional relationships.

For instance, in the field of "qualitative physics" or "qualitative modelling" the goal is to model people's knowledge about the behaviour of medium sized objects and relations among them. This goal is sometimes replaced by one of simply devising elegant non-quantitative models independently of how humans actually think. The point of such modelling efforts is to avoid the bog of intractability (by carrying out calculations on quantities) and attempt to mirror the efficiency of so-called qualitative reasoning (de Kleer & Brown, 1984; Forbus, 1988). Similarly, modelling comprehension of discourse involves semantic relations and attributes and it needs to take into account people's qualitative modes association and reasoning.

When talking about "predictive" models it is helpful to distinguish between predicting the particular trajectory of an item in a domain, given certain initial conditions, and predicting the kind of trajectory which the item will follow. The first kind of prediction involves saying something about a certain token—a concrete item fixed in space and time; the other kind of prediction says something about a type, rather than a token. Whether a type prediction is successful depends on whether the people who are doing the modelling have chosen the appropriate categories and relations (compare Plato's advice that when trying to understand reality we should carve it at its joints, just like a good cook will cut up fowl by their joints). Our point is not that non-quantitative is easier than quantitative modelling, but that it is a feasible approach which will typically be the appropriate one to select when seeking to develop predictive models of design. We might note that the so-called object-oriented programming paradigm seems to be a particularly promising and suitable approach to testing complex qualitative models by simulations.

The need for predictive models in HCI is made more acute by the fact that information technology has to provide increasingly complex systems which at the same time must be capable of adjustment to the changing conditions of work, production and organisation. In the following section we shall review some major trends in current developments in information technology and we shall focus on the outstanding an ever increasing degree has to be tailored to the individual need rapid growth in the vast variety of functions which information technology can support.

2. SOME CURRENT TRENDS IN
INFORMATION TECHNOLOGY

The widespread introduction of information technology is currently changing human work conditions quite markedly, and this development is likely to continue and even accelerate. The significance of this for HCI research is difficult to underestimate—although it is impossible to predict which will be the actual major lines of HCI research, say, in the next decade.

The level of mechanisation and automation is steadily increasing: information systems are used more and more for planning and control of integrated manufacturing and for small as well as large-scale administration systems. Computer-based interfaces become inserted between humans and their work domain and work content, and advanced communication networks serve to integrate the operation of large-scale distributed systems in the service and production sectors. On the background of this seemingly unstoppable development, the important human factors issues can no longer be directed at "human-computer interaction", taken in its literal sense, i.e. directed at the computer and/or interface as a separate entity. Instead they must be focused on the mutual influence of information technology on work conditions, work organisation and management structures.

Traditional work environments have been planned for efficient production over comparatively long periods. They have developed to produce more or less standardised products that stayed in the market for years. Thus, planning criteria have been efficiency, economy, and reliability, and it follows that the types of human activity called for in such environments have been heavily dependent on knowhow and skills evolving through long and relatively stable periods. Similarly, the analysis and description of work in these environments has centred on what is sometimes called "task analysis" in the sense in which it denotes decomposing the flow of prescribed activity into a sequence of modular elements.

By way of contrast, in modern work settings, advanced information technology is a primary source of many fundamental changes. For example, computer integration of manufacturing systems increasingly offers a pronounced flexibility of production which enables quick and effective response to a sudden change in specific customer demands. Such types of production, including the required management and organisational structures, depend, as already indicated, on the services provided by large information systems. However just as importantly, such services can only be made good use of if those involved—managers and workers—are capable of flexible and rapid adaptation to new requirements. That is, the stability and repetitive tasks which are characteristic of traditional work environments are largely replaced in flexible production environments by dynamic work settings involving tasks that are discretionary and require problem solving rather that standardised procedural responses.

The transitions from traditional to modern work environments that rely on advanced information technology and the ensuing consequences for organisations and for the tasks of managers and workers have been described by several authors. For instance, R.S. Kaplan (1989), writing about management accounting required for advanced technological environments, makes the following point, typical of recent literature on the subject:

Managers and workers, attempting to achieve continuous improvements in their operations, need information to detect problems quickly and to guide their experimentation and learning activities. Knowledge no longer exists centrally, to be imposed on local operations; improvements are suggested and made locally. The focus of the operational control system has shifted from adherence to centrally determined standards to providing timely, accurate, and relevant information for local learning and improvement activities.

For similar observations see: Drucker, 1988; Gunn, 1987; Rasmussen et al., in press).

This is not the place to go into details of the transition from traditional to modern work environments. Rather, we shall briefly outline some of the implications of the trends involved in this transition:

1. There is, as already mentioned, a trend towards large-scale integrated information systems (at least company-wide, but external data and knowledge bases will be made more and more use of as well). One of the implications for HCI research is that it will be increasingly inadequate for system designers to consider the modules of the information system in isolation from each other. Another is that the modules can no longer be designed around the requirements of a narrow group of users; for instance, to set up an accounting system used to involve a requirement analysis that started at the accounting department and went little further. In contrast, a work environment in which many user groups need to access and understand information and to exploit the powers of distributed databases necessitates a much wider elicitation and analysis of requirements.

2. The rapid pace of technological change will alter the practice of long-term planning, and it will impose severe demands on the basic

qualifications of employees. An important implication of this is that information system designers can no longer rely on gradual empirical adjustment of systems—but will have to adapt themselves to the demand for reasonably reliable, predictive models of the behaviour of information systems.

3. The steady trend towards automating an increasing number of routine tasks will transfer people from direct work processes to higher levels of supervisory control. This means that the work force will need to be able to use the services of information systems to make improvised decisions about re-scheduling work, re-allocating resources etc. Again, the implication for design is, as we observed earlier, that a much greater part of human activity will centre on discretionary decision-making, and therefore, the information system has to be able to provide support of this. For instance, an important function of the system may be to provide results of contemplated, simulated decisions and plans; i.e. a "what if?" facility that enables users to experiment with a variety of scenarios and decisions.

4. The introduction of integrated information systems involves effective communication networks among most work groups. A tighter coupling among cooperating (groups of) decision-makers goes hand in hand with the fact that any decision may have ramifications for a number of other work groups. An important implication for information system design is that work groups will need a quick way of coordinating their current "agendas"—i.e. they need the information system to display implications for their own work stemming from recent decisions of management and of other groups, and they need facilities for negotiating about decisions (cf. Bjørn-Andersen and Ginnerup's contribution in this volume). The need for supporting, as it might be called, "agenda broadcasting" is of particular importance in organisations that have to work (perhaps only intermittently) in a high-tempo mode. Agenda broadcasting serves to present all agents with current goals and it lends itself particularly well to realisation in information networks. Put in general terms, there is a crucial need to establish useful, predictive models of dynamic decision-making among cooperating agents.

3. SOME CURRENT PROBLEM AREAS AND BASIC RESEARCH ISSUES IN HCI

While the five papers in this volume go into greater detail in specific areas and issues, we would like to outline a few research issues that cut across customary boundaries. These do not pretend to be representative of HCI research but they serve to illustrate the broad scope of current efforts.

3.1 Ecological Interface Design

Throughout millennia, evolution has granted humans an extremely effective perceptual motor system serving control of their dynamic interaction with the environment. Being able to interact dynamically with the environment and its inhabitants was a key to primitive man's survival. Thus, the evolutionary process has resulted in the development of capabilities for very efficient feature extraction, classification and dynamic coordination of the motor system with the environment. Some of the characteristics of this perceptual motor system are "hardwired" whereas some depend on adaptation to the characteristics of the environment during a learning phase.

In man-made environments, humans will not necessarily be able to benefit from this long evolution. When new work conditions arise (e.g. when new tools are introduced), further adaptation is necessary to supplement the product of natural evolution. In general, many degrees of freedom are available to humans when they plan and engage themselves in work situations. These degrees of freedom, however, will be reduced through adaptation. A normal set of practices will evolve, thereby removing the need for conscious choice and decisions. One can view activities in man-made environments as consisting of two phases: one is a phase of adaptation during which activity is being guided by exploratory behaviour; the second is the adapted phase, in which behavioral patterns have reached a state of equilibrium. Which of these phases is more important depends on the characteristics of the work domain.

In stable work domains with moderate-sized artifacts and characterised by slow changes, the adaptation phase is transient and is eventually overcome through training and experience. The major part of work falls into the equilibrium phase of stereotypical working patterns governed by surface features of the environment; i.e. activity is guided by stereotype cue action procedures. As a result, faced with traditional tools and systems, users are not, in general, concerned with the system's internal physical functions, but rather with the surface features of the work environment. In case of difficulties, trial and error exploration is acceptable; i.e. the cost of an error can be expected to be less than the value of the information gained. Consider the example of a radio receiver. Everybody will know how to operate it without knowing its functional properties. Cue action association will serve the user of even an unfamiliar manufacture; if not, trial and error exploration will most often succeed.

In this context, design of interfaces can basically be an empirical craft. It can be performed by human factors specialists who need not necessarily be familiar with the internal functioning of the gadget. However, this condition has radically changed as regards modern high-tech systems.

There are a number of properties of high-tech environments that raise complications for interface design. Automation of work processes moves workers to situations requiring decisions about novel problems, as we have described earlier. Therefore, owing to the constant shift in task demands, stereotypical activity patterns will only replace, to a very modest degree, exploration of opportunities and boundaries of acceptable interaction. In other words, the second phase of activities characterised by equilibrium is never actually reached. Instead, task demands are in a state of flux, requiring continual adaptation efforts on the part of workers.

These severe demands on workers in high-tech environments impose a need for interface design which represents the internal functions of the work domain. This need has most clearly been identified in high-hazard industries such as nuclear power and chemical processing; but, in the future, it will no doubt be characteristic of many other kinds of advanced systems. We suggest that efforts to address this need be classified as "ecological interface design"—a concept that characterises efforts to match the graphical design of interfaces to the great human capabilities for efficient feature extraction and categorisation, and for fluent, dynamic motor-coordination with the natural environment. In brief, the concept embraces the efforts to design interfaces for direct perception and manipulation specifically for high-tech environments. (cf. Beltracchi, 1987; Flach & Vicente, 1989; Hutchins, Hollan, & Norman, 1986; Vicente & Rasmussen, 1989. See also Shneiderman, 1982; 1983.)

3.2 Communication of Values and Intentions

The current surge in large-scale distributed information systems means, as we mentioned earlier, that cooperating groups of human agents need to negotiate decisions that have ramifications for several work groups. Such negotiation and distributed decision-making demand in turn that the information system providing the services to support this type of dynamic activity must meet requirements which are largely unknown within traditional work environments. As described in the previous section, the ability of organisations and companies to yield flexible and quick responses to client demands depend essentially on the use of advanced information technology. At the same time, however, cooperating work groups, whose important means of communication become tied to a large-scale distributed information system, must now somehow acquire a picture of the current priorities of other work groups and management—just as they have to be sure that their own changes in priorities or agenda will be perceived by the others.

This is a far smaller problem for traditional work environments where current goals are much less changeable and where directives typically are issued from above; but it does impose severe problems exactly in those environments where quick, flexible response at all levels of work is a necessity and where frequent revisions of agenda and even work practice are required (cf. our earlier remarks about the importance of "broadcasting current agenda").

Therefore, HCI research will have to devote considerable attention to how humans cope with situations that require coordination of decisions—and how they may be supported in this. In particular, it will be of importance to make principled studies of how agents may be supported in relating long-term, overall goals to short-term goals or current agenda; or to put it differently, how the current practice of a work group relates to the overall and more or less permanent abstract goals of the organisation (e.g. preservation of customers' confidence, short-term profitability, safety, employment).

One of the great difficulties within this area is that values and norms are largely tacit or inexplicit, so they may not be revealed by normal elicitation techniques. People's judgments about what they or their group ought to do in a given work setting or what their guiding goals and sub-goals really are appear to be governed by only partially conscious processes. Indeed, even considered judgement about norms and values seems to issue from a balancing of unreflective intuition against more reflective considerations.

3.3 Some Methodological Issues

A major problem of HCI research is to arrive at generalisable results and at models of design that are actually predictive. This problem is exacerbated by at least two related factors.

Firstly, HCI is committed to studying the complex interaction of three things (cf. section 1.2), human agents, information systems, and work settings. However, we are unlikely to arrive at general and quantifiable theories—as, say, physics or microbiology; (cf. section 1.5) covering such complex interaction. Hence, we have to make do with results—properly analyzed and structured in terms of a useful taxonomy—derived from simulations and from accumulated empirical observations (cf. Rasmussen et al., 1990; Brehmer et al., in press). Yet, as has often been observed when comparing the results of simulations of models with real life environments, there is no principled way of establishing that the application is valid. That is, we can never rule out that among those innumerable particularities of the environment that are not represented in the model, there will be some that play a decisive role in and therefore invalidate our model-based predictions.

Secondly, HCI research proceeds, as do all disciplines concerned with the study of human intentional activity, along two different tracks. One is concerned with empirical studies of particular organisations and cultures or of particular tools and interfaces. Followers of this track are often sceptical about the possibility of attaining useful or explanatory general statements about particular socio-technical systems. This may be called the "particularist" approach. In contrast, those following the other track—the generalists—do not share such scepticism, and they aim at arriving at regularities and even lawful connections. Looking at another field, we find a revealing illustration of this dichotomy among historians and philosophers who theorise about the nature of historical explanations: What is a historical explanation? Does it necessarily involve some alleged regularity governing human nature and culture, or is it rather an interpretation of the motives and reasons underlying unique acts? (e.g. Dray, 1957; Danto, 1979).

The friendly opposition between these two lines of research is not something that HCI should be embarrassed about. Cognitive science studies which (in part) concern higher mental functions and which focus on how they manifest themselves in real life can neglect neither the particular nor the general. There is, we submit, little reason to apologise for the fact that so far there has been no marriage between the ethnographic or field study approach and the more common empirical, regularity seeking approach of generalists. On the contrary, both approaches are necessary and a number of more concrete HCI issues may profitably be studied by both approaches (cf. Montmollin's contribution in this volume). While it is true that predictive models can only be attained by pursuing the generalist line, it is equally true that the viability of applying some general results to a concrete environment or work setting can be made only on the basis of close scrutiny of particularities.

4. THE CONTRIBUTIONS OF THIS VOLUME

The five papers contained in this volume describe areas which together cover a broad spectrum of current HCI research. A systematic reader might most profitably read them in the sequence in which they are reproduced, but they can be read independently of each other. Casual readers may start with any paper and section that attract their immediate interests, or they may first want to peruse the following overview.

Thomas Green in his paper reviews user modelling from the perspective of human information processing. The author distinguishes three research paradigms within this area—the science, engineering and system design paradigms—stressing that his paper is devoted to describing user modelling from the science perspective.

Green points out that cognitive science is characterised by two research traditions—modelling behaviour and testing hypotheses—and he observes that within HCI a relatively greater effort is devoted to modelling than to empirical testing. This, he suggests, reflects "the fact that developments in HCI have stretched our conceptual apparatus, taken from classical psychology and from cognitive science, to a point where we find it difficult to find explanatory terms". A somewhat similar point is alluded to by several authors in this volume, highlighting the need for new concepts and models to describe, explain and predict how humans perform in real-life conditions when coping with complex systems.

The author structures his survey into five main sub-areas each of which he describes in terms of recent developments, prospects and research needs. First, *perception of the environment*. This aspect of HCI is concerned with how users perceive, and also how to represent and present, complex information so that users may understand it (e.g. the current state of a large process industrial plant or the current state of a large computer program being used). This is a promising area, where a much greater interdisciplinary effort is likely to pay off—especially in seeking to find principles for representing visually complex physical processes or symbolic structures, or for representing complex phenomena at varying levels of abstraction selected by the user. Second, the author reviews briefly some contributions from *task analysis*, noting that recent developments have placed increasing emphasis on identifying the necessary knowledge that users need to have about the domain of work. Third, he describes *action-based user modelling*, having remarked that the study of users' perception must be carried out concurrently with the study of their actions. He outlines some current European efforts as well as Norman's well-known classificatory analysis, and he sees the prospects in this area as being determined by the fact that there is convergence of action-based user modelling with other areas of cognitive science, viz. the approaches based on planning and on the analysis of errors and slips. Fourth, the area of *knowledge-based models*, which is concerned with modelling the user's knowledge of the domain and the system is, as the author stresses, an extremely active and potentially fruitful field. Being closely allied with engineering-oriented research into knowledge-based systems, this line of research attracts interest and, therefore, funding from a broad variety of sources, some of which have little concern with HCI. The author encourages cooperation between approaches focusing on human information processing and on formal modelling and approaches which seek to describe and explain the very broad but central notion of what users "understand" when faced with their work domain and an information technological interface. As with Montmollin's paper, Green urges extensive observational studies that will describe the latter. Finally, the area of *formal and cognitive modelling* concerns computer executable or formal models of cognitive performance. As the author points out, developments here have so far mainly been within the science paradigm and have not yet been of substantial practical use for system design.

In his final section Green reviews some main points of recent discussions concerning a very basic methodological question about the development of HCI, namely, whether user modelling is currently best served by information processing models and a "hard science" approach or by approaches that in a number of less formal ways attempt to describe and model the cognitive processes of users. The author, who has devoted much of his research to formal task action grammars, does not recommend a one-sided approach but notes in a "compatibalist" spirit that there is no unavoidable conflict here: "In any reasonably difficult form of progress there is surely no single path that all must follow". We agree (cf. section 3.3), seeing no incompatibility between pursuing within the same discipline both an information processing (or computationalist) line of research as well as extensive field studies calling for methods which are broadly interpretative—but not therefore necessarily less rigorous.

Gerrit van der Veer in his paper focuses on individual differences in relation to learning with or about computers. The author stresses from the outset that for the near future there is no possibility of replacing human teachers with computerised tutors, but that the computer may be applied as a tool by student and teacher offering special possibilities for adjusting to individual learning behaviour. The paper reviews recent work on computers, learning and individual differences on the one hand, and interface design methodology with a special emphasis on learning, training and metacommunication aspects on the other.

In his first section on "Individual differences, learning and computers", the author surveys a number of empirical investigations of students' or users' performance at and learning of computer-related tasks. Typically, these investigations either establish or refute possible correlations between different types of traits of users or students and their proficiency at some computer tasks. Learning depends in large measure, but not exclusively, on adaptation to individual differences.

The most successful way of matching tutor and student to each other is determined by the possibilities for changing the student's characteristics, the author observes. To structure the results of the empirical investigations surveyed, van der Veer sets up a classification of the dimensions of changeability of cognitive functions. These four dimensions are intended to reflect the ease or difficulty with which students' traits may be changed in a learning situation. The most stable traits are personality factors (intelligence, introversion *vs.* extroversion, fear of failure, creativity). Next come cognitive styles (field dependence, problem-solving styles), which are less stable. This is followed by strategies (such as a heuristic or an algorithmic approach, serialism *vs.* holism), which are even less stable and thus more liable to be influenced by current external factors. Finally, knowledge and skills (the content of episodic memory, the details of actual knowledge represented, rules and skills), which are the most readily changeable aspects of cognition. This type of research delivers an important input to HCI, indicating both ways in which the design of complex information systems may be shaped to cater to individual differences and preferences, as well as ways in which users may best be trained to master existing systems.

Next, van der Veer outlines a "cognitive ergonomic approach" to questions on learning involving computers. This involves several concepts central among which are the following: (1) the concept of a computer user's mental model—that is, the set of knowledge structures which a user applies in the interaction with a computer, the knowledge used to predict the systems' reactions to the user's own input; (2) the scientist's conceptualisation of the user's mental model; (3) the conceptual model of the work or target domain which is, ideally, a correct, accurate and consistent description of the elements and structure of this domain; and (4) the concept of the "user's virtual machine" (by "virtual" the author means "that the machine [i.e. the computer used as a tool for performing a set of well-defined tasks] must be seen only in relation to the defined task space, in the way in which the machine is able to perform these tasks and in the way in which the user can specify the delegation of tasks to the system"). He recommends therefore that the specification of the user interface be regarded as a conceptual model, intended to be a complement to the intended mental model of the user. Relying in particular on work by Norman and Moran, van der Veer proposes: (a) that Moran's multi-level representational framework should be applied to give an adequate description of the virtual machine or the user interface and that this description may be transformed into a teacher's model, tuned to a certain task domain and user group; (b) that metaphors may be designed for teaching, consistent with the different levels of the conceptual model; (c) that a method may be developed for establishing a scientist's conceptualisation of the users' mental models as they result from teaching; and (d) that different users will have different mental models depending on their prior knowledge of the task domain and similar domains and on their preferred style of representation of information (verbal or visual).

The author's ergonomic approach is aptly illustrated in the final section of his paper combining design techniques and methods for representing the user's virtual machine with the mental model concept. The representation of systems, interfaces and models of systems are analysed from two different aspects, the "human factors" approach and the "informatics" or systems design approach. Van der Veer's proposed framework is at the same time an illustration of how results from research in learning and individual differences may be usefully applied in order to shape and guide ideas about interface design and to conceptualise the interrelations between interface and systems design.

Montmollin devotes his paper to a review of some recent and current research in human activities in actual, complex work environments. During a period when information technology is widely applied to work places in the form of integrated work stations offering support in multiple functions and leading to a reversal of the earlier specialisation into more diverse and discretionary task requirements, it is important to consider not only human-computer interfacing, but human-task interfacing. In this development towards much less proceduralised work settings, the study of human performance in actual work becomes an important prerequisite for understanding the role of information technology in work contexts. The present review of recent and current research, especially in the French speaking parts of Europe, is illuminating for one particular and noteworthy European approach to the problem.

Montmollin draws several distinctions to define the scope of his review. He explicitly wants to focus on the description of human activities as observed during actual work. This is in contrast to the classical "task analysis" which is frequently normative in nature, being focused on proper system design and training. Furthermore, his review does not address human behaviour in general but deals with the specific area of industrial process control, i.e. it is directed at the study of process operators. Thus, Montmollin notes that "all ergonomic studies conclude that operators never conform with the prescribed tasks" (i.e. the authorised, procedural description of task requirements). In general, many degrees of freedom can be found when meeting task requirements, and the form of activity chosen by a person reflects task requirements in the light of the person's subjective performance criteria. As Montmollin concludes: "Real work is a dialectic interaction between normative tasks and intelligent activities".

This is an important issue. Analysis of actual activities identifies the subjective choice of an individual among the existing degrees of freedom in task requirements. Therefore, if requirements can be modelled in a form identifying the acceptable, alternative ways of coping with a task, the actual choice as revealed by the activity analysis will serve to identify subjective criteria of choice. This may well be a fundamental dimension in the design of support systems. The required "normative work analysis", going beyond the simple procedure description becomes, therefore, an indispensable counterpart to activity analysis. Such work analysis will depend on expertise in the individual domain rather than psychological expertise. (This area is not represented in the present collection—for one particular approach, see Brehmer et al., in press.) The complex interaction between work requirements and subjective choices is similarly reflected in Montmollin's discussion of the impossibility of reducing the specific, complex activities observed (the "local stories") into a limited number of universal, broad characteristics.

Therefore, he concludes, activity analysis is more oriented towards time than towards distinctions among types. In other words, human activity can only be modelled on the background of the ecological complexity and based on careful field studies—and not from analysis of selected features in psychological laboratories. Consequently, he objects to the usefulness of studying intelligent behaviour by means of the well-formed micro-worlds of AI.

Next, Montmollin argues that interface design is not only an ergonomic problem of matching the communication to human perceptual abilities, but rather the more important task of communicating the work content and requirements to operators. He warns that to follow sophisticated engineers who "try to 'facilitate' (in their opinion) the work" may very well lead to control of the interface instead of the process itself. This observation points to the need for development of what we broadly referred to earlier as "ecological interface design". Since the processes to be controlled by operators are in fact invisible, and since the operators are assumed to control the process itself (e.g. a thermodynamic process of a power plant) and not the individual pieces of visible equipment, the interface design problem is, in fact, to make visible at the interface the very processes to be controlled. This, in turn, will require a significant integration and interpretation of the large set of measured data. Operators today frequently suffer from data overload, seldom from information overload.

Concerning the background to this general discussion, Montmollin gives a review of recent research seeking models of operators' activities, categorised in terms of cognitive processing activities, cognitive structures, and kinds of competence. Finally, he briefly discusses research into human errors.

Discussions of human-computer interaction are very often focused on the interaction of an individual user and their work terminal. This is a natural consequence of the usual preoccupation with interface design. It is a major argument of the papers in the present collection that the essential issue is the idea of the computer as a mediator between humans and their actual work content; hence, it becomes of crucial importance to analyse the implications of modern information technology on cooperative work performance. This is the topic taken up by Bjørn-Andersen and Ginnerup.

They begin their review by agreeing with Montmollin's observations, that the critical issue in HCI at present is the support of work, in particular cooperative work, rather than the design of the individual screen layout. The authors' professional background is research into business and administration and this quite naturally gives their paper a focus on office environments. Although the approaches may seem dissimilar, the authors' review of the relevant research is based on a number of premises which largely overlap those of Montmollin.

Bjørn-Andersen and Ginnerup emphasize the need to view the individual agents in the context of what they try to achieve. This requires that the usual procedure-oriented task analysis be supplemented by a focus on goals and functions—in particular because office work does not often depend on any standard operating procedures—indeed, the exception is the rule, while most time is spent on handling non-proceduralised tasks in a cooperative setting. On this view, the role of the discourse systems that people use in different social settings and the informal social networks that evolve during work become essential issues. Following the conclusions of the first international workshop on computer support for cooperative work, the authors consider as key issues: the nature of cooperative work groups; the nature of support technology; and the nature of their mutual relationships. What is the proper balance between humans and machines; how does technology affect group structure; and how does technological innovation affect organisations?

On this basis, they review present research under the three major headings of: (1) social and organisational aspects of computing; (2) a communication perspective; and (3) a decision-making perspective.

Considering the organisational perspective, they invoke the influential tradition from the sixties and classify the different approaches to understanding and modelling the nature of cooperative work according to the scientific background, i.e. as to whether an organisation is seen as a rational, a human activity, a socio-emotional, or a socio-political system.

In their review of research, the authors emphasize, on the one hand, the approach of Checkland, who views organisations as being mostly confronted with very complex, unstructured problems in poorly defined environments, and on the other, Flores and Winograd's concern with organisations as structures of commitment and communication. Concerning computer-based support of decision-making, they emphasise that the management philosophy behind the design of decision support systems addresses the problem of making explicit what is normally implicit in the reasoning processes involved. It does so in order to facilitate problem structuring in ill-defined decision situations by directing the agents' attention to the critical decision set, and ruling out distracters. With respect to support of group decision-making, the authors point to the danger that explicit emphasis on decision-making may be "exaggerated given what we know about organisational functioning as often resembling some kind of loosely coupled system". This note of warning matches the recent concern of decision research with "dynamic decision-making". On this approach, the classical view of decision-making as a resolution of separate conflicts by "problem formulation, data collection, formulation of alternative solutions, and finally decision and choice" is to some extent repudiated. Instead, decision-making is viewed as a continuous, fluent activity having the character of control of the states of affairs in a rather loosely coupled work domain which is simultaneously subject to controlling actions of other decision-makers. (Elaborations on this view of decision-making may be found in several of the papers in Rasmussen et al., in press).

Following this line of reasoning, another aspect can be added to the research represented in Bjørn-Andersen and Ginnerup's review. Being primarily based on business and administration research, as we noted, their review focuses on office activities and organisation in a rather context-free setting, not relating functions to the content of "management", i.e. to what is actually being "controlled." In many cases, however, the activities in an organisation and its functional structure will be very much shaped and constrained by the basic activity of the company or organisation in question. This is, for instance, clearly the case for companies based on "tightly coupled" technology such as chemical process industries and advanced manufacturing plants. In this type of work environment, cooperative work, organisation, and design of information systems will be influenced significantly by the properties of the "technical core" of the company. The close relationship between the technical functionality and the dynamic decision-making viewed as a control problem indicates an increasing need for a cross-disciplinary effort involving social science, management science, control theory, decision research, and subject matter domain expertise for analysis of cooperative work, organisation, and design of information systems.

Many promises have been issued from artificial intelligence (AI) quarters regarding the benefits to be gained from AI research results for the design of decision support systems and improved computer-based tools in general to support work activities in complex settings. The topic of Hollnagel's review is the role of artificial intelligence research for such facilitation of human-computer-work interaction. He begins his review by pessimistically noting that the review will have to consider the potential influence on HCI rather than the actual one, since it is not clear, he notes, whether there really has been an actual influence of AI on HCI.

To assess this potential influence, the author engages in a critical review of definitions of both AI and HCI. He considers three definitions of AI that have been offered or, more precisely, three different approaches to the goal of establishing an understanding of the principles that makes intelligence possible and that will enable the recreation of human intelligence in machines. Each of the three approaches—AI through emergence, simulation, and formalisation—is criticised by the author on a number of points. Instead, he offers as a useful substitute a "pragmatic" definition of AI which states in brief that the chief goal of the field is to make computers more useful. This approach or definition of AI as a discipline focuses on the use to which AI systems and tools can be put; hence, it stresses that: "(1) they can use general knowledge and principles to infer heuristic rules from data, and (2) that they can apply these rules to solve the problems they are given".

Turning next to HCI, Hollnagel, in much the same spirit as Montmollin in his review, confronts the classical ergonomic approach to human-computer interaction—characterised by a fairly narrow concern with interfaces and separate optimisation of individual tools, and he contrasts this with an approach which is directed at a more general concern with human-machine interaction and which therefore considers deliberately and much more explicitly the content of work. He, like Montmollin, points to a difference between the general North American approach with an emphasis on behavioral studies and syntax and the European approach, with its focus on the semantics of work and on what may be called "hermeneutical" points of view.

The author discusses what he calls the "technology gap" between technical invention and conceptual understanding, i.e. the gap between the continuous and accelerating development in information technology and the slower, stepwise development of the conceptual background. While agreeing that the gap is real, he concludes that it is not necessarily harmful. The fact that HCI is largely technology driven, and not concept driven, is not a genuine problem, the author observes—because it actually represents "an asset, i.e. a redundancy or richness in the technology which makes it easier to implement conceptual solutions, offering a richer implementation environment and more possibilities for the designer". However, as he goes on to note, the essential concern of HCI research should be at the functional task level rather than the technological or the HCI-implementation level.

In his discussion of the nature of HCI, Hollnagel echoes the increasingly influential thesis that the computer should be viewed as the mediator in actual work; that humans act through the computer rather than with the computer: "the point of view taken here [is that] the computer is to be considered as a sort of tool, as a means to an end. The purpose of HCI is consequently to assist in the specification, design, and implementation of that tool..." Following the philosopher Don Ihde, the author describes how the computer may serve in an "embodiment relation" allowing or inviting the user to focus exclusively on the domain or the task at hand. (Compare the notions of "direct manipulation" and "direct perception" and our remarks in section 3 about "ecological interface design".)

On this background, Hollnagel reviews the role of AI on HCI in terms of the cognitive functions that can be supported by appropriate tools. Noting that the human-computer relationship at its best should be one of embodiment, he discusses three types of AI enhancements for cognitive functions: (1) perception and discrimination; (2) interpretation (including expert systems); and (3) planning and control (including qualitative modelling and reasoning). In addition to these AI enhancement areas, he reviews briefly AI efforts in user modelling and natural language understanding. Finally, Hollnagel argues in his conclusion that if HCI is to be successful it should "look outward, to the task". Indeed, one of the most pervasive themes in the present volume is that the interaction between humans and computers has to be conceptualised in terms of the work and tasks for which humans use computers.

ACKNOWLEDGEMENTS

We are grateful to Len Goodstein and John Paulin Hansen for offering useful remarks to a draft of this chapter. We also gratefully acknowledge comments made by Paul Booth prompting an expansion and, we hope, clarification of our remarks about qualitative and predictive modelling.

REFERENCES

Anderson, J.R. (1987). Methodologies for studying human knowledge. *Behavioral and Brain Sciences, 10* (3), 467-505.

Beltracchi, J.R. (1987). A direct manipulation interface for water-based rankine cycle heat engines. *IEEE Transactions on Systems, Man, and Cybernetics. SMC-17,* 478-87.

Brehmer, B., Leplat J., & Rasmussen, J. (in press). Use of simulation in the study of complex decision making. In J. Rasmussen, B. Brehmer & J. Leplat (Eds.), *Distributed Decision Making: Cognitive Models for Cooperative Work.* Chichester: John Wiley.

Danto, A. (1979). *Analytical Philosophy of History.* Cambridge: Cambridge University Press.

de Kleer, J., & Brown J., (1984). A qualitative physics based on confluences. *Artificial Intelligence, 24,* 7-83.

Dray, W. (1957). *Laws and explanation in history.* Oxford: Oxford University Press.

Drucker, P. F. (1988, Jan/Feb). The coming of the new organization. *Harvard Business Review,* 45-55.

Flach, J. M., & Vicente, K. J. (1989). *Complexity, difficulty, direct manipulation and direct perception.* Manuscript submitted for publication. (Available from University of Illinois, Urbana-Champaign, Dept. Industrial & Mechanical Engineering.)

Forbus, K. D. (1988). Qualitative physics: Past, present, and future. In H. E. Shrobe (Ed.), *Exploring Artificial Intelligence.* San Mateo, CA: Morgan Kaufmann.

Gunn, T. G. (1987). *Manufacturing for competitive advantage. Becoming a world class manufacturer.* Cambridge, MA: Ballinger.

Hutchins, E. L., Hollan, J. D., & Norman, D. A. (1986). Direct manipulation interfaces. In D. A. Norman & S. W. Draper (Eds.), *User Centred System Design: New Perspectives on Human-Computer Interaction* (pp. 87-124). Hillsdale, NJ: Lawrence Erlbaum Associates Inc.

Kaplan, R. S. (1989, August 25). Management accounting for advanced technological environments. *Science, 245,* 819-823.

Newell, A., & Card, S. (1985). The prospects for psychological science in human-computer interaction. *Human-Computer Interaction, 1,* 201-242.

Norman, D. (1987). Cognitive engineering - cognitive science. In J.M. Carrol. (Ed.), *Interfacing Thought.* Cambridge, MA: MIT Press.

Rasmussen, J. (1986). *Information processing and human-machine interaction. An approach to cognitive engineering.* Amsterdam, New York: North-Holland.

Rasmussen, J., Pejtersen, A.M., & Schmidt, K. (1990). *Taxonomy for Cognitive Work Analysis.* (Risø-M-2871). Roskilde, Denmark: Risø National Laboratory.

Rasmussen, J., Brehmer, B., & Leplat, J. (Eds.). (1990). *Distributed decision making: Cognitive models for cooperative work.* Chichester: John Wiley.

Rasmussen, J. (in press). Information technology and cognitive work. In R. Amalberti, M. de Montmollin, & J. Theureau (Eds.), *Modèles de l'Analyse du Travail.* Paris: Dunod.

Simon, H. (1981). *The sciences of the artificial.* Cambridge, MA: MIT Press.

Shneiderman, B. (1982).   The future of interactive systems and the emergence of direct manipulation. *Behaviour and Information Technology, 1,* 237-256.

Shneiderman, B. (1983).   Direct manipulation: A step beyond programming languages. *IEEE Computer, 16* (8), 57-69.

Vicente, K., & Rasmussen, J. (1989).   Coping with human errors through system design: Implications for ecological interface design. *International Journal of Man-Machine Studies, 31,* 517-534.

CHAPTER TWO

User Modelling: The Information Processing Perspective

T.R.G. Green
*MRC Applied Psychology Unit, 15 Chaucer Road,
Cambridge, UK.*

1. INTRODUCTION

1.1 Background: Science, Engineering, or Design?

This chapter is concerned with human information processing considered as an applied problem in human-computer interaction. More particularly, it is concerned with attempts to model human-information processing in this area.

This heavily applied area weaves together three strands: engineering, science, and system design. The distinction is familiar, but the need to observe it is particularly important in this area: many of its most exciting and visible advances are engineering developments, whereas the scientific advances have been rather sparse, leading to an understandable tendency to associate HCI with the former component. It is, therefore, worth exploring it in more depth.

The problems of mis-spelling provide a good illustration of the three paradigms. A number of spelling "correctors" for word processors are on the market. Potential spelling mistakes in a document are detected by looking each word up in a stored dictionary; words not found are flagged as potential errors. (Nothing can be done about mis-spellings yielding genuine, but unintended, words, such as "not" for "knot".) Guesses are offered for each potential error by generating a list of candidates, each of which is found in the stored dictionary. Typically, these candidates are generated by simple transformations of the input: for the input string "noe", the spelling checker I am using now offers "one" (transposition of neighbouring letters), "nor" (changing one letter), "no" (discarding one letter), "note" (inserting one letter), and other words found by the same four operations.

The science relevant to mis-spelling is that of cognitive psychology. Mis-spellings caused by slips of the hand are describable by theories of action, such as the Norman and Rumelhart (1983) simulation of skilled typing in which certain typing errors were modelled, notably letter transposition (as in "experiemnt"). "Genuine" mis-spellings, such as "kahky" for "khaki", are describable by theories of the mental representation of sound-to-spelling rules, the mental representation of known spellings for familiar words, the nature of working memory, lexical access to words, etc. (Wagner & Torgesen, 1987). The aim of this approach is to elucidate the "mental architecture".

The engineering component of existing spelling correctors specialises existing computer science knowledge of fast search techniques in ordered lists and applies it to the particular case of searching dictionaries. It also includes solving the individual problems of file storage on particular computer systems, developing means to communicate with the user, etc.

Finally, the system design of spelling correctors ought to (but often does not) draw on task analysis to discover what the user wants to do, and on scientific knowledge to form a "requirements specification" indicating what the system ought to do to assist the user. Existing spelling correctors hardly draw at all on the cognitive psychologist's knowledge of sound-to-spelling rules, and so they are really "mistyping correctors" rather than spelling correctors; moreover, if the user genuinely does not recognise the correct spelling the system design will never be fully dependable. The system component also deals with the inter-relationship of different parts of the design solution to each other.

Long (1986) analyses the distinction in terms of types of representation and the activities leading from one representation to another. In the scientific paradigm, the real world is analysed into an intermediary representation, which is then generalised into one of the familiar science representations (from the human sciences, computer science, or one of the other sciences); predictions drawn from the science representation are generalised in the form of a validation representation, from which we draw an integrated understanding of the real world. The engineering paradigm, on the other hand, uses an engineering representation, which is fed by the same process of analysing the real world but is also fed by particularising the current scientific representation; and finally, the system design paradigm draws on both the science and the engineering paradigms, forming its own representation in which specifications, designs, implementation details, and evaluations are contained.

The aim of the present paper is to consider only the scientific aspects of the area, and more especially the cognitive science rather than the computing science aspects. Nevertheless, some of the relevant material has a flavour of engineering or design, and has been included to make clear the present state of the field.

Paradigms within Cognitive Science: Modelling and Testing

Cognitive science is heir to two traditions: modelling behaviour and testing hypotheses. In the area of human information processing within human-computer interaction, I attach more weight to modelling than to empirical testing. This is not a value judgement about the worth of empirical testing as such; in "classical" cognitive psychology it is the fundamental mainstay of research. But in the area of human-computer interaction, a study of papers at any conference will show that they are split into many sub-groups. More often than not, papers that report empirical studies deal with comparisons among advances in engineering technique. Those papers that contribute to the science of understanding human information processing are more often built around new models, with only rather loose empirical testing.

This phenomenon reflects, I believe, the fact that developments in HCI have stretched our conceptual apparatus, taken from classical psychology and cognitive science, to a point where we find it difficult to find explanatory terms. Cognitive psychology develops hypotheses and models about the fine detail of mental architecture, but works in rarefied conditions, where, for instance, subjects rarely have a choice of sensible strategies. How frequently do subjects have to plan a course of action several steps ahead in cognitive psychology experiments? The answer is, almost never, unless planning is the topic of study. Yet in real situations, planning ahead is frequently important. Parallel to the contribution of cognitive psychology to the study of individual "architectural components", such as working memory, we need to study performance in situations that are both more complete and more demanding. This is where the existing conceptual apparatus breaks down, and where models of information processing in HCI can potentially make a contribution to cognitive science as a whole.

This review, therefore, is mainly devoted to developments in modelling the performance of users, rather than to reporting empirical studies. These are the developments that have a scientific output rather thn contributing to engineering or to design practice.

Structure of the Survey

The main developments in this area are classified into: (1) perception of the environment; (2) task analysis; (3) action-based user modelling; (4) knowledge-based user modelling, and (5) formal user modelling. Each sub-area is described in terms of recent developments and prospects. A final section briefly discusses some methodological issues. Divisions are always baneful: a few words on each "county" will help elucidate the map.

1. The perception of which we speak here refers to understanding what is on offer from a very large program text, or a VLSI design, or a text displayed by computer, or the applications program itself. This is a weak area at present.

2. The analysis and description of user's tasks is not classically regarded as a problem in human information processing.   However, the information processing demands of real artefacts (whether computer-based or not) cannot readily be understood without an analysis of the task as viewed by the user, and therefore task analysis of one type or another is central to the tradition of applied psychology.

Current developments in this area include, first, close analysis of the user's tasks and the requisite knowledge. This work is not strictly in our area (except when it is based on a model of human information processing, as is sometimes the case) but it alerts us to the all-important fact that understanding the behaviour of a person as part of a system is impossible unless we also understand what the person is attempting to accomplish and how—which may not be evident from armchair analysis. In particular such notions as "system complexity" cannot be metricated without reference to the user's understanding of the system.

3. An alternative line of development aims not to analyse but to model the user's representation of knowledge, or the process of using the knowledge. Here we shall first cover the substantial tradition of descriptive models based on human information processing.

4. More recently there has been considerable interest in adopting techniques drawn from cognitive science and especially from the area of knowledge representation techniques. "Mental models" of devices and "plans" or "schemas" in the generation of instructions and programs form a central topic in this area.

5. A small number of formal or computational models have been presented. These models knowingly trade generality for precision, helping us to explore what we really mean by loose terms or what the consequences of particular cognitive architectures might be.

2. SURVEY OF CONTEMPORARY RESEARCH

One must both perceive the world, and act on it; the first section, 2.1, discusses the former, then I turn to the latter. The division is only convenient for exposition. In actuality perceiving and acting are not so easily separated. They are especially hard to separate in tasks where users are trying to create external versions of complex mental structures.

2.1 Perception and Interpretation of the User's Environment

Recent Developments
In this section we consider mainly the problem of how to use existing display technology to represent, firstly, complex entities on which the user is working, such as argument structures of complex prose, and, secondly, the current state of the computer program being used, e.g. what mode it is in—"display-based problem-solving", as it is known.

Much of this section describes possible links to other areas of cognitive science. In some cases, such as the problems of information management, HCI seems to be raising problems that are ahead of the mainstream of cognitive science; in other cases, such as the applications of parsing models, recent mainstream advances have yet to be imported and applied specifically to the HCI domain. Whether such an importation would be appropriate is not always clear, which demonstrates that the limits of applicability of cognitive science theories need to be more sharply defined than they are at present.

i) Systems are obviously hard to use if they do not convey enough information of the required type—this is a truism with its roots in the skills literature and the frequent demonstrations of the need for knowledge of results. Riley and O'Malley (1984) showed how the user's mental model of the machine was modified or distorted by systems which hid crucial state information; discovering what information is actually required is not always easy. What is needed here (from the science base) is an understanding of how mental models are formed and used, and (from the system design base) practical experience in designing systems intended to support effective mental models by displaying the appropriate information.

ii) A major problem in handling complex information is to display its internal structure. The treatment of structure perception aptly demonstrates the relationship between the study of human information processing in HCI and in mainstream psychology. Within cognitive psychology the perception of structure in the environment is treated rather separately for the major examples of linguistic, visual, and auditory structure; the emphasis is on the processes of perception. Within HCI, in contrast, the emphasis is on how to choose a structure that will be comprehensible and relevant to the user's task, and in many cases the theme is how to map from one structure—usually symbolic or abstract—into another, usually visual. The immediate need is for better understanding of the processes of perceptual grouping and organisation, especially in visual structures (Pomerantz, 1985).

Program texts form a prime example of large symbolic structures— imagine 10,000 lines of material, with little redundancy—but there are many other cases, such as VLSI design, designs for large buildings, engineering specifications, and timetables for large organisations. How can they be comprehended? For programs, there is evidence that mapping the internal structure into a perceptual form, for instance by using indentation and colour coding, aids comprehension, not only in programming languages (Cunniff & Taylor, 1987; Gilmore & Green, 1988) but also in command languages (Payne et al., 1984) and in the layout of spreadsheets (Saariluoma & Sajaniemi, 1989). At MCC in Austin, Texas, the problems of browsing very large databases have been tackled by Fairchild et al. (1988) using advanced graphic displays. In their SemNet system perceptual cues such as size, colour, and orientation are being applied to very large displays of nodes in "database-space", through which the user can "fly". A number of techniques have been used to position the nodes well, so that related nodes are close together; by "looking around" at a node, the user can observe other nodes that are likely to be relevant. No evaluations have been reported but it is thought to be helpful.

On a smaller scale, there have been attempts to display the internal structure of English text—see for instance the work of Wright and Lickorish (1988) on reading text from VDU screens. Strong generalisations do not seem to be readily made in this area.

There is no clear theory here, and an input from other areas of cognitive science is needed. An urgent question is whether existing models of natural language parsing can be sensibly applied to artificial languages. It is true that most of these models are built around the syntactic constructions appearing in natural languages, specifically English, and in many cases the structure of the parser appears to have been designed by the author simply to get the right behaviour. Nevertheless, a few models are attempts to derive a parser by considering broader principles of cognition (Kempen & Vosse, 1989; Levelt, 1989). Are these models applicable to parsing Pascal programs?

Technical prose structures? Spreadsheet displays? Flow charts? Or only to natural languages, because of a postulated modularity of linguistic expertise? There is room here for a promising convergence.

There is a large and rapidly growing literature on attempts to make complex structures more comprehensible by "folding" them (e.g. by eliminating unnecessary detail). This work is almost entirely derived from the engineering paradigm and has paid very little attention to the analysis of the user's tasks or to the structure of the user's knowledge. Structure-based editors for programs and "hypertext" displays for prose (e.g. "Notecards"—Halasz et al. 1987) are typical examples. In both cases the symbolic structure is not only pruned, but is also mapped into a visual structure which is intended to reinforce the symbolic structure and make it easier to perceive. Unfortunately there is no existing literature analysing how to perform this mapping effectively. I see this as an urgent research objective, requiring interdisciplinary cooperation.

A particular problem is the display of temporal phenomena. Computers are now capable of much more effective graphics and are now being interfaced to small devices such as robots and turtles. Yet again, work in this area is fragmented. Computer science and HCI conferences contain individual reports on schemes for program animation; elsewhere are techniques to illustrate the temporal behaviour of mechanical devices, etc.

iii) The management of such large information structures is a problem in itself, especially during the design activity. Except for the fact that the work was done by computer scientists and was not based on a serious model of cognition, it would be reasonable to claim that one of the major successes of applied psychology over the last two decades has been the development of "structured programming" techniques, which have permanently changed the structure of programming languages and the "methodologies" of software design. Similar ideas have been applied to VLSI design—again coming not from cognitive scientists but from practitioners. However, the structured programming school was based on a view of design in which the design was systematically developed, and its advocates strongly urged that the problem should be fully understood before starting the design phase. Empirical studies of design (e.g. Carroll & Rosson, 1986; also see under Action-based Modelling, discussed later) show that design is a cyclical process in which periods of development are separated by fresh attacks and new approaches. In general, the question of how to support large-scale design has not been effectively tackled by cognitive scientists, but this is an area that is increasingly important and where the time is ripe for some effective contributions.

iv) Finally, one aspect of the user's environment, and more especially of how it is perceived by the user, concerns "situated actions". This topic has been developed much more broadly in the US than in Europe, notably by Suchman (1987). Rather than attempting to abstract action from its circumstances and reconstruct it as a rational plan, the approach is to study how people use their circumstances to achieve intelligent action. It is difficult to foresee how important these ethno-methodological developments will eventually become.

More directly relevant to our theme is work showing how information processing models of perceptual activities must take into account context or situation. Examples are Wright's (1989) discussion of how readers develop strategies for NOT reading, and Bouwhuis's (1989) treatment of reading as goal-driven behaviour. These considerations reinforce the warning above that the division between perception and action is only an expository convenience.

Prospects

Our perception of the environment in which we interact has not achieved the same degree of rigorous modelling that our actions have received (as discussed later,) except, of course, for the contribution of grammatical theory. Techniques for displaying internal structure by mapping it into a visual structure need to be gathered, taxonomised, and made subject to general statements. At the syntactic level, I find fascinating the problems of applying human parsing models to the artificial languages designed for computer interaction, trying to explain why some languages are unexpectedly difficult; but the real question here is how such models can be extended to cover much more complex objects. VLSI circuits, for instance, are rule-bound, like symbol strings, and may turn out to be susceptible to parsing approaches—but at present I know of no such work, and much needs to be done to develop existing knowledge.

2.2 Task Analysis

Recent Developments

Work mentioned in this section aims to describe in systematic terms the tasks performed by users. Recent developments have placed increasing emphasis on identifying the knowledge components of tasks, and this may well be the most interesting direction, showing signs of a convergence with other areas of cognitive science.

i) Johnson, Diaper and Long (1984) have developed TAKD, "Task Analysis for Knowledge Description", which aims to elucidate the knowledge that users must learn in order to perform particular tasks in a specified domain. Much of the emphasis in this work has gone into methods of knowledge elicitation for real world tasks, e.g. by structured interviews with users. Following this, an initial task description is generated, in natural language. The actions and the objects mentioned in the initial task description are then referred to generic actions and objects in a simple "knowledge representation grammar".

TAKD has little or no information processing content. Nevertheless, such developments are important to assist in identifying the components of tasks that information processing models cope with. Related work from the same group (at the Ergonomics Unit, London University) has offered analyses of the task content of tele-shopping by viewdata (Buckley & Long, 1985), showing that the analysis can be extended to new areas. Combined with a simple model of human information processing, existing designs were critiqued.

ii) An intensive study of knowledge requirements, making greater use of information processing analyses, has been offered by Wilson and MacLean (1986) for the case of a particular applications program: VisiOn. This was largely empirical work, based on repeated observation of a number of users over the course of learning, and subsequently attempting to model the behaviour of the users. The major import of this work is the challenge it poses to the science paradigm—namely, how to explain mistakes. The users' performance contained systematic types of mistake and misunderstanding, which were related to a simple model of their knowledge and how it was used. Wilson et al. speak of mismatch between "ideal system knowledge" and "non-ideal" knowledge. The ideal knowledge describes the system knowledge of a perfect user, who knows precisely how to operate the system and never draws on any other source of guidance for actions. The "non-ideal" knowledge refers to cases where users base actions on guesswork involving previous experience with similar systems, comparisons between the command set and natural language, knowledge of what graphs and other domain-specific entities "ought" to look like, etc.

At present this work has not generated predictive user models, but its message is clear. Users draw on a very wide range of background knowledge, and their actions are guided by "non-ideal" knowledge as well as by ideal knowledge. The challenge to the science paradigm is to find ways of incorporating such knowledge into the user models described in the next section.

iii) There is a strong tradition of research combining elements of task analysis with elements of information processing theory, substantially predating the computer revolution in the workplace. Hacker is noted for his well-developed model of action structures within a system, and has developed this work more recently with special reference to the sharing of function between people and computers (Hacker, 1986). Rasmussen and Rouse (1981) are equally well-known for studies in error detection, and their book contains 35 papers on models and theories for fault detection. We shall outline Rasmussen's own approach next.

Prospects
Tools for browsing, writing, drafting designs, home shopping, programming, and financial modelling have all been designed on the basis of inadequate information about the user's tasks. So, too, on a larger scale, have the notorious control rooms of nuclear reactors. The need for task analysis is quite evident as a system design requirement, but it only contributes to our topic here insofar as it relates to human information processing.

The most interesting developments are those that combine elements of task analysis with those of cognitive modelling and thereby span two fields. There are signs that task analysis is leaving its mark in other areas, at least at the level of thinking concerning what users want to do and how they are trying to do it. Examples such as Bouwhuis's (1989) treatment of reading as goal-directed behaviour, cited previously, show how treating a cognitive activity in isolation is no longer adequate. The following section shows many examples of efforts to combine a form of task analysis with an account of how users achieve actions.

2.3 Action-based User Modelling

Recent Developments
The major interface between cognitive psychology and human-computer interaction lies in attempts to describe user activity within the standard framework of human information processing. Within the science paradigm, this exercise is rewarding for both sides, partly because the artificial universe of human-computer interaction is better-defined than the "real" world, and partly because so many different "worlds" exist that the standard framework is severely tested.

i) There is a considerable history of work in the area of fault detection and action theory where implicit or explicit cognitive models are assumed, as mentioned earlier. Because of the particular nature of these topics, neglected aspects of human information processing are brought to the fore. Rasmussen has developed a "stepladder" theory of decision-making which he and his co-workers have applied to a wide variety of real-life situations: process control, emergency management, CAD/CAM, office systems, and library systems (Rasmussen, 1986a, b). In this model, decision-making proceeds from the bottom of one leg of the stepladder, up a series of steps to the hinge, and down the other leg. The first leg represents succeeding steps in the process of understanding the state of the system; the hinge at the top represents the evaluation of performance criteria; and the second leg represents the refinements by which an actual sequence is formulated.

Decision-making need only traverse the full path in the hardest cases. One important quality of this model is that it describes the circumstances in which the passage up one leg and down the other can be cut short. One of the steps on the downward leg, in particular, is the perception of "what to do" as a recognisable task. If, on the upward leg, this step can be reached by a direct jump, without going up to the hinge, the user can save much mental effort. (In this respect, the theory prefigures, at a descriptive level, the work on "knowledge compilation", e.g. Anderson, 1982). Other short-cuts are also specified.

The second important quality of this model is that it has been successfully applied to a very wide range of activities. In some cases, counter-intuitive design advice emerges: for instance, Rasmussen (1986a, p. 21) points out that much effort is spent on presenting control room operators with analytical, bottom-up information about the system, with relatively little attention to the need for top-down, intentional information on reasons behind design decisions, and that this lack of information can be crucial—or even fatal—when operators have to make control decisions, e.g. about whether to overrule an interlock protection.

ii) A descriptive analysis of user activity by Norman (1986) promises to have seminal effects on the field. Although it contains little that is new (it closely resembles the approach taken by Rasmussen, see earlier), it has been closely tied to the developing fields of cognitive science—at least at a conceptual level. Norman describes the "gulf of execution" between the goals formed by the user and the actions required in order to achieve them, and the "gulf of evaluation" between the system's overt response and the user's relating that response to the original goals. Seven stages of activity are described, most of them mental: establishing the goal, forming the intention, specifying the action sequence, executing the action, perceiving the new system state, interpreting that state, and, finally, evaluating that state with respect to the goals and intentions.

Although extremely high-level, this theory of action has some degree of benefit to the system designer, in that it is possible to interpret different interface styles in terms that reveal their strengths and weaknesses. Menu systems, for instance, support the stages of intention formation and action specification, but can slow down the stage of action execution because many sequential actions may be required.

iii) A much lower-level attempt to describe all interaction within the information processing framework has been made by Barnard (1987) in his "interacting cognitive sub-systems" work. Barnard's aim is to identify the "cognitive resources" required for each of a wide range of user activities, to describe the known features of the information processing that characterise each such resource, and to describe the communications between resources that are necessary to perform each specified activity. The user's performance on a particular activity will be determined by the set of resources required and their pattern of communications.

The resources, or cognitive sub-systems, include visual, acoustic, propositional, and effector resources. Each resource processes information in a particular mental code, but it can translate its own code into the codes required for other resources to use. Estimates of times are available for some of the operations specified in this model, allowing much more detailed predictions to be made than is usual.

iv) There have been several moves to apply recent research on action planning and the control of complex behaviour to the domain of human-computer interaction. Young and Simon (1987) have developed a model of planning which can move smoothly from the backward chaining typical of STRIPS-like systems to the "routine cognitive skill" typical of GOMS-like systems. Whitefield (1984) has applied the "blackboard" planning model, first developed by Hayes-Roth and Hayes-Roth (1979), to the use of a computer-based design tool for use in CAD. The blackboard model was specifically designed to model opportunistic behaviour, in which a person who is trying to achieve several goals simultaneously can take advantage of an unexpected opportunity to pursue a goal that has temporarily been shelved; to achieve this ability to snatch an opportunity, it is necessary to postulate quite a complex cognitive architecture. Whitefield's empirical work showed that the behaviour of CAD designers could indeed be modelled in these terms. It also showed that even experienced users of computer-based tools can spend extraordinary lengths of time in neither achieving their externally-set tasks ("content problems"), nor in thinking, but in getting their systems to do things ("interaction problems").

Hoc (1986) also supports the blackboard model, generally now described as "opportunistic" planning. One of the most interesting features of his work is that it is able to relate the task constraints, the tools and facilities offered to the user, and the model of planning. In Hoc (1988) he describes how experienced programmers working with tools intended to support one style of planning had very considerable difficulties when attempting to solve problems that imposed constraints of a different type. Work by Guindon et al. (1988) and Visser (1990) lends further support from studies of highly experienced software designers, whereas Hartson and Hix (1989) show similar findings from the design of user interface systems. The old-fashioned "waterfall" model of design (in which design develops from broad outlines to low-level details) has failed to meet with reality.

v) Errors and slips have been analysed in terms of action theories by Norman (1981), Reason (1987), and others. (The classical distinction is between a mistake, when an inappropriate action is planned and executed, and slips, when an appropriate action is planned but is wrongly executed.) Most of these models are purely analytical, but this is an important area; if we understood how actions are developed from knowledge, we could discover how they go wrong—and if we knew how they went wrong, we could at least avoid designing systems where slips are especially frequent. Unfortunately, attempts to produce different frequencies of slips in the laboratory (Bellamy & Green, 1986; Gillie, 1984) have been less successful. The current state of knowledge in how to design HCI systems to minimise error, and to help users recover from error, is summarised informally by Lewis and Norman (1986).

An interesting development has been presented by Amendola et al. (1987), who have attempted to model not just the human operator's cognitive processes but also the machine that is affected by the human actions, in a single tightly-coupled system. The cognitive side of their model separates high-level decision-making, such as situation assessment; low-level decision-making, determining actual intentions; and errors. By separating the error mechanism, they can use identical principles to model either high-level errors or low-level errors; thus the traditional distinction between "mistakes" and "slips" is maintained but is explained by a single mechanism.

Finally, Rizzo et al. (1987) point to an area that is comparatively neglected: the detection of one's own errors. Their data show that, as is to be expected, mistakes are harder to detect than slips, but also that a complex variety of other factors need to be considered. Whether our concerns are those of science, engineering, or design, this is an area that deserves more attention.

Prospects
Action-based modelling in human-computer interaction is converging with other areas of cognitive science in two ways: first, the approaches based on planning, and second the analysis of slips and errors, which may coalesce with recent developments in the origin of slips in speech, typing, and other areas.

From the point of view of the engineering and system design paradigms, these approaches leave something to be desired. They are all descriptive, and "soft" rather than "hard" science. They are not easy to apply without a very considerable background in the field, and they therefore only have effect on actual design in those organisations which can support human factors specialists. Thus the descriptive approaches could easily find themselves in slack water!

One solution might be to codify the content of a descriptive model of information processing in the form of an expert system for the use of interface designers. Designers would describe the main features of a proposed system and be informed by the expert system of the main aspects of human information processing that would be relevant. Such an approach has been explored by Barnard et al. (1987), who have developed a prototype system for demonstration purposes. This promises to be an extremely effective approach.

There is at present no real substitute for "soft", descriptive models. Attempts to create formal models, especially executable models, described in the following section, are necessarily restricted to handling what can be done easily at the present moment. All the descriptive models agree with common sense, for instance, that visually salient objects are usually processed earlier and faster; but as we have no computational vision models that can be plugged into models of user behaviour, there is no way to incorporate this simple fact in the formal models—nor many other equally important facts of a similar type.

Within the scientific paradigm these descriptive cognitive models, applied to human-computer interaction, are not as visible as they could be; the main interest of the scientific community is in extending knowledge of the architecture of cognition and its components and performance, rather than on applying existing knowledge. The problem here is not so much in the research needs and objectives as in the infrastructure of the science base.

There is a need for more research into programming which treats it as a topic in human information processing. This is required firstly for scientific reasons; we have the chance to study complex planning in a well-controlled and well-defined environment of a degree of complexity that can be determined by the experimenter, and to examine the effects of many different types of constraint. We can also obtain subjects of many different degrees of experience. Secondly, it is also an urgent need within the system design paradigm. Programming, in a mild form, has already reached the average office, in the form of global search-and-replace facilities in word processors; even humble WordStar allows quite complex commands to be given. Soon, small packages of instructions ("macros") will become commonplace in many of the artifacts we use. Turning to professional use of programming facilities, as more of our social fabric becomes controlled by computers, it becomes more necessary to provide human-engineered support tools and to design human-engineered programming languages.

No mention has been made of the different aims of the models discussed here. Whitefield (1986) shows how different models have subtly different purposes, as well as differences in their explanatory adequacy. For the development of research, all aims are acceptable.

2.4 Knowledge-based Models

Recent Developments

i) The vast literature on memory engendered by psychology has so far proved to have relatively little impact on human-computer interaction—at least in the form of memory research, rather than knowledge representation research. A notable exception, however, is the work of Klix (see his review paper, 1986), who describes functional principles to allow effective modes of information storage and retrieval. By mimicking these in the design of computer software Klix (1986, p.114) hopes that it will "make the capability of computers more transparent and familiar especially to naive users since their own mental activity works in a related way". His principles are claimed also to lead to cognitive learning capabilities such as the detection of fruitful analogies, generalisation of rules, and inference.

ii) The problem of analogy and metaphor has not been solved within cognitive science. It is hardly surprising, therefore, although all workers are agreed that it is an important issue in human-computer interaction, that it has not been systematised. Fruitful and effective metaphors have been devised, such as the famous "desk-top" metaphor, which appear to help learners in the early stages to work out how the system works; but it is not clear that making the metaphor more perfect would actually assist them still further. How perfect a metaphor would be desirable? Are metaphors desirable at all, or do they lead to problems? There have certainly been voices pointing out the difficulties, in the present stage, of determining the limits to the effectiveness of analogy and metaphor (Carroll & Mack, 1985). The research need here is for an improved understanding of the process of analogy.

It is not even clear that contemporary theoretical tools are adequate for describing the process of metaphor. Streitz (1986) analyses metaphor in terms of nested models for example, and argues that further progress demands methods of comparing representations which at present we do not possess.

iii) "Mental models" of the system, another contribution from cognitive science (Gentner & Stevens, 1983), are proposed as high-level explanations of differences between users, effects of metaphor, etc. There has been difficulty in clarifying exactly what the term "mental model" might be taken to mean, or how to investigate the mental model held by a particular user, but it is certainly the case that one's conception of how a system works is an actively constructed representation that may well be wrong. Young (1981) has analysed some particularly simple devices, ordinary pocket calculators, in these terms. The received wisdom at present, based on results by Halasz and Moran (1983), is that a good mental model is very important when unexpected problems arise but that otherwise it makes little difference to performance.

Others have extended the analysis to human-computer interaction, and, notably, both Ackermann and Stelovsky (1987), and Payne (1988) have examined the role of mental models in the way users develop improved methods for performing tasks. Ackermann and Stelovsky focussed on the individual differences between mental models, and have reported studies in which users tailored the system to resemble their own mental model more closely. The results of tailoring varied enormously between users; however, the topic of individual differences is being treated elsewhere. Payne has concentrated on the conditions that encourage users to construct one mental model rather than another, with particular reference to "deep" or "figurative" knowledge rather than "shallow" or "operational" knowledge; the argument is that a user who "understands" a particular operation only as a step in a routine method, without understanding its effect and its role in the method ("operational" understanding), will be unable to use that operation in the construction of new methods. This suggests that the received view is somewhat over-simplified, and that mental models are also important in the development of expertise, as well as in coping with the unexpected.

iv) The particular case of knowledge representation in programs has received much study from the group of researchers centered around Soloway at Yale. The central topic here is the growth of expertise. Much of their work has been loosely based on errors made by novice Pascal programmers; their interpretation has been based on Schankian notions of "plan" and "schema". Many of their papers appear in Soloway and Iyengar (1986). The most rigorous theoretical analysis in this school has been developed by Rist (1986) who attempts to illustrate how programming knowledge is represented and used by both novices and experts. Black et al. (1987) show how the analysis can be unified with a model of users' knowledge of command languages, and how the approach relates to more traditional work on story grammars.

Empirical testing has been scarce in this area, although Détienne (1989) reports convincing studies of Pascal experts supporting the "plans" analysis. Gilmore and Green (1988) consider the problems of extending the analysis beyond Pascal; their BASIC programmers showed no evidence of plans, but Davies (1990) restored some credibility by showing that the effect depended on training. Pennington (1987) found that Cobol program fragments were better primed by textual neighbours than by plan-related "neighbours". Plans are evidently only a partial model.

v) The problem of understanding has recently become a large, though extremely ill-defined, issue in cognitive science, attempting to bring together what is known about many of the topics mentioned earlier. The collection of papers edited by Norman and Draper (1986) includes a large section dealing with naive theories of computation, what users need to understand, how users can gain understanding from watching events, and models of computation. This area is so exploratory and so much more concerned with the search for concepts than with solid demonstrations or empirical tests that it is difficult to summarise, but it will certainly be profoundly important in the next decade. One of the most impressive papers here is Lewis's model understander (Lewis, 1986), which uses a few simple heuristics to gain an understanding of a system by watching demonstrations. Another idea that may prove to be seminal is Whiteside and Wixon's (1985) attempt to use developmental psychology as a framework for understanding "user growth" in HCI.

vi) The role of application domain modelling bears only tangentially on human information processing in HCI, just as task analysis does. Yet from the system design perspective, it is just as essential. Among many recent papers on aspects of this topic, Dzida and Valder (1984) show how knowledge engineering techniques can be applied. They use set theory and allied algebraic techniques to model the components of a work act, a structure combining a result (with an attribute), a tool, an object, and a parameter that provides attributes of an object. Operators are used to take objects from an initial state to a resulting state, and eventually a substantial fragment of the user's knowledge, it is hoped, can be represented in these terms. They have applied their techniques, at an armchair level, to the work of a real estate agency, but little empirical comparison has been reported between what has been modelled and what users "really" know, either from this or from other, similar, developments.

Dix and Runciman (1985) describe a different approach, in which they attempt to prove or disprove desirable properties of interface designs using formal methods. Examples of properties they can define at present are "reachability" (whether one system state is reachable from another) and "reversibility".

Notice that this is another example of convergence, this time with ideas from the knowledge representation literature. Elsewhere in this report many other approaches to knowledge representation will be discussed. It is not yet evident which may be the most appropriate for "export" to the field of human-computer interaction as an applied tool.

Prospects

The technical ability to represent knowledge in computer-usable form is increasing vastly. With it, we are gaining an increased understanding of human knowledge representation and domain modelling—topics which are dealt with elsewhere. The area is extremely active and promises to be very fruitful. The exact interpretation of Klix's statement quoted earlier, that a successful system should mimic human knowledge representation, is unclear (after all, many of our most successful artefacts, such as wheels, succeed precisely because they complement human abilities, not because they mimic them), but his emphasis on the importance of the area cannot be faulted.

From the engineering paradigm viewpoint, the ability to represent knowledge effectively will clearly lead to many new uses for computer systems, and is one of the most important prospects of the next decade. Whether we shall make sufficient progress in the next decade to use knowledge which is effectively seen as a system design problem is open to doubt; but there are many proposals and demonstrations of not-too-complex knowledge-based systems, such as Wilensky's Unix consultant (1982), which utilise intuitive models of human information processing to good effect.

The study of knowledge representation in programming has been dominated by the desire to understand the shift from novice to expert and by the increasing interest in intelligent computer-based instruction. Both are treated elsewhere in this report, as aspects of learning. But the knowledge representations they engender should form part of the input to work on support environments for programming and related activities (see previously).

The research on understanding still needs a clear and straightforward research objective. Both from the scientific viewpoint and the system design viewpoint, it is important to understand what "understanding" means, but until the issues are clarified it is hard to predict the direction research will take.

2.5 Formal and Computational Cognitive Modelling

Recent Developments

Much recent work aims explicitly to use a form of cognitive theory as the basis for a formal or computational model, preferably one that can be executed. Indeed, the emphasis in most cases has been on achieving an executable model rather than a truly formal one. These developments at present lie mainly in the science paradigm; practical use for system design is still a hope rather than an actuality.

Developments in this area so far appear to have been exclusively based on the symbol-processing model of human information processing, deriving ultimately from production systems or from linguistic grammars. There has been no equivalent to the recent growth of connectionist models in other areas of cognitive science (see, for instance, the review of neurocomputational studies of learning and memory in Phillips & Baddeley, 1989).

Within the realm of symbol-processing models, it is important to distinguish between performance models and "cognitive-competence" models (Payne & Green, 1986). Performance models actually simulate the performance of the subject—see (i) and (ii) as follows. Cognitive-competence models (henceforth, competence for short) specify what the user knows how to do, but not the operations of, say, working memory; see (iii).

i) Most work in this area acknowledges its debt to the pioneering work of Card, Moran and Newell (1983). Their work is very consciously related to the engineering paradigm, in that they attempted to create usable approximate theories by which designers could calculate preferred solutions to design questions. Their analysis was based mainly on times for "routine skills" such as text editing, and their work assumed that performance was virtually errorless. A substantial part of their effort lay in applying a simple model of the human operator to the hand motions on a keyboard or with a mouse, but this part of their work has little information processing content.

Their most seminal contribution was the idea of the "unit task", a task for which the user can provide a "method". As seen by Card et al., methods are ways to achieve goals, and can invoke sub-goals or operators. A method for deleting a word would invoke a sub-goal involving locating the word and then an operator for deletion, using whatever was the appropriate instruction on the given text editor. Since words can be located in various ways (e.g. by visual browsing or by invoking a search command), their model incorporated selection rules to choose the appropriate method in given conditions.

Notice that this model, known as GOMS (Goals, Operators, Methods, and Selection rules), relies on the cognitive science developments of its time. It is essentially a production system incorporating a goal stack to guide control. It was not implemented by the authors as a running program but was extensively used as an explanatory device in discussing performance.

GOMS has proved very successful in many areas. Recent applications cover spreadsheet usage (Olson & Nilsen, 1988), S-R compatibility, and transcription typing (John & Newell, 1989).

ii) Kieras and Polson (1985) have developed the GOMS model as an implemented production system, with additional theoretical apparatus, under the title of "Cognitive Complexity Theory". This is a very extensive development and has generated many papers (see Polson, 1987). They have developed style rules to differentiate between models of novice users and models of expert users; reported tests of predictions of learning times derived from their model; and have pushed hard for a version of their model that can be used as a system design aid. Related work by Ziegler et al. (1986) has also provided empirical support.

Kieras and Polson use a specialised production system as their cognitive model of the user. The productions correspond to the "methods" of Card et al. It turns out that, when expressed in this form, the model becomes rather verbose, since each sub-goal must make a note in working memory when it is invoked and must delete that note when it completes its task. Kieras and Polson put the fragmentation of knowledge to good use, however, in their "common elements" theory of transfer. Essentially they argue that a production learnt for one task is still available to be utilised in the learning of subsequent tasks. So learning will be fast when the methods for achieving tasks learnt later share production rules with tasks learnt earlier. By counting the number of common elements, they can obtain a prediction of learning time. Recent papers have shown surprisingly good agreements between theory and prediction, although there are still some methodological problems to be sorted out.

A serious difficulty with this approach is that the "cognitive architecture" and the specific knowledge are entwined in the same model, in such a way that they cannot be separated. The model's "knowledge" of how to perform tasks using a particular device is described in terms of making notes in working memory, invoking sub-goals, and the rest. In consequence, it is difficult to say what, exactly, is the implied model of human information processing. From an engineering point of view, the lack of separation means that it is not yet possible to build a model of the cognitive architecture, supply it with a representation of knowledge about a particular device, and observe its interaction. Each new device requires a new, hand-crafted model.

iii) The next type of cognitive model we shall describe is a competence model, aimed only at representing the user's knowledge. Like competence models in linguistics it is based on a grammatical representation. Although the first work using a grammar was by Reisner (1981) we shall not describe that, since her grammars only modelled the system, not the user's view of the system.

Payne and Green (1986) have considerably extended the grammatical approach. Their system uses semantic features to describe user's tasks: in this way, similar tasks can be expected to be described by similar features. The grammar is a "mapping" grammar, rather than a generative grammar, and it maps task descriptions into action sequences using rewrite rules in which feature values (a) determine the applicability of left-hand rules, and (b) carry through information, rather like parameters to subroutines.

Task-action grammar (TAG) is considerably more succinct than the production system model, partly because it achieves a complete separation between the representation of knowledge and the cognitive architecture which actually makes use of the knowledge. It is also psychologically more complete because it represents syntactic-semantic consistency; it is capable of representing "family resemblances". TAG also contains a notational device which can be used to represent reliance on users constructing mappings from semantic features to spatial features of the device, or to lexical features of the user's vocabulary.

Payne and Green (1989) report an empirical test which supports the consistency arguments, whereas Bowden et al. (1989) showed that still better results were obtained if genuinely orthogonal languages were used. Little empirical research has been based on the TAG model outside the laboratory but some efforts have been made to analyse real-life systems (Green, Schiele, & Payne, 1988) and to extend its semantics (Tauber, 1987). A particularly interesting development has been the work by Hoppe (1988) on "task-oriented parsing", the recognition of users' plans by an active help system based on an extended version of task-action grammar.

iv) Lastly we come to "programmable user models" based on "unified cognitive architectures" (Young et al. 1989). Before practically useful executable models can be achieved, it is necessary to create performance models which separate the description of the device from the model of the cognitive architecture. The same model can then be supplied with descriptions of different devices, in a suitable formalism, and the performance can be predicted. To do this, the architecture must be sufficiently general to allow representation of an adequate amount of knowledge about the device and the task domain, and it must be capable of creating, discovering, or being told, methods to accomplish the required tasks on the given device.

This approach relies heavily on the concept of a cognitive architecture. Young et al. have adopted the "SOAR" cognitive architecture offered by Newell (1989). Earlier production system models regarded problem-solving as an exploration of a state space (the "problem space") in which operators changed the state. SOAR extends this view, introducing a multiplicity of problem spaces; an impasse at one level (e.g. SOAR finds that two operators are equally appropriate) may be resolved by exploring a deeper problem space which contains operators for refining the choice criteria. A clever chunking mechanism ensures that SOAR remembers the circumstances and adds appropriate knowledge to the upper level; on meeting the same impasse in the future, SOAR will proceed without even noticing the impasse. This form of failure-driven learning is the converse of the success-driven learning postulated in Anderson's ACT*, where frequently-used productions become "proceduralised".

Newell's development of SOAR is ambitious, even provocative, proposing it as an example of a "unified theory of cognition" able to account for a wide range of cognitive phenomena with a single mechanism. To his credit, he and his team have done well to meet the many challenges implicit in such a claim. Making a really successful inroad into modelling cognition with a single architecture would obviously be a development of the first importance to psychology as a whole, not just to the sub-discipline of human-computer interaction. One immediate consequence within HCI would be to resolve the dilemma between competence modelling and performance modelling (see the comparison between "task-action grammar" and "cognitive complexity theory" mentioned earlier); if the architecture is pre-defined, then the complaint that performance models do not distinguish between the psychological component and the knowledge component no longer applies.

An unforeseen development from SOAR was the discovery that the learning mechanism could also be applied to the perception side as well as to the action side. The effect of this "data chunking" is to allow structures to be perceived with minimal computational effort (Rosenbloom, Laird, & Newell, 1989). At present the consequences of this development are still being explored, but in view of the impoverished state of perceptual research within HCI noted earlier all progress must be welcomed.

Young et al.'s development of "programmable user models" attempts to show that a variety of observable "scenarios" in human-computer interaction can be described in one breath, as it were. It can be viewed as an effort to bring the idiosyncratic modelling developments in HCI under the shade of a single umbrella, one that is wide enough to allow the information processing component of HCI to be seen as a specialisation of cognitive information processing in general.

Prospects
Comparison with earlier sections will show that many features mentioned there are still well outside the scope of computable modelling. The work on Norman's "gulf of evaluation", for example, finds almost no echo in the process models we have described. Nor do the complexities of different forms of perceptual coding, described in Barnard's "Interacting Cognitive Subsystems", or the concepts of "mental models", metaphor, etc. Opportunistic planning and the continued, deliberate interleaving of many tasks and sub-tasks have been modelled in AI territory but no extensive application to realistic HCI tasks has been made, and although this topic may soon be tackled (using blackboard planning systems, or possibly using versions of linguistic models, as suggested by Edmondson, 1989) it will take some time to achieve results.

For these and similar reasons, deep reservations about the true effectiveness of all types of formal or computational approaches to cognitive modelling have been voiced. Briggs (1988) has recorded the experiences of well-motivated novices learning a word processing system. She doubts whether any formal evaluation technique could have foreseen the bizarre fictions invented by users to explain unexpected behaviours of the system. Whiteside and Wixon (1987) mention "observations we have seen of users actually trying to use diskettes. On one prototype, a pair of users successfully inserted a diskette, not into the drive, but into a seam in the plastic case that they mistook as the drive-slot." So much, they say, for formal GOMS-based models in which the action, "insert the diskette" is a unit task comparable to "press the space bar". Formalist modelling will not be able to handle such occurrences in the foreseeable future.

Despite these reservations it is widely hoped, from the engineering paradigm viewpoint, that developments in models of users will provide useful means for the early evaluation of designs. From the science viewpoint, these models are interesting and challenging applications of cognitive theory to well-specified domains, thereby helping to test and develop the underlying theories. For these reasons, this area is one of great activity.

3. PERSPECTIVES ON
INFORMATION-PROCESSING
MODELS IN HCI RESEARCH

It is hardly surprising that not all development in the HCI field is led by information processing models. For instance, the rapid development of hypertext (Conklin, 1987), of techniques to record argumentation and design rationale (Fischer et al., 1989; MacLean et al., 1989), and of collaborative work systems (Greif, 1988), exist independently (so far) of information processing models. Disquiet has been growing as to whether information processing is as relevant to the development of HCI as had previously been thought, and a powerful debate has started up in learned journals.

The positions adopted in that debate are motivated by the desire to improve design. The advancement of science for its own sake is not an issue. In terms of the three strands of HCI research outlined in the Introduction, most of the debate comes under the rubric of system design and therefore does not come strictly within the scope of this paper. Mention of some of the major positions may nevertheless be useful. However, because some of the protagonists see the advancement of science as the best route to improving design, whereas others disagree, the outcome of the debate may profoundly affect the direction of HCI research, according to the view of scientific achievements that is eventually adopted.

i) The clearest statement of the information processing position comes from Newell and Card (1985, p.237), arguing strongly for a scientific approach—and not just any science, but a hard science.

"Our sole concern is with the quality of future interfaces. We think psychological science has major contributions to make, but that, as soft science (compared to computer science) its actual influence could well be marginal. The only chance we see of preventing this is to harden the science ... Striving to develop a theory that does task analysis by calculation is the key to hardening the science."

They point to GOMS-like approaches as examples of such theories.

ii) Do information processing models of "typical" users, in the GOMS mould, give "leverage"? Curtis (1986) argues that in the area of the psychology of programming, the largest source of variation in performance is accounted for by individual differences, and that improvements in professional programming can be most effectively made by identifying and supporting "super-programmers" or "super-designers". Information processing theories, by implication, have at best a very limited role.

iii) Landauer (1987) has argued for a less "hard-nosed" approach, an iterative relationship between cognitive theory and system development in which the applied problems encountered in system development can serve as a source of theoretical development, and existing theory can serve as a guide to system development. This is a very familiar position in applied psychology, but Landauer correctly points out that in system development there has been little indication of cognitive psychology seriously influencing the designers. He suggests organisational solutions to this gap, principally the technique of iterative testing, in which new designs are repeatedly tested and modified against realistic tasks in realistic contexts.

iv) Carroll and Kellogg (1989) reject Card and Newell's approach because, they claim, if we are to concentrate on "hard" science, the result will be to enforce a concentration on low-level details, such as task time or error rate, or to "view artifacts through the filter of an isolated theoretical abstraction (e.g. a 'grammar-in-the-head')". They opt for a view in which system designers are not expected to be guided by cognitive theory, but are seen as cognitive theorists themselves, because almost every aspect of an HCI design can be viewed as a "claim" about the user's psychology. They analyse a familiar programming system, Apple's Hypercard system, and suggest how some of the key techniques can be interpreted as psychological claims. For instance, Hypercard comes with a large supply of examples and built-in functions, and Carroll and Kellogg list a variety of ways in which these can be viewed as making psychological claims. One of their suggestions is that: "Examples and built-ins assert that planning and acting is simplified by being able to directly incorporate appearance and behaviour of components (e.g. a button and its function). A corollary claim is that modifying is easier than creating from scratch: users can borrow a button that already behaves in the desired way, but modify its appearance." (This may seem obvious, but remember that most programming systems do not come with plentiful examples to be borrowed!) Thus, their argument is that HCI artifacts are in themselves psychological theories, and that interpretation of these artifacts is a process of scientific understanding, leading to "seeing a design in psychological terms".

v) Finally, there are suggestions that the entire cognitive enterprise may be misguided! Whiteside and Wixon (1987) suggest that some of the most common assumptions in cognitive modelling of information processing (e.g. that users have goals) should be challenged. After outlining a number of such theories, they continue (p.360): "We invite the authors to ponder what the consequences might be for theoretical and practical work if one did not grant that almost all of human behaviour can be characterized in terms of goals and plans." Instead of modelling, they suggest hermeneutic interpretation: "Formal modelling seeks explanation in terms of a supposed underlying true structure. Interpretation seeks a more relative truth, one that is sensible and appropriate to the situation at hand, but not absolute or timeless." They seek "a more tentative, holistic, and contextualist framework" than formal modelling can provide.

The purpose of this paper is, of course, not to discuss how to create better HCI artifacts, but to review how information processing models have been developed and used. We can therefore excuse ourselves from entering into this debate in any serious way, merely noting that in any reasonably difficult form of progress there is surely no single path that all must follow, and that synthesis comes from the encounter between push and shove.

REFERENCES

Ackermann, D., & Stelovsky, J. (1987). The role of mental models in programming: From experiments to requirements for an interactive system. In M. Tauber & P. Gorry (Eds.), *Visual aids in programming*. Berlin: Springer-Verlag.

Amendola, A., Bersini, U., Cacciabue, P.C., & Mancini, G. (1987). Modelling operators in accident conditions: Advances and perspectives on a cognitive model. *International Journal of Man-Machine Studies, 27,* 599-612.

Anderson, J. R. (1982). Acquisition of cognitive skill. Psychological Review, 89, 369-406.

Barnard, P. J. (1987). Cognitive resources and the learning of human-computer dialogues. In J.M. Carroll (Ed.), *Interfacing Thought: Cognitive Aspects of Human-Computer Interaction*. Cambridge, MA: MIT Press.

Barnard, P., Wilson, M., & MacLean, A. (1987). Approximate modelling of cognitive architecture: Towards an expert system design aid. *Proceedings of CHI 87.* New York: ACM.

Bellamy, R., & Green, T.R.G. (1986). "Damn it, I've done it again": An investigation of action slips. *Proceedings of the 3rd European Conference Cognitive Ergonomics*, Paris: INRIA.

Black, J.B., Kay, D.S., & Soloway, E.M. (1987). Goal and plan knowledge representations: From stories to text editors and programs. In J. M. Carroll (Ed.), *Interfacing Thought*. Cambridge, MA: MIT Press.

Bouwhuis, D.G. (1989). Reading as goal-driven behaviour. In B.A.G. Elsendoorn & H. Bouma (Eds.), *Working Models of Human Perception*. Academic Press.

Bowden, E.M., Douglas, S.A., & Stanford, C.A. (1989). Testing the principle of orthogonality in language design. *Human-Computer Interaction, 4,* 95-120.

Briggs, P. (1988). What we know and what we need to know: The user model versus the users model in human-computer interaction. *Behaviour and Information Technology, 7*, 431-442.

Buckley, P. K., & Long, J. B. (1985). Effects of system and knowledge variables on a task component of "teleshopping". In P. Johnson, & S. Cook (Eds.), *People and computers: Designing the interface*. Cambridge: Cambridge University Press.

Card, S. K., & Newell, A. (1985). The prospects for psychological science in human-computer interaction. *Human-Computer Interaction, 2*, 251-267.

Card, S.K., Moran, T.P., & Newell, A. (1983). *The psychology of human-computer interaction*. Hillsdale, NJ: Lawrence Erlbaum Associates.

Carroll, J. M., & Kellogg, W. A. (1989). Artifact as theory-nexus: Hermeneutics meets theory-based design. *Proceedings of CHI 89*. New York: ACM.

Carroll, J.M., & Mack, R. L. (1985). Metaphor, computing systems, and active learning. *International Journal of Man-Machine Studies, 22*, 39-57.

Carroll, J.M., & Rosson, (1986). Usability specifications as a tool in iterative development. In R. Hartson (Ed.), *Advances in Human-Computer Interaction: Vol 1*. Norwood, NJ: Ablex.

Conklin, E. J. (1987). Hypertext: An introduction and survey. *IEEE Computer, 2* (9) 17-41. Reprinted in Greif (1988).

Cunniff, N., & Taylor, R.P. (1987). Graphics and learning: A study of learner characteristics and comprehension of programming languages. In H.-J. Bullinger, & B. Shackel (Eds.), *INTERACT 87*. North-Holland: Elsevier.

Curtis, B. (1988). The impact of individual differences in programming. In T.R.G. Green, J.-M. Hoc., G.C. van der Veer, & D. Murray (Eds.), *Working with computers: Theory versus outcome*. London: Academic Press

Davies, S.P. (1990). The nature and development of programming plans. *International Journal of Man-Machine Studies, 32*, 461-481.

Détienne, F. (1990). Program understanding and knowledge organization: The influence of acquired schemata. In P. Falzon, J.-M. Hoc, & Y. Waern (Eds.), *Psychological Foundations of Human-Computer Interaction*. Springer-Verlag.

Dix, A. J., & Runciman, C. (1985). Abstract models of interactive systems. In P. Johnson, & S. Cook (Eds.), *People and computers: Designing the interface*. Cambridge: Cambridge University Press.

Dzida, W., & Valder, W. (1984). Application domain modelling by knowledge engineering techniques. In B. Shackel (Ed.), INTERACT 84. North-Holland: Elsevier.

Edmonson, W.H. (1989). Asynchronous parallelism in human-behaviour: A cognitive science perspective on human-computer interaction. *Behaviour and Information Technology, 8*, 3-12.

Fairchild, K.M., Poltrock, S.E., & Furnas, G.W. (1988). SemNet: Three-dimensional graphic representations of large knowledge bases. In R. Guindon (Ed.), Cognitive science and its applications for human-computer interaction. Hillsdale, NJ: Lawrence Erlbaum Associates.

Fischer, G., McCall, R., Morch, A. (1989). Design environments for constructive and argumentative design. *Proceedings of CHI 89*. New York: ACM.

Gentner, D., & Stevens, A.L. (Eds.). (1983). *Mental models*. Hillsdale, NJ: Lawrence Erlbaum Associates.

Gillie, T. (1984). *Slips: An applied psychological approach*. Unpublished MA thesis, Sheffield University.

Gilmore, D.J., & Green, T.R.G. (1988). Programming plans and programming experience. *Quarterly Journal of Experimental Psychology, 40A* (3), 423-442.

Green, T.R.G., Schiele, F., & Payne, S.J. (1988). Formalisable models of user knowledge in human-computer interaction. In G.C. van der Veer, T.R.G. Green, J.-M. Hoc, & D. Murray (Eds.), *Working with computers: Theory versus outcome*. London: Academic Press.

Greif, I. (Ed.). (1988). *Computer-supported collaborative work: A book of readings*. San Mateo, CA: Morgan Kaufmann.

Guindon, R., Krasner, H., & Curtis, B. (1988). Breakdowns and processes during the early activities of software design by professionals. In G. Olson, E. Soloway, & S. Sheppard (Eds.), *Empirical Studies of Programmers: Second Workshop*. Norwood, NJ: Ablex.

Hacker, W. (1986). What should be computerized? In F. Klix, & H. Wandke (Eds.), Man-Computer Interaction Research: Macinter-1. North-Holland: Elsevier.

Halasz, F.G., & Moran, T.P. (1983). Mental models and problem-solving in using a calculator. *Proceedings of CHI 83*. New York: ACM.

Halasz, F. G., Moran, T. P., & Trigg, R. H. (1987). Notecards in a nutshell. *Proceedings of CHI 87 (ACM)*. New York: ACM.

Hartson, H.R., & Hix, D. (1989). Toward empirically derived methodologies and tools for human-computer interface development. *International Journal of Man-Machine Studies, 31*, 477-494.

Hayes-Roth, B., & Hayes-Roth, F. (1979). A cognitive model of planning. *Cognitive Science, 3*, 275-310.

Hoc, J.-M. (1986). *Psychologie cognitive de la planification*. Grenoble University Press. Also available in translation as *The Psychology of Planning*. London: Academic Press.

Hoc, J.-M. (1988). Towards effective computer aids to planning in computer programming. In G.C. van der Veer, T.R.G. Green, J.-M. Hoc and D.M. Murray (Eds.), *Working with computers: Theory versus outcome*. London: Academic Press.

Hoppe, H.U. (1988). Task-oriented parsing: A diagnostic method to be used by adaptive systems. *Proceedings of CHI 88*. New York: ACM.

John, B.E. & Newell, A. (1989). Cumulating the science of HCI: From S-R compatibility to transcription typing. *Proceedings of CHI 89*. New York: ACM.

Johnson, P., Diaper, D., & Long, J. B. (1984). Tasks, skills, and knowledge: Task analysis for knowledge based descriptions. In B. Shackel (Ed.), *INTERACT 84*. North-Holland: Elsevier.

Kempen, G., & Vosse, T. (1989). Incremental syntactic tree formation in human sentence processing: An interactive architecture based on activation decay and simulated annealing. *Cahiers de la Fondation Archives Jean Piaget*.

Kieras, D.E., & Polson, P.G. (1985). An approach to the formal analysis of user complexity. *International Journal of Man-machine Studies, 22*, 365-394.

Klix, F. (1986). Memory research and knowledge engineering. In F. Klix, & H. Wandke (Eds.), *Man-Computer Interaction Research: Macinter 1*. North-Holland: Elsevier.

Landauer, T. K. (1987). Relations between cognitive psychology and computer system design. In J. M. Carroll (Ed.), *Interfacing thought*. Cambridge, MA: MIT Press.

Levelt, W.J.M. (1989). *Speaking: From intention to articulation*. Cambridge, MA: MIT Press.

Lewis, C. (1986). Understanding what's happening in system interactions. In D.A. Norman, & S. Draper, (Eds.), *User-centered system design*. Hillsdale, NJ: Lawrence Erlbaum Associates.

Lewis, C., & Norman, D. A. (1986). Designing for error. In D.A. Norman & S. Draper, (Eds.), User-centered system design. Hillsdale, NJ: Lawrence Erlbaum Associates.

Long, J. B. (1986). People and computers: Designing for usability. In M.D. Harrison, & A.F. Monk (Eds.), *People and computers: Designing for usability*. Cambridge: Cambridge University Press.

MacLean, A., Young, R.M., & Moran, T.P (1989). Design rationale: The argument behind the artifact. *Proceedings of CHI 89*. New York: ACM.

Newell, A. (1989). *Unified Theories of Cognition: The William James Lectures*. Harvard University Press.

Newell, A., & Card, S.K. (1985). The prospects for psychological science in human-computer interaction. *Human-Computer Interaction, 1*, 209-242.

Norman, D. A. (1981). Categorisation of action slips. *Psychological Review, 88*, 1-15.

Norman, D. A. (1986). Cognitive engineering. In D.A. Norman, & S. Draper, (Eds.), *User-centered system design*. Hillsdale, NJ: Lawrence Erlbaum Associates.

Norman, D.A., & Draper, S. (1986). *User-centered system design*. Hillsdale, NJ: Lawrence Erlbaum Associates.

Norman, D. A., & Rumelhart, D. E. (1983). Studies of typing from the LNR research group. In W. C. Cooper (Ed.), *Cognitive aspects of skilled typing*. Springer-Verlag: New York (chap. 3).

Olson, J. R., & Nilsen, E. (1988). Analysis of the cognition involved in spreadsheet software interaction. *Human-Computer Interaction, 3*, 309-349.

Payne, S.J. (1988). Using models of users' knowledge to analyse learnability. In J.B. Long, & A.D. Whitefield (Eds.), *Cognitive ergonomics and human-computer interaction*. Cambridge: Cambridge University Press.

Payne, S.J., Sime, M.E., & Green, T.R.G. (1984). Perceptual structure cueing in a simple command language. *International Journal of Man-Machine Studies, 21*, 19-29.

Payne, S.J., & Green, T.R.G. (1986). Task-action grammars: A model of the mental representation of task languages. *Human-Computer Interaction, 2* (2), 93-133.

Payne, S.J., & Green, T.R.G. (1989). The structure of command languages: An experiment with task-action grammar. *International Journal of Man-Machine Studies, 30*, 213-234.

Pennington, N. (1987). Stimulus structures and mental representations in expert comprehension of computer programs. Cognitive Psychology, 19, 295-341.

Phillips, W.A., & Baddeley, A.D. (1989). Learning and memory. In A.D. Baddeley, & N.O. Bernsen (Eds.), *Cognitive Psychology. Research Directions in Cognitive Science: European Perspectives. Vol. 1*. Hove, UK: Lawrence Erlbaum Associates Ltd.

Polson, P.G. (1987). A quantitative theory of human-computer interaction. In J.M. Carroll (Ed.), *Interfacing thought*. Cambridge, MA: MIT Press.

Pomerantz, J. R. (1985). Perceptual organization in information processing. In A.M. Aitkenhead, & J. M. Slack (Eds.), *Issues in cognitive modelling*. Hove: Lawrence Erlbaum Associates.

Rasmussen, J. (1986a). *A cognitive engineering approach to the modelling of decision making and its organization*. Unpubublished manuscript, Risø National Laboratory, Roskilde, Denmark.

Rasmussen, J. (1986b). *Information Processing and Human-Machine Interaction*. North-Holland: Elsevier.

Rasmussen, J., & Rouse, W.B. (Eds.). (1981). *Human detection and diagnosis of system failures*. Plenum: New York.

Reason, J. (1987). Generic error-modelling system (GEMS): A cognitive framework for locating common human error forms. In J. Rasmussen, K. Duncan, & J. Leplat (Eds.), New technology and human error. John Wiley.

Reisner, P. (1981). Formal grammar and design of an interactive system. *IEEE Trans Software Engineering, 7*, 229-240

Riley, M. & O'Malley, C. (1984). Planning nets: A framework for analyzing user-computer interactions. In B. Shackel (Ed.), *INTERACT 84*. North-Holland: Elsevier.

Rist, R. (1986). Plans in programming: Definition, demonstration, and development. In E. Soloway, & S. Iyengar, (Eds.), *Empirical Studies of Programmers*. Norwood, NJ: Ablex.

Rizzo, A., Bagnara, S., & Visciola, M. (1987). Human error detection processes. *International Journal of Man-Machine Studies, 27*, 555-585.

Rosenbloom, P.S., Laird, J.E., & Newell, A. (1989). The chunking of skill and knowledge. In B.A.G. Elsendoorn, & H. Bouma (Eds.), *Working Models of Human Perception*. Academic Press.

Saariluoma, P., & Sajaniemi, J. (1989). Visual information chunking in spreadsheet calculation. International Journal of Man-Machine Studies, 30, 475-488.

Soloway, E., & Iyengar, S. (Eds.). (1986). *Empirical Studies of Programmers*. Norwood, NJ: Ablex.

Streitz, N. (1986) Cognitive ergonomics: An approach for the design of user-oriented interactive systems. In F. Klix, & H. Wandke (Eds.), *Man-Computer Interaction Research: Macinter 1*. North-Holland: Elsevier.

Suchman, L.A. (1987). *Plans and situated actions: The problem of human-machine communication*. Cambridge University Press.

Tauber, M. J. (1987). On mental models and the user interface. In G.C. van der Veer, T.R.G. Green, J.-M. Hoc, & D.M. Murray (Eds.), *Working with computers: Theory versus outcome*. London: Academic Press.

Visser, W. (1990). More or less following a plan during design: Opportunistic deviations in specification. *International Journal of Man-Machine Studies, 33*, 247-278.

Wagner, R.K., & Torgesen, J.K. (1987). The nature of phonological processing and its causal role in the acquisition of reading skills. Psychological Bulletin, 101, 192-212.

Whitefield, A. D. (1984). A model of the engineering design process derived from Hearsay-II. In B. Shackel (Ed.), INTERACT 84. North-Holland: Elsevier.

Whitefield, A.D. (1986). Human-computer interaction models and their use in computer system design. *Proceedings of the 3rd European Conference on Cognitive Ergonomics*. Paris: INRIA.

Whiteside, J., & Wixon, D. (1985). Developmental theory as a framework for studying human-computer interaction. In H.R. Hartson (Ed.), *Advances in Human-Computer Interaction I*. Norwood, NJ: Ablex.

Whiteside, J., & Wixon, D. (1987). Improving human-computer interaction - a quest for cognitive science. In J.M. Carroll (Ed.), *Interfacing thought*. Cambridge, MA: MIT Press.

Wilensky, R. (1982) Talking to Unix in English. *Proceedings: AAAI-2*, Carnegie-Mellon.

Wilson, M.D., & MacLean, A. (1986). Assessing cognitive aspects of learning and using computer systems. *Proceedings: ECCE 3, Third European Conference on Cognitive Ergonomics*. Paris: INRIA.

Wright, P., & Lickorish, A. (1988). Colour cues as location aids in lengthy texts on screen and paper. *Behaviour and Information Technology, 7*, 11-30.

Wright, P. (1989). The need for theories of NOT reading. In B.A.G. Elsendoorn, & H. Bouma (Eds.), *Working Models of Human Perception*. Academic Press.

Young, R.M. (1981). The machine inside the machine: Mental models of pocket calculators. *International Journal of Man-Machine Studies, 15*, 51-85.

Young, R.M., & Simon, T. (1987). Planning in the context of human-computer interaction. In D. Diaper, & R. Winder (Eds.), *People and computers III*. Cambridge: Cambridge University Press.

Young, R.M., Green, T.R.G., & Simon, T. (1989). Programmable user models for predictive evaluation of interface designs. *Proceedings of CHI 89*. New York: ACM.

Ziegler, J.E., Hoppe, H.U., & Fähnrich, K.P. (1986). Learning and transfer for text and graphics editing with a direct manipulation interface. *Proceedings of CHI 86*.

CHAPTER THREE

Human-Computer Interaction from the Viewpoint of Individual Differences and Human Learning

Gerrit C. van der Veer
Department of Psychology and Department of Computer Science, Free University, Amsterdam

INTRODUCTION

In the next decade the number of computer users may be expected to increase at an explosive rate. New uses of computers will reflect a variety of applications and of task domains, and a growth in structural complexity. The amount of expertise about these systems and the frequency of use will differ greatly between users and above all, user characteristics in the fields of cognition, strategies, styles and competence will be very diverse in the new user population.

There is still no end to technical development. Nowadays an explosion may be perceived in the introduction of microcomputers in job situations, in schools, and even in the home. Tremendous effort is invested in developing a fifth generation of computer systems, with new architectural concepts, more possibilities for adaptation and new "intelligent" ways of interacting with human partners. First drafts for a functionality and an architecture of the 6th generation are already being discussed. This might restrict the validity of scientific knowledge to a limited period of time.

Knowledge gained through cognitive psychological research may be applied to situations of learning in human-computer interaction (HCI). An overview of the state of the art in cognitive psychology, including a thorough review on learning and memory, will be found Volume 1 edited by Alan Baddeley. General aspects of human information processing in HCI is the topic of the contribution by Green (this volume). The current contribution focuses on individual differences in relation to learning with or about computers. To this end, an overview will be presented in part 1, showing the relevance of internal and external conditions of learning for the effects of the use of computers in learning situations.

It has to be emphasised that, for the immediate future, a teacher is irreplaceable in view of his unique human competence to deal with a wide variety of educational problems in interaction with considerable individual differences. In this respect the computer may be applied as a tool, with special possibilities to adjust to individual learning behaviour. In the future both the tool in itself, and the knowledge about its application will certainly improve, but human expertise is needed to realise the possibilities fully. But even if training technology is only developing gradually, the advantage of using a computer system is that the fast, flexible closed loop features can be employed to learn about the learner (Patrick & Stammers, 1981).

Users of a computer application need a clear and consistent knowledge structure of the system they interact with. This knowledge only concerns that part of the machine, that is directly relevant to the task delegation by the user to the system, the virtual machine or user interface. The cognitive ergonomic approach that will be illustrated in part 2 combines methods for the representation of the user interface or virtual machine, with the concept of mental model. The basic ideas are:

a. The mental model is an important cognitive aspect of the human-computer interaction (Norman, 1983);

b. specifying the virtual machine means defining explicitly the conceptual model for the user interface in a knowledge-based way;

c. the conceptual model can be described in a multi-level approach derived from Moran (1981), which should also apply to the user's mental model;

d. this conceptual model should be presented to the user, taking into account relevant characteristics of human learning and user variables.

Designers of the user interface and application interface should be aware of the fact that the future users of their systems will have to learn and understand the system. To this end, part 3 contains an investigation of the representational problems and possible solutions in an interdisciplinary approach to the design aspects of human-computer interaction. We try to solve the problem users face when confronted with a system they do not know in all its details (and which they may never be able to know completely), by the following method:

a. If there is an existing system we want to start with, then describe the user interface as part of the conceptual model of the application;

b. starting with the functionality of the goal system (from the task analysis and description of "natural" semantics), define the conceptual model for the user interface component of the intended computer application in such a way that it is acceptable from cognitive psychological and cognitive ergonomic viewpoints, taking care of interactions at the user interface, individual differences, and learning processes. This will include the construction of metacommunication (both implicit and explicit), and the development of metaphors to induce valid mental models;

c. with the help of feasible definition languages, construct a user interface according to the conceptual model as defined, providing mechanisms for adaptation to user differences.

1.INDIVIDUAL DIFFERENCES, LEARNING, AND COMPUTERS

The success of education is related to adaptation to individual differences. Whether optimal learning results can be expected may to a certain extend depend on the matching of the learning situation (including teaching style, level of difficulty, speed of presentation) to the characteristics of the student. Matching means tuning "tutor" and student to each other. This process may take two different directions:

a. Adaptation may take the form of educating the pupil in the direction of an "average" student, to which the learning conditions are optimally fit, or to a "good" student, who has mastered the necessary basic skills and obtained sufficient prior knowledge for participating in the learning discourse;

b. the learning situation may be adjusted to the individual student, accepting the fact that the end product of learning effort will not be of a uniform nature for different students. Both the resulting general level and the quality of knowledge and skills will divert.

Often the optimal teaching strategy combines elements of both. The most successful way of adaptation is determined by the possibilities for changing the students' characteristics.

1.1. Changeability of Individual Differences

Research on the possibilities to use computers in learning situations, and in situations where computing is the object of teaching, has shown a variety of results, with occasional cases of success and failure. At least some of these phenomena seem to be due to the fact that several of the characteristics at which individual students may differ are easy to affect, whereas in the case of other attributes an educator has to invest a lot of effort to produce a fair change. Some traits even seem to resist any influence from the outside world. In order to structure these observations, van Muylwijk, van der Veer, and Waern (1983) introduced a model of changeability of cognitive functions which is illustrated in Figure 3.1.

The dimension of changeability represents an indication of the ease with which cognitive functions may be changed. On the extreme left are located personality factors such as intelligence, introversion/extraversion and the negative fear of failure. These are generally considered to be stable features. It seems almost impossible to change them in a reasonable amount of time. As far as such stable personality traits define the learning process, adaptation of the learning environment is obvious.

stable, resistant to change			*mainly defined by current influence from the outside world*
←——————————————————————————————————————→			
personality factors:	*cognitive styles:*	*strategies:*	*knowledge structure:*
Intelligence	Field (in)dependence	Heuristic/ systematic	Episodic memory
Extraversion/ introversion	Visual/verbal		Semantic representation
Fear of failure	Operation/ comprehension learning	Serialist/holist	Rules
Creativity			Skills

FIG. 3.1. Dimension of changeability.

In the traditional educational situation, organised in levels of ability, only intelligence has been treated in this way.

At the extreme right-hand side, knowledge and skills are positioned. The content of episodic memory, the details of actual knowledge represented, rules, and skills are the result of influences of the environment (external conditions) in combination with more stable personality characteristics (internal conditions). In this model any cognitive faculty that is to the left of another is a determinant of qualities that are more to the right, in combination with outside influences. The development and adaptation of knowledge structure and strategies is a feasible goal for education, provided individual differences are taken into account.

In the middle of the dimension of changeability is the domain of cognitive styles such as field-dependence; problem-solving styles such as the concepts elaborated by Pask (1976); the domain of strategies such as a heuristic or algorithmic approach (De Leeuw, 1983); serialism or holism. Strategies are conceived as domain-specific and adjustable while cognitive styles are rather stable products of talent and education.

1.2. Computers and Adaptation in Learning: Internal and External Conditions

While illustrating the interaction between internal conditions (individual differences in cognitive functions) and external conditions (teaching on computers, facilities incorporated in computer systems and strategies of computer use) in learning, the dimension of changeability will act as a guideline.

In our analysis we can only present fragmentary knowledge. Most results stem from isolated studies and experiments. Black and Moran (1982) point to the fact that the results of research in the field of learning in the case of human-computer interaction are strongly dependent on the experimental situation and the representativity of the tasks. Experimental results should "be checked in more realistic situations". We propose an approach to cover systematically the domain of potentially relevant individual differences, testing their interaction with a computerised learning environment in real-life situations.

Our analysis will begin with the most readily changeable aspects of cognition.

1.2.1. Knowledge and Skills
The practice of elementary skills has been a very important contribution of the computer, ever since its introduction in education (cf. Suppes, 1979). This emphasis on exercises is in agreement with the increasing

attention of individual differences: skill training and exercises aiming at extending or reinforcing the personal knowledge structure are chosen by teachers both for remedial purposes, and for individual (self-paced) practice after the introduction of new material in the group. This form of computer use may replace group-wise exercises (which teachers tend to consider old-fashioned) and is more practical than individual coaching by the teacher of his many pupils.

Considerable gain in learning domains such as mathematics and logic is found when a computer program adapts the amount of detail of feedback and help to the actual behaviour of individual student. The success seems to be due to the possibilities of structuring the feedback: the hints provided by the programs may decrease in generality if more and more help is needed. In this way students will always be encouraged to solve at least part of the problem by themselves. However, if their attempts are unsuccessful, the problem can be split for them. In order to apply this method, it is a condition that the problem can be structured in a logical way (as seen from the point of view of the problem-solver).

In understanding text a different situation exists. Perfetti (1983) makes a distinction between two components of the process of human understanding of written language, supported by empirical evidence: (a) decoding, or pattern recognition, leading to the identification of the written units (words, phrases); (b) understanding, or integration of this decoded input with available knowledge. There is, however, an interaction between these components. Understanding will only be possible as far as the decoding process has been successful, whereas decoding might be improved by "guesswork", derived from understanding the environment of the fragment to be encoded. For bad readers the first aspect of reading behaviour requires a fair amount of attention at the expense of the second component, as both have to be effectuated within the limited capacity of the working memory. Perfetti reports positive effects of computer application in the domain of the first aspect only.

Practice of skills in interaction with a computer makes sense only if the activity of the program is directed at identifying or decomposing the real problem. Training higher level skills (understanding coherent text) in a situation where conditional lower ones (coding written material) are only partly mastered, requires more than just exercises on understanding. It will be necessary to account for differences in the availability of the basic skills, asking for a flexibility of adaptation that in some cases is difficult to effectuate in a computer program. However, the processing of natural language and the analysis of the semantics of a user's response would require a state of artificial intelligence that is not yet realised in actual educational situations.

From observations by Bernaert (1978) it may be concluded that it is often preferable to leave the introduction of new material to the teacher. Aspects of inter-human interaction, too delicate to analyse, let alone provide in a computer program, are essential to help the student build an initial representation of the domain to be mastered. After the introduction, the computer may be allocated the task of presenting exercises and allowing students to practise at their own pace. If, however, there exists a situation in which the computer should be used for introduction of new material, one should not allow novices to select the order of the units, but let the program guide them in a tutorial way. Only after they have received sufficient instruction and examples (and formed a reasonably valid mental model of the domain), should they be allowed to take control, choosing their own way of exploration.

1.2.2. Strategies of Learning

Strategies are readily changeable, although this takes time and effort. There are cases in which a teacher or a teaching computer program is preferred to adjust to the student. In other situations it might be better to have the student change their strategy.

a. Adaptation to Differences in Student Preferences for Strategies.

Van der Veer and Beishuizen (1986) show that the preference for strategies, like the distinction serialism/holism (Pask, 1976), depends on the task domain. They give an overview of the possibilities of application of these notions to computerised learning situations for adult students. Students profit considerably from a teaching strategy of a computer program (presenting verbal material in an order dependent on the inferred knowledge of the individual student of the separate elements of the domain), if this strategy matches the strategy of the student. None of the teaching strategies is generally to be preferred, nor is any of the learning strategies. A necessary condition for adaptation in this case is, to start with, an indication of the preferred strategy of individual students (for which testing procedures have to be available), or, alternatively, to have the students choose for themselves (from options that indicate clearly the kinds of teaching sequence available, and the possible reasons for choosing any of them).

In tasks concerning search in databases, individual strategies again may be distinguished. Beishuizen (1984) found that the search process can be facilitated by a computer coach that advises the searcher to be consistent in using a preferred method, although, generally speaking, individual approaches may be equally successful as long as they are maintained consistently. Adaptation to the individual computer user through coaching by the program (a kind of metacommunication, initiated by the computer program) again requires either the diagnoses of the preferred strategy or the presentation to the user of a reasonable opportunity to decide how they might like to be guided.

b. Education Towards Optimal Strategies.   In   learning   to   write computer programs, a distinction can be made between learning to structure one's problem solution (programming) and learning to code the solution into a computer language. Van der Veer (1983) found that the coding behaviour of novices showed striking individual differences; it proved to be systematically related to the amount of experience in mathematics. University students with no mathematical background used abbreviations and one-letter identifiers whenever possible, deteriorating the readability of their programs, and giving themselves the idea that they had only learned tricks. Students with some years of mathematical education wrote programs which were understandable and they mentioned having learned a useful way of attacking problems from the programming course. In another study on learning simple coding languages, the time needed for mastering the language turned out to be positively related to the amount of mathematical background, although students with or without a considerable amount of mathematical experience did not differ in performance on additional programming exercises after the language was mastered. The conclusion from these studies is that it might be useful to prevent the use of one-letter commands and object names (which means not adapting to individual preferences), and on the other hand, not to worry too much about the variability in prior experience with abstract notation. Experience with a simple coding language designed in view of these results showed that even primary school children are able to master the skill of coding, using names that are workable to them and that help them to remember the meaning of identifiers and procedures—provided their creativity does not prompt them to choose names with which the semantics associated are incompatible with the meaning in the program.

In studies on the application of structured diagrams ("real programming" in the sense of creating algorithmic solutions to problems) again differences were found in relation to mathematical background, resulting in differences in learning speed (van der Veer, van Beek, & Cruts, 1987). If, however, the choice of examples and the structure of the introduction did not suggest to novices that programming is related to symbol manipulation or mathematical skills, the dropping-out of students could be prevented, and learning to apply this graphical tool as a strategy in programming was possible for a wider range of students.

In the field of problem-solving, tutorial computer programs either emphasise a more heuristic approach, or teach an algorithmic approach to certain problems. The latter strategy always leads to correct solutions within the problem domain, but this gain is of restricted value. The transfer to problems of a related type, or to a related domain, shows that the same algorithm will not necessarily be valid, and on all occasions the algorithmic method loses its optimality as soon as transfer to a more remote domain is involved, whereas a heuristic strategy, even in these cases, may be applied. De Leeuw (1983), when experimenting with problem domains of arithmetic and logic, found transfer of problem-solving strategies to be facilitated by computer programs that were based on a heuristic approach (which was initially inferior for the learning results on the original domain, although a heuristic strategy showed improved performance in the long run).

1.2.3. Cognitive Styles: Adaptation to Individual Differences

This kind of individual differences is the result of a long-term interaction between stable personality characteristics and educational and cultural influences. In human-computer interaction one should not expect to be able to influence them, so adaptation to styles seems to be the only way to take differences into account.

a. Learning Styles from Conversation Theory.   Pask (1976) developed from his conversation theory several dimensions of cognitive style that describe relatively permanent ways of integrating new information (among other things applicable in human-computer situations): tendency to learn (amount of effort invested in collecting information); operation learning (tendency to or possibility of attending to details and tools to construct procedures); and comprehension learning (concentration on global relations, induction of general rules and descriptions). When somebody has the capacity to choose between these last two style dimensions in accord with the demands of the actual situation, Pask speaks of versatility.

Van der Veer and Beishuizen (1986) found positive relations between these styles and performance both in real-life courses on programming languages and in experiments on learning coding languages. Once a computer language is mastered, these individual differences seem to be less important, but when problems of an obscure abstract nature have to be solved, non-versatile subjects turn out to be deficient. In constructing exercises for programming courses, this should be taken into account.

b. Field Dependence.   The tendency to actively structure the situation (field independence) in contrast to being affected by irrelevant aspects in the environment (field dependence) is an important determinant of problem-solving behaviour. Field independent problem-solvers are able to apply a method in new, related domains. They perceive analogies and differences between old and new problem types, and they are more accurate in drawing schemes as an aid to problem-solving (De Leeuw, 1983). Field dependent students on the other hand, need more assistance during the problem-solving process, with levels of feedback varying from very general remarks to problem-specific hints. Facilities like this can be provided in computer environments. Adaptation to individual differences in this respect may be characterised as providing additional structure in the environment in which the students work.

1.2.4. Personality Factors
These group of factors are the most stable characteristics of cognitive behaviour. It does not make sense to invest effort in changing them by applying sophisticated tools if there is no theoretical base for this. Adaptation to the personality or the ability level of the pupil is the only possible way to give a fair chance to weak students in a human-computer situation. At this extreme of the dimension of changeability, observations will be presented of two variables: general ability level and "negative fear of failure".

   a. General Ability Level.   Bernaert (1978) and Kok (1984) present examples of situations in which the application of adequate computer-assisted teaching strategies compensate to a certain extent for the lack of ability of less intelligent students. For other types of student-computer interaction, intelligence is an important source of variation (Beishuizen & Brazier, 1984): in learning a programming language constructed especially for primary school children, there is a significant correlation between coding performance and intelligence, consistent with reports on the Brookline LOGO project (Watt, 1979). In both projects, however, even the weak students were capable of showing a certain level of creative behaviour in using a programming language, showing hidden talents that remained unexploited in traditional educational situations.

   b. Negative Fear of Failure.   Negative fear of failure may be characterised by a paralysing effect on achievement in situations throughout which the performance is observed by others, or is perceived as highly important for inter-human relations (examinations, public performances, competitions). De Leeuw (1983) investigated the extent to which fear of failure might be compensated for. Extensively structuring the situation is one form of compensation. Generally speaking, the students with negative fear of failure asked for more help. There is a positive effect of learning with computers: the computer is perceived as a non-human object, and students experience this as a safe situation, without the kind of competition that is so often threatening in other situations.

1.3. Current European Work

There is a large amount of European research on learning in relation to HCI. Barnard (1987) presents an overview of work on the impact of cognitive resources on learning in human-computer dialogues. Ideas on individual differences in cognitive functions, in relation to human computer interaction, have a relatively long tradition. Pask et al. (Pask, Kallikourdis & Scott, 1975; Entwhistle, 1978) describe issues such as knowledge representation, strategies and cognitive styles, in relation to learning in computerised environments. Hammond and Allinson (1988a) describe individual differences in the knowledge and choice of different available search facilities. Studies on the effect of individualisation in human-computer interaction have recently led to an overview of possibilities and effects (e.g. Ackermann, 1986; Ackermann & Ulich, 1987; Greutmann & Ackermann, 1987), and to ideas for application in industry (Frese, 1987). A taxonomy of adaptation in HCI is presented by Edmonds (1986). Clowes et al. (1985) and Benyon et al. (1987) show effects of adaptation on changing needs of the user, and give some ideas of the application of user profiles. Quilici et al. (1986) illustrate the relation of adaptation (aiming at the user's model of the system) to planning failures of users.

Benyon (1985) presents a prototype self-adaptive user interface, aimed at the needs of users and their changing requirements over time. The emphasis in this study is on the large and, thus far, much neglected "intermediate" class of users (between novices and experts) who still need a lot of attention (cf. Cooper & Hockley, 1986; Gardiner, 1986). Ulich (1987) also directs his research on individual differences for this intermediate group, investigating the interaction between HCI and related work activities, and personality development.

2. TEACHING COMPUTER SYSTEMS

In this section a cognitive ergonomic approach to questions on learning involving the use of computers and computer applications will be illustrated. The theoretical notions we apply are derived from Norman's analysis of system and models of the system (Norman, 1983); from

Moran's analysis of the user interface in different levels (Moran, 1981); from our analysis of individual differences and of the application of metaphors for teaching; and from van der Veer, Tauber, Waern, and van Muylwijk's analysis of the virtual machine and the role of teaching the user interface (van der Veer et al., 1985). Relating these notions we derive the following theses:

a. Application of Moran's levels of representing the user interface results in a description of the virtual machine or user interface. This description may be transformed into a teacher's conceptual model, tuned to a certain task domain and user group;

b. metaphors may be designed for teaching, consistent with the different levels of the conceptual model;

c. a method may be developed to acquire a scientist's conceptualisation of the mental models that results from teaching, in particular concerning the quality of the mental model, and of the user's way of representation;

d. users will differ in their mental models, depending on their *a priori* knowledge of the external task domain and of related systems, and depending on their preferred style of representation of information: verbalising or visualising.

2.1 System and Models of the System

Norman (1983) makes a distinction between a system, the conceptual model of the system, the mental model of the system, and the scientist's conceptualisation of the mental model:

a. Target System.   This refers to the physical object, e.g. a computer system.

b. Conceptual Model.   This involves a correct description of the target system, as far as the human-machine interface is concerned; an accurate and consistent representation, that is invented or developed by a teacher and/or designer. This includes both relevant aspects of hardware, of screen and keyboard (meaningful for the user, e.g. audible signals on hitting keys that do not have a meaning in the current mode, blinking cursors), and application software, as far as the user interacts with these. The aim of teaching a novice is to transmit this model.

c. Mental Model.   This concept denotes the knowledge structure the user applies in his interaction with the computer. The user predicts reactions of the system to his own behaviour. Decisions and planning are based on the mental model, as are explanations of unexpected system behaviour. This model evolves during interaction with the target system, especially in the initial learning phase. A user "understands" a system if predictions based on his mental model are consistent with the behaviour of the user interface of the target system. Or, in other words, if his mental model maps completely to the relevant part of the conceptual model, e.g. the user virtual machine. Unexpected effects and errors point to inconsistency between the mental model and the conceptual model.

d. The Scientist's Conceptualisation of the Mental Model.   This is the idea the psychologist or researcher has about the mental model of the user.

Streitz (1986) further developed these notions, especially aiming at the functionality of a system S(f); the user's mental model of the realised system U(S(f)); and the scientist's conceptualisation of the mental model Sc(U(S(f))). He presents empirical evidence for the importance of cognitive compatibility between the system's functionality and the mental model.

2.2. The User Interface

The central point in teaching a human-machine system is the definition and representation of the user interface (van der Veer, Tauber, Waern, & van Muylwijk, 1985). There are many different points of view about what exactly the interface is. Interfaces are connecting two communicating actors (independent system components) and can be regarded as the set of mutual suppositions.

When the computer is used as a tool for performing a set of well defined tasks (a task space), the user needs a set of assumptions about the "user's virtual machine" (UVM). Virtual means that the machine must be seen only in respect to the defined task space, in the way in which the machine is able to perform these tasks and in the way in which the user can specify the delegation of tasks to the system.

Therefore the user interface must be regarded as a whole in a conceptual sense, as the representation of the virtuality of the machine. The specification of the user interface can be regarded as a conceptual model, intended to be a complement to the intended mental model of the user (Rohr & Tauber, 1984).

2.3. Representation of Conceptual Models

Moran (1981) proposed a representational framework in his "Command Language Grammar" (CLG), enabling the description of the conceptual model of the user interface on the one hand, and the intended mental model of the user on the other hand. An important aspect in the CLG is the description of knowledge about the human-computer interaction in four levels. The first two levels refer to the functionality of the system. The lowest CLG level is the Interaction level. In our analysis we need to represent physical aspects of interaction as far as they are meaningful to the user, and thus we replace this level by a key-stroke level.

a. Task Level.   This level concerns the actual tasks for which the system may be used, their relations, and the integration of sub-tasks to be delegated to the system and sub-tasks delegated to other instances or completed by the human user. The task delegated to the computer system is defined by an object world (containing objects, object structures and the state of the world) and a set of operations working on the object world (producing new objects, changing the state of the object world). All tasks of the virtual machine may be defined by means of the task space. The conceptual model consists of a complete review of the possibilities in this respect.

At the task level it should be noted that a user always regards a computer system as a tool to perform a task. Applying a system, at this level, may be described as the delegation of sub-tasks to the machine. Knowledge of the target system (the mental model) involves understanding which sub-tasks may, and which may not, be delegated. This means that a user not only needs a list of sub-tasks that the system can perform, but also requires an explicit account of how these sub-tasks can be delegated as part of an envisaged task. The particular task may be a familiar one or one which has been added due to the new possibilities offered by the system. In either case, the user needs to relate the system to the task in question. It may be difficult to incorporate sensible metacommunication at task level in the user interface (van der Veer, Tauber, Waern, & van Muylwijk, 1985). Teaching and documentation will have to supply this, outside the system.

b. Semantic Level.   Based on the task space is the semantic level of the human-machine interaction. This consists of the representation of the object world in the interface, the representation of the operations provided by the system to manipulate the system's object world, and of the relations between the relevant objects. The semantic level is the description of the functions of the system regarding the task space.

Semantics may be generalised for different systems for the same task domain or different implementations or releases of one system.

Singley and Anderson (1985) showed strong positive transfer in learning a new editor with the same semantics as a known one. There is a problem about the relation between task level and semantic level however. The UVM's objects and their relations cannot always be consistently analogous to the objects and relation in the user's task space. If the system is designed without sufficient reflection upon the user's problems in developing a mental model, the structure of the semantic level may be incongruous with the structure of the task level.

The task level maps down into the conceptual operations and conceptual entities within the semantic level of the users' virtual machine. As users learn about a system, their mental models are revised. If a system recognises that a user cannot achieve a task successfully then some remedial interaction (metacommunication) concerning the semantics should be taken. On a simple view, this could take the form of a change in the error messages and related information. This metacommunication can also be adaptive (Fischer, Lemke, & Schwab, 1984) and the construction should aim at improving the ease of learning of an application system. Hence there is a strong and complex interaction between the application system and the metacommunication (Rich, 1983).

c. Syntactic Level.   This level gives the commands available for accomplishing the conceptual operations defined at the semantic level. System objects must be described and system operations must be evoked by the user. This linguistic component of the interface is captured at the syntactic level. It defines the commands and their meaning (procedures or operations triggered by the command); the context in which commands are valid; the descriptors for the objects; the "state" variables (remembered by the system between two commands); and the organisation of the output devices. The syntactic level is strongly system-dependent. If the communication is not in a kind of "natural language", it is useless to define the syntax in analogy to human language. However, if one has to use different systems, negative transfer may result if the different syntaxes are built on different kinds of structure, or even lack any kind of consistency. The conceptual integration of knowledge on a semantic level and a syntactic level also increases by consistency in syntactic rules. Inconsistency in systems for different commands with related semantics leads to a disadvantage for the user (Green, 1984).

There are many guidelines (Shneiderman, 1980) provided at this level regarding, for example, uniformity and consistency in command language syntax. The syntax level includes naming conventions and the use of mnemonics in commands, and these are particularly important to users. Unless the link between the syntax level and the semantic level is established through transparent intermediaries (e.g. visual metaphors and icons), users can have considerable difficulty. These can be overcome by metacommunication.

d. Key Stroke Level. In Moran's terminology, this level is called the "interaction level", but we prefer the label "key stroke", because "interaction" is in other contexts often used to denote the entire human-computer interaction including all four levels. On this level, the commands must be specified by actions like key strokes or pointing activities, followed by perceptible system behaviour (e.g. sounds to indicate "illegal" commands, locking keys in certain contexts, changes on the screen, reaction time of the system, attention-provoking cues like blinking of screen messages). This level of the user interface is always (terminal) hardware dependent.

The dialogue interactions through physical devices is defined at this level and maps directly into the syntax level. Dialogue modes (e.g. natural language, menu, command, graphical), are partially equivalent at a syntax level and it is possible to separate this level out for implementation.

In teaching a computer application, the actual goal of the learning process will not always be a mental model that is complete at all levels. When the aim is to acquire an overview of the functional properties of a new system, e.g. for the purpose of decision-making at an organisational level, knowledge at task level and at semantic level are most important; when the aim is to educate users to become experts on a system, the syntax level is also important; if the task of a user is to do a terminal operator's job supervised by a task expert, interaction level and syntax level are most important.

2.4. Development of Mental Models

The development of cognitive representations of computing systems or user interfaces is a process in which structures in semantic memory are built or changed. The process of acquisition or change of mental representations is generally considered to be strongly based on analogies: known concepts and structures are related to the new situation. This process can be activated if the teacher refers to existing semantic knowledge and schemes. Metaphors may be used to activate knowledge and act as analogies. These metaphors should be presented as such, not as actual representations of the new system (Simons, 1980). The choice of appropriate metaphors is crucial for the development of adequate mental models (Carroll & Thomas, 1982; Carroll, 1983; Clanton, 1983; Houston, 1983). Several distinct metaphors might be referred to for the same conceptual model, each illustrating a few aspects of the new system to be learned (Rumelhart & Norman, 1983). In generating metaphors it should be kept in mind that the capacity of the working memory is restricted to a limited number of chunks (units of meaning that may be handled as one item and are only expanded when necessary). Metaphors that are too rich in composition distract too much attention and may obstruct the learning process. These have to be broken down into manageable sub-structures when presented to the student.

Metaphors are often proposed as a way to establish an adequate mental model of computer systems or of computing. A metaphor in principle consists of well-known concepts, activated as an analogy to a new concept or situation. With the help of the semantic relations already present, this should organise the thinking and learning, hence the name "advanced organiser". Foss, Rosson and Smith (1982) present the traditional example of the filing cabinet applied to learning an editor; Peelle (1983) describes different categories of metaphors and related approaches to be used in education about computers; Lawson (1982) presents elaborate examples of some metaphors, intended for a first introduction to computer systems.

Halasz and Moran (1982) point to dangerous aspects of this approach, especially when the student is left alone and encouraged to reason analogically. In using a single analogy, the teacher will soon discover that the metaphor requires adjustment, adding new (and often bizarre) features to it or, alternatively, combining various metaphors that are not normally associated. Waern (1987) presents examples of difficulties with the typewriter metaphor for the purpose of introducing text editor systems. Maass (1983) advocates systems transparency in this respect.

On the other hand, metaphors might still be useful as analogies to the conceptual models to be taught, according to Halasz and Moran (1982), if the student is clearly aware of the fact the metaphors are only valid in respect to certain aspects of the system or process to be modelled. In that case, several distinct metaphors might be referred to for the same conceptual model, each illustrating a few aspects of the new system to be learned. The teacher has to be active in directing the associations of the students, and in drawing the analogies, at the same time pointing to the limits of applicability of each metaphor.

The analysis and description of the virtual machine often reveals inconsistencies in the user interface, due to the fact that the system has been assembled from a set of originally independent tools, combined with new facilities that were designed on behalf of the integration. The inconsistencies will be especially evident for syntax details of commands in relation to the semantics, for naming of objects and actions, and for texts supporting metacommunication. The teacher may have the choice of solving this problem by deliberately defining a consistent teacher's conceptual model, deviating from the target system, pointing to the occasions of mismatch between the conceptual model he presents and the actual user virtual machine, calling these exceptions, or even bugs in the design of the system.

2.5. Individual Differences in the Acquisition of Mental Models

Novice users of a system differ on a number of relevant features:

a. A Priori Knowledge.   Users who possess adequate mental models of systems that are relevant in the same or in analogous task domains as the system at hand have a good base for analogical reasoning (Waern, 1983). These systems may be computer systems, but for a lot of task domains computerless systems (e.g. office systems) exist that cover the same tasks.

b. Style of Information Processing.   Individual style of information processing not only results in preferences for different modes of presentation of learning material and of metaphors, it also leads to individual differences in the organisation of semantic knowledge and in different representations of this knowledge (i.e. in individually different mental models). It has been shown that the distinction between verbal and image representation style is relevant (van Muylwijk, van der Veer & Waern, 1983), as may be the difference between the dimensions of operation learning and comprehension learning, or between the strategies serialism and holism.

c. Stable Characteristics.   Other individual differences that might be relevant in the way novice users acquire a mental model are more stable characteristics like field dependency, general intelligence and spatial ability (Rothkopf, 1986).

In evaluating the resulting changes in the cognition of the novice user, we encounter the problem of the observability of representations of mental models. A feasible solution for "the scientist's conceptualisation of the mental model" (Norman, 1983; Streitz, 1986) consists of retrospective interviews and a "teach back method" (asking the student to express to somebody else an overview of what has just been learnt).

Other variables of interest concern transfer of the knowledge and strategies acquired: to other systems, to other levels of the conceptual model, and to a later phase in the use of the system.

2.6. European Effort and Prospects

European studies on teaching the conceptual model of a system include Du Boulay, O'Shea and Monk (1981). The cognitive aspects of novices' use of computer systems is reviewed by Allwood (1986). Allwood points to the large variability within this group of users in their representations of the system, in comparison to experts. Du Boulay and O'Shea (1981) mention the effect of programming language type on the semantic errors of novices. This may relate to the mechanism of development of mental models (Allwood and Wikström, 1986). Payne and Green (1986) define a task-action grammar (TAG), providing a formal description of the decomposition of simple tasks into actions by the user on the user interface. In this way they model the mental representation of an "ideal" user's interaction with a system, and enable the derivation of indications of learnability of computer applications (as functions of the set of rewriting rules).

A large amount of both theoretical and empirical work has been done by Barnard and colleagues. Just to give some examples: problem-solving as characteristic for users' initial behaviour, and fragmentary mental models as the primary source of failures are described by Barnard, Maclean and Hammond (1984). Wilson, Barnard and Maclean (1985) report an analysis of the learning of command sequences in menu systems. Hammond and Allinson (1988b) report work on constructing metaphors for teaching complex systems, and their analysis of metaphor use is based on a level approach derived from Moran.

The development of knowledge about teaching computer systems and the effect of metaphors and of the UVM on users' mental models, knowledge representation and skills, still needs a lot of investment. Research will have to aim at large-scale and longitudinal field studies on application systems, not only focusing on either novices or experts, but taking the situation of intermediate users and occasional users into consideration.

On the other hand, controlled experiments have to be conducted on realistic examples of learning applications and transfer between systems and languages, localising the effects of representation model, choice of metaphors, and individual differences in learning characteristics and experience.

3. DESIGNING FOR THE MENTAL MODEL

Users of a computer application need clear and consistently structured knowledge of the system they interact with. This knowledge only concerns the part of the machine that is directly relevant to the task delegation by the user to the system: the UVM. The cognitive ergonomic approach that will be illustrated in this section combines design techniques and methods for the representation of the user virtual machine with the mental model concept. The question of how to represent systems, interfaces, and models of systems will be analysed from two different aspects, the "human factors" approach and the "informatics" approach. Figure 3.2 presents a schematic representation of the different concepts and their relations in these two domains.

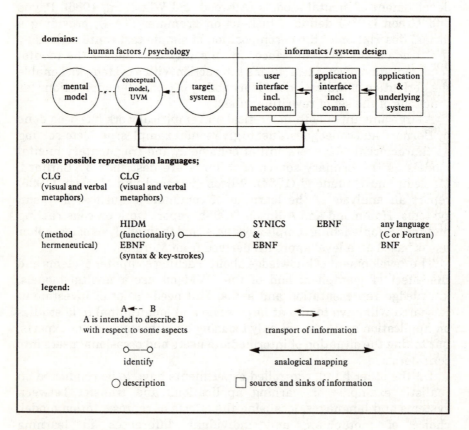

FIG. 3.2. Relations between representations.

3.1. The Domain of Human Factors (Psychology)

The relation between the target system and the conceptual model may be defined as follows: The conceptual model is intended to describe the target system with respect to some aspects. The same definition is valid for the relation between the conceptual model and the mental model. The UVM is a special kind of conceptual model, defined for a circumscribed user group and a specified task domain.

In order to analyse and define the conceptual model, and to analyse the mental representation of users, representation languages are necessary (the aim of these representations is scientific analysis, not direct communication to the user. For that last goal, a translation of formal representation to metaphors has to be made). The representations applicable for these different concepts will differ, relevant to the nature of the models (or the system). The four levels of Moran's CLG provide a framework for description of both the mental model and the conceptual model. CLG failed, however, as a design tool (Browne, Sharratt, & Norman, 1986), providing no slots for heuristics at the semantic level. Later on Sharratt (1987) replaced parts of CLG for a prototyping tool. In order to collect information on actual mental models a hermeneutic method of analysis may be useful (van der Veer, 1989). For the representation of the functionality (task level and semantic level) of the conceptual model, the "Heidelberg Interface Description Method" (HIDM, Tauber, 1988) may be used. This is a formal representation of the UVM and the interaction language, derived from TAG, and employing concepts that are borrowed from psycho-linguistic description methods (Jackendoff, 1983). For both the syntax and keystroke level a multi-party grammar is needed, e.g. an extension of the BNF notation (EBNF, Innocent et al, 1988). For our purposes it is irrelevant to give an exact description of the target system.

The development of the conceptual model may start from two different sources: either an existing system is described with respect to its relevance to the user, or a conceptual model is defined from the analysis of the functionality of some intended human-computer interaction.

In any case, an analysis has to be made of metacommunication aspects of the user interface. This concept denotes all communication between the user and any source of information on how to interact with the system. It includes on-line help facilities and on-line coaching, and also documentation, teaching, and consultation of available experts. The design of metacommunication will have to start from knowledge of the user group and of possible relevant user variables, and has to take into account human learning mechanisms. The metaphorical aspects of the intended metacommunication will have to refer to existing semantic knowledge and schemes.

3.2. The Domain of Systems Design (Informatics)

In this domain the components of the system to be designed or to be adapted are linked by lines of information flow. Therefore a protocol must be adopted to ensure the integration of this communication. The components may exist as independent processes, or groups of processes. In other cases the components may be combined in a single process. We apply a distinction between system, application, interfaces, and different types of communication.

a. User Interface.   The user communicates only directly with the user interface. The user interface includes both explicit metacommunication, and implicit metacommunication aspects of mnemonics and tokens.

b. Application and Application Interface.   The application interface includes all communication between the user and the application regarding task delegation. All communication between the user and the application interface goes through the user interface, where tokens and mnemonics may be transformed on behalf of implicit metacommunication.

c. The System.   The user interface and application(s) are supported by a computer-based system. Functions like data storage and retrieval are processed by the host system. Such functions may introduce time delays at the application interface, and hence at the user interface.

d. Communication.   Information is communicated between the user, the user interface, application and system relating to data objects and control. Information may come from different system layers following strict protocols, finally arriving at the application layer. Some information may relate to the state of the system/application/user interface. For example, if a network breaks down, higher levels are informed, including the user. Communication between the system and the user is normally through the user interface.

e. Metacommunication.   This refers to the communication of information between a user and the system about how to communicate. Within the process of interaction, users may be given help about entities in the system space. For example, help requests and error messages are often explicitly about the syntax or the semantics of commands. The mnemonic or icon chosen to represent a token (command or prompt) in the user interface may implicitly refer to semantic aspects of the object or command that is denoted. One of the aims of metacommunication is to adapt the user interface to the user's needs. User interfaces may be designed that contain a special module for advice-giving or coaching. Carroll and McKendree (1987) give an analysis of intelligent metacommunication systems and point to the deficiency in current research and theoretical structure in this respect.

Metacommunication may also refer to information on the interaction that is exchanged outside the system proper. Alty and Coombs (1980), Coombs and Alty (1981) and Lawson (1982) found that documentation and advisory services (metacommunication) especially for novices tend to be totally unsatisfactory. Analysis of their findings shows that the novices' questions and the explanations provided (from the domain of informatics) seem to refer to incompatible semantic knowledge representations of task delegation to the system. Allwood (1986) points to the importance of better error message systems and better design of manuals.

For every component of an informatics system there are different languages for description. An interface description method (Guest, 1986) will be needed for the user interface (including metacommunication), and a multi-party grammer like EBNF (Innocent, 1982) for the application interface (including communication about the task delegation by the user to the application). Several languages will generally be available for defining the system. It should be noted that an interface description language like SYNICS (Guest, 1982) has EBNF as a sub-set of its pattern match. This can provide the ability to implement the application interface in an environment that facilitates rapid prototyping.

3.3. The Relation Between the Two Domains of Representation

There is a complete, analogical mapping of the conceptual model (including the user virtual machine) of the "human factors domain" to the user interface and the application interface of the "informatics domain" and vice versa. In fact they represent exactly the same, but are merely seen from two different points of view. Depending on the case, this mapping may start from the systems designer describing a system on behalf of the users, or from a human factors specialist defining an intended conceptual model to the designer. EBNF notation may bridge the gap between the two disciplines, enabling them to communicate in a uniform and unambiguous way.

As the mental model is intended to describe the conceptual model with respect to some aspects, it can be said to be aiming to describe the user interface and application interface.

The target system is a concept that can be used in the "psychological domain" to refer to everything in the "systems designer domain", including the physical aspects of the computer system.

3.4. Adaptation and the User Interface

Adaptation in human-computer interaction is directed at adjustment to individual differences. Optimal interaction is only to be expected if the user interface (including the metacommunication) closely matches the characteristics of the user. There are situations in which matching is impossible, since the abilities needed to perform a certain task are beyond an individual's potentialities. Selection of users (possibly self-selection) is the only way to solve this problem. Matching means tuning the system and the user to each other. This process may take two different directions:

a. Adaptation may take the form of an educational activity, taking care of individual differences among users, their special wishes, abilities and problems, aiming at changing the human partner and at improving the individual's possibilities. The educational activity can take place either within or outside the computer system. Within the system, education can take the form of a tutorial, separated from the main activity (in fact creating a new application part), or, alternatively, it may consist of adaptive help- and error-messages, related to the user's main activity, thus comprising real metacommunication (located in the user interface), aiming at adaptation of the user's knowledge and skills towards the requirements for adequate communication with the system;

b. The interface may react to the individual user's task delegation in a flexible way; the system adapts itself to the user. In this case the designer will have to accept the fact that the mode and quality of interaction will not be of a uniform nature for different users. To accomplish adaptation, the user interface must be constructed with a built-in model of the user, tailored to the relevant characteristics of each individual user. The required data about the user can be obtained by asking each user (before the session is started, or on request during the session) or by diagnosing the user during the session. The adaptation of the interface can then take place either by the user (customisation), or automatically by the system. Customisation should be preferred in order not to confuse users about the characteristics of the user's virtual not to confuse users about the characteristics of the user's virtual machine. In this case different options are offered to the user, for instance for help, undo, documentation and renaming. The system may even offer users a choice of interaction formats. Automatic adaptation may be recommended for cases where the system detects simple, recurring errors in the user's interaction behaviour. A user who consistently writes "flie" instead of "file", for instance, could be helped by a system which understands what is meant and does not ask every time the misspelling occurs.

Often the optimal situation combines elements of both directions. The most successful way of adaptation is determined by the possibilities and desirability of changing the user's characteristics and by properties of the task domain.

3.5. European Efforts and Prospects

Design of user interfaces and of human-computer dialogues is related to characteristics of the user. Hammond and Barnard (1984) illustrate the impact of novice user knowledge on their learning behaviour and use of computer systems. To this end they report both field studies and laboratory research. The direction of research is turning towards the design of application systems and the design in relation to individual differences. In most cases the aim is to provide a flexible user interface (Tauber, 1988), and not a variety of different systems for different users. Frese (1987) studies human-computer interaction on office systems; Allwood and Eliasson (1986) study text editing in relation to individual differences; Mayes et al (1987) investigates the effect of cognitive styles and prior computing experience on the user behaviour at user-driven adaptive interfaces; Heim (1987) illustrates possibilities to design an application generator in such a way as to decrease the negative effects of the lack of special abilities of users learning a 4th generation application.

An interdisciplinary approach is indispensable in this domain (Baecker & Buxton, 1987). The framework we propose should enable designers of a user interface and human factors specialists, to communicate about design guidelines, and about design rules for a generalised user environment (Monk, 1985). This communication between the two disciplines should be the basis for the design architecture and the content or functionality of the modules. The framework (Brünning & Milbredt, 1988) is structured in modules. It presents the idea of separate machines or "acting agents" (i.e. distinguishable functions from the human factors point of view) working on circumscribed data collections, also called channels or "descriptions".

a. The acting agents, represented in the figures by rectangles, may be called machines that are defined only by their functionality from the point of view of human factors (communication on task delegation, metacommunication, coaching, diagnosis, help, inference of user plans);

b. The descriptions, indicated by ellipses, denote collections of knowledge the acting agents will have to apply (a model of the user, knowledge of external task domain, semantics, syntax, lexicon, history of the interaction, the "blackboard"). Descriptions of this type enable agents to store and retrieve information in an order that is free to the choice of the agent. These descriptions have the function of sources and sinks of information. The content will have to be provided, depending on their character, by acting agents like teachers, external task domain specialists, psychologists, and designers of the application interface. Some types of descriptions may be provided by acting agents inside the user interface (e.g. a log analyser producing a user model). The structure of a description has to be distinct from its content. The structure (or script) has to be defined by an acting agent, as a special activity that might be called an existential event.

Some of these objects can be materialised in different languages, e.g. a communication module in SYNICS or any state transition diagram implementation, a process inference machine in PROLOG, applying HIDM descriptions to parse the log.

Information transport is denoted by a single arrow (A denotes an agent, and D a description), where A → D means that A may send information to D, and where A ← D means that A requires input from D. Several agents may transport information to the same description, and several may collect information from it. In cases when two acting agents exchange information via a simple channel (of the type first-in-first-out), we expand the notation by an arrowed circle Ai---O--→Aj, indicating that Ai sends information to Aj (indicating that from the point of view of human factors the information transfered does not need to be described in any level of detail).

For the control structure related to this design framework, different solutions might be proposed (e.g. Winston's chapter on control metaphors, 1984; and ANSA architecture guidelines, Herbert & Monk, 1987). This has to be elaborated by systems designers in relation to technical development and architecture of systems and networks. A fundamental requirement will be the preservation of modularity, to enable the exchange of acting agents or descriptions for reasons of prototyping, research, improvement, and application to new task domains, or, for the same task domain, to new target systems.

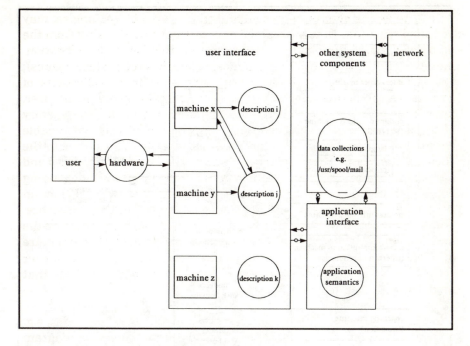

FIG. 3.3. User interface and relation to environment.

Figure 3.3 shows the overall framework indicating the user interface in relation to the user, the application and the underlying system and network. This is related to Figure 3.2. For the purpose of illustration, some examples of information transport are indicated in the user interface, which is only filled in an abstract way.

The description called "application semantics" denotes the semantics of the UVM. These are defined by the designer of an application interface. They need to be formally described, e.g. with HIDM. Although this description is located in the application interface, it will be consulted by different acting agents that are located inside the user interface proper.

Figure 3.4 shows details of a possible user interface containing the functionality of communication between user and application, and metacommunication of various types. Only some acting instances that might be located inside the user interface are mentioned, with examples of sources of information they might need:

Monitor Machine.   The function of this agent is to guard the integrity of the doorkeeper activities (e.g. no loops), to support the traffic going

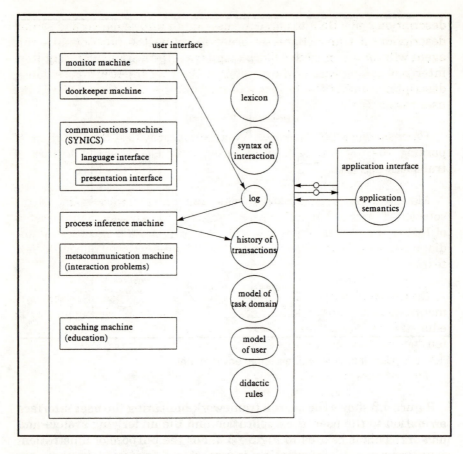

FIG. 3.4. Possible structure of a modularised user interface.

on in the user interface's control mechanism, and to maintain the log collection.

Doorkeeper Machine. The main function of this agent is the reception and distribution of communication, and to control priorities. A possible structure for the doorkeeper might be a blackboard or a bus architecture to all acting agents inside the user interface (apart from the monitor), resulting in an object-centered control mechanism.

Communication Machine. The communication of task delegation transactions between the user and the application interface is the function of this agent. Therefore it may request information from semantic, lexicon and syntax descriptions. It may apply HIDM description and EBNF to parse the user input into semantic and syntax description of transactions. In order to refine the functionality, this agent will contain modules like a language interface and a presentation interface, taking care of the parsing of the user input into a semantic description, and of the format and mode of the messages towards the user respectively.

Process Inference Machine.   This agent provides the function of parsing the log into a (session-based and user specific) history of transactions.

Metacommunication Machine.   The function of this agent is the solution of interaction problems, cf. a "passive" help system in the sense of Fisher, Lemke, and Schwab (1984). It will contain modules for the diagnostics of the user's problem and for the production of adequate help texts.

Coaching Machine.   In fact this is a special type of metacommunication machine, with the functions of coaching and education of users. This will have to be modularly designed in its turn (an "active" help system, cf. Fischer et al, 1984; Carroll, 1987).

The set of associated descriptions may contain:

Lexicon.   This will mostly be defined by a designer, but it could be an experienced user in certain situations. The lexicon may include non-verbal concepts: icons, interaction tokens like movements with a mouse or "glove", and sounds have to be defined in the lexicon.

Syntax of User-machine Interaction.   Defined by designers of HCI language, the representation language for the syntax might be a multi-party grammar like EBNF.

Log.   This denotes a substraction from processes going on at the monitor, preserving all relevant aspects of interaction in its "raw" appearance.

History of Transactions.   This history is defined by a process inference machine, as a result of the analysis of the original log. It contains a list of transaction between user and system.

Knowledge of External Task Domain.   For the definition of a model of the task domain a cooperation between a human factors specialist and a designer (often complemented by an expert at the task domain) will be needed. In case of complicated functionality and an elaborate body of task knowledge, special methods of knowledge engineering and expert systems design have to be applied. In relatively simple cases a formal method like HIDM might be applicable.

The Machine's Model of the User.   This might be defined, for example, by a teacher, or by the actual user, but a much more flexible method is to have certain aspects of it defined and continuously maintained by a diagnostic agent (see Carroll, 1987).

Didactic Rules for Coaching.   An expert on teaching seems to be the best source for this description.

In future research on the user interface, the different modules will have to be isolated in their functions. The modular approach enables the designer to adapt a simple prototype for those elements in the structure that are not the object of experimentation in a single study, at the same time providing a complete system for the user. Separate experimental studies should be combined with field studies on integrated user interfaces for real life applications.

REFERENCES

Ackermann, D. (1987). Handlungsspielraum, Mentale epräsentation und Handlungsregulation am Beispiel der Mensch-Computer-Interaktion. *Inauguraldissertation*. Zurich: ADAG Administration & Druck AG.

Ackermann, D., & Ulich, E. (1987). On the question of possibilities and consequences of individualisation of human-computer interaction. In M.Frese, E. Ulich, & W. Dzida (Eds.), *Psychological issues of human-computer interaction*. Amsterdam: North-Holland.

Allwood, C.M. (1986). Novices on the computer: A review of the literature. In B.R.Gaines, & D.R. Hill (Eds.), *International Journal of Man-Machine Studies, 25* (6), 633-658.

Allwood, C.M., & Eliasson, M. (1986). Analogy and other sources of difficulties in novices' very first text editing. *Göteborg Psychological Reports, 16*, No. 6.

Allwood, C.M., & Wikström, T. (1986). Learning complex computer programs. *Behaviour and Information Technology, 5*, 217-225.

Alty, J.L., & Coombs, M.J. (1980). Face-to-face guidance of university computer users-1. A study of advisory services. *International Journal of Man-Machine Studies, 12*, 389-406.

Baecker, R.M., & Buxton, W.A.S. (1987). *Readings in human-computer interaction : a multidisciplinary approach*. Los Altos, CA: Morgan Kaufmann.

Barnard, P.J., Maclean, A., & Hammond, N.V. (1984) User representations of ordered sequences of command operations. In B. Shackel (Ed.), *Proceedings of*

Interact '84, First IFIP Conference on "Human-Computer Interaction". Amsterdam: Elsevier.

Barnard, P. (1987). Cognitive resources and the learning of human-computer dialogs. In J.M. Carroll (Ed.), *Interfacing thought: Cognitive aspects of human-computer interaction* (pp. 112-158). Cambridge, MA: MIT Press.

Beishuizen, J.J. (1984), Informatie verzamelen in een bibliotheek: Coaching en zoekstrategie ën. In A. Dirkzwager, S.D. Fokkema, G.C. van der Veer, & J.J. Beishuizen (Eds.), *Leren met computers in het onderwijs.* Den Haag: S.V.O.

Beishuizen, J.J., & Brazier, F.M.T. (1984). Leren programmeren op de basisschool. In A. Dirkzwager, S.D. Fokkema, G.C. van der Veer, & J.J. Beishuizen (Eds.), *Leren met computers in het onderwijs.* Den Haag: S.V.O.

Benyon D. (1985). Monitor: A self-adaptive user interface. In B.Shackel (Ed.), *Proceedings of Interact '84, First IFIP Conference on "Human-Computer Interaction".* Amsterdam: Elsevier.

Benyon D., Innocent P., & Murray D. (1987). System adaptivity and the modelling of stereotypes. In H.J. Bullinger, & B. Shackel (Eds.), *Proceedings of Interact '87, the second IFIP Conference on Human-Computer Interaction.* Amsterdam: Elsevier, 245-253.

Bernaert, G.F. (1978). *Sturing in het onderwijsleerproces, cognitieve capaciteit en leersituatie.* Den Haag: S.V.O.

Black, J., & Moran, T. (1982). Learning and remembering command names. *Proceedings of the Conference on Human Factors in Computer Systems, Gaithersburg.*

Browne, D.P., Sharratt, B., & Norman, M.A. (1986). The formal specification of adaptive user interfaces using CLG. In M. Mantei, & P. Orbiton, (Eds.), *Human Factors in Computing Systems. Proceedings of CHI 86.* New York: ACM.

Brüning, H., & Milbredt T. (1988). *Architecture description by "Black Forest" diagrams.* Darmstadt (FRG): Darmstadt Institute of Technology, Department of Computer Science.

Carroll, J.M. (1983, December). Presentation and form in user-interface architecture. *Byte,* 113-122.

Carroll, J.M., & Thomas, J.C. (1982). Metaphor and the cognitive representation of computing systems. *IEEE Transactions on Systems, Man, and Cybernetics, 12,* 107-116.

Carroll, J.M., & McKendree, J. (1987). Interface design issues for advice-giving expert systems. *Communications of the ACM, 30* (1), 14-31.

Clanton, C. (1983, December). The future of metaphor in man-computer systems. *Byte,* 263-270.

Clowes, I., Cole, I., Arshad, F., Hopkins, G., & Hockley, A. (1985). User Modelling techniques for interactive systems. In P. Johnson & S. Cook (Eds.), *People and Computers: Designing the Interface.* Cambridge: Cambridge University Press.

Coombs, M.J., & Alty, J.L. (Eds.). (1981). *Computing skills and the user interface.* London: Academic Press.

Cooper, P., & Hockley, A. (1986). The evaluation of an adaptive interface. In *IEEE colloquium on adaptive interface.* (Digest no. 110). London: IEEE.

Edmonds, E.A. (1986). Towards a taxonomy of user interface adaptation. In *IEEE Colloquium on adaptive interfaces.* (Digest No. 110). London: IEEE.

Entwhistle, N.J. (1978). Knowledge Structures and styles of learning: A summary of Pask's recent work. *British Journal of Educational Psychology, 48.*

Fischer, G., Lemke, A., & Schwab, T. (1984) *Active help systems*. HCI84, BCS.

Foss, D., Rosson, M.B., & Smith, P. (1982). Reducing manual labor: An experimental analysis of learning aids for a text editor. *Proceedings of the Conference on Human Factors in Computer Systems*, Gaithersburg: ACM.

Frese, M. (1987). The industrial and organizational psychology of human-computer interaction in the office (rev. ed.). In C.L. Cooper, & I.T. Robertson (Eds.). *International review of Industrial and Organizational Psychology*. London: John Wiley.

Gardiner, M.M. (1986). Psychological issues in adaptive interface design. In *IEEE Colloquium on Adaptive Interfaces*. (Digest No. 110). London: IEEE.

Greutmann, T., & Ackermann, D. (1987). Individual differences in human-computer interaction: How can we measure if the dialog grammar fits the user's needs? *Proceedings of the 2nd IFIP Conference on Human-Computer Interaction*. Amsterdam: North-Holland.

Green, T.R.G. (1984). Cognitive ergonomic research at SAPU, Sheffield. In G.C. van der Veer, M.J. Tauber, T.R.G. Green, & P. Gorny (Eds.), *Readings on cognitive ergonomics—mind and computer*. Heidelberg: Springer-Verlag.

Guest, S.P. (1982). Software tools for dialogue design. *International Journal of Man-Machine Studies, 14*, 263-285.

Guest, S.P. (1986) *Software tools for dialogue design*. Phd Thesis, Leicester Polytechnic.

Halasz, F., & Moran, T. (1982). Analogy considered harmful. *Proceedings of the Conference on Human Factors in Computer Systems*, Gaithersburg: ACM.

Hammond, N.V., & Barnard, P.J. (1984). Dialogue design: Characteristics of user knowledge. In A.F. Monk (Ed.), *Fundamentals of human-computer interaction*. London: Academic Press.

Hammond, N., & Allinson, L. (1988a). Travels around a learning support environment: Rambling, orienteering or touring? In E. Soloway, D. Frye, & S.B. Sheppard (Eds.), Proceedings of CHI 88, *Human factors in computing systems*. ACM: New York.

Hammond, N., & Allinson, L. (1988b). The travel metaphor as design principle and training aid for navigating around complex systems. In D. Diaper, & R. Winder (Eds.), *People and computers*, III. Cambridge: Cambridge University Press.

Heim J. (1987). Intelligence, creativity and personality in the mastery of a 4th generation application generator. *Abridged Proceedings of the HCI International 87*.

Herbert A.J., & Monk J. (1987). The ANSA reference manual. Cambridge: Advanced Networked Systems Architecture.

Houston, T. (1983, December). The allegory of software. *Byte*, 210-214.

Innocent, P.R. (1982) Towards self adaptive interfaces. *International Journal of Man-Machine Studies, 16*.

Innocent, P.R., Tauber, M.J., van der Veer, G.C., Guest, S., Haselager, W.F.G., McDaid, E., Oestreicher, L., & Waern, Y. (1988). Representation of the user interface - comparison of descriptions of interfaces from a designers point of view. In R. Speth (Ed.), *Research into networks and distributed applications - EUTECO 88*. Amsterdam: North-Holland.

Jackendoff, R. (1983). *Semantics and cognition*. Cambridge, MA: MIT Press.

Kok, E.J. (1984). Effectiviteit van computeronderwijs—getalstructuur. In A. Dirkzwager, S.D. Fokkema, G.C. van der Veer, & J.J. Beishuizen (Eds.), *Leren met computers in het onderwijs*. Den Haag: S.V.O.

Lawson, H.W. (1982). *Understanding Computer Systems*. Rockville, MD: Computer Science Press.

Leeuw, L. de (1983). Teaching problem solving: An ATI study of the effects of teaching algorithmic and heuristic solution methods. *Instructional Science, 12*, 1-48.

Maass, S. (1983). Why systems transparency? In T.R.G. Green, S.J. Payne, & G.C. van der Veer (Eds.), *The psychology of computer use*. London: Academic Press.

Mayes, J.T., Brooks, A., Russell, P., & Alty J.L. (1987). Predicting interactive processes at a user-driven adaptive interface. *Abridged Proceedings of the HCI International 87*.

Monk, A. (1985). *Fundamentals of human-computer interaction*. London: Academic Press.

Moran, T.P. (1981). The Command Language Grammar: A representation for the user interface of interactive computer systems. *International Journal of Man-Machine Studies, 15*, 3-50.

Norman, D.A. (1983). Some observations on mental models. In A.L. Stevens, & D. Gentner (Eds.), *Mental Models*. Hillsdale, NJ: Lawrence Erlbaum Associates.

Pask, G., Kallikoudis, D., & Scott, B.C.E. (1975). The representation of knowables. *International Journal of Man-Machine Studies, 7*.

Pask, G. (1976). Styles and strategies of learning. *British Journal of Educational Psychology, 46*, 128-148.

Patrick, J., & Stammers, R.B. (1981). The role of computers in training for problem diagnosis. In J. Rasmussen, & W.B. Rouse (Eds.), *Human detection and diagnosis of system failures*. New York: Plenum Press.

Payne, S.J., & Green, T.R.G. (1986). Task action grammars: A model of the mental representation of task languages. *Human Computer Interaction, 2*, 93-133.

Peelle, H.A. (1983). Computer metaphors: Approaches to computer literacy for educators. *Computers and Education, 7*, 91-99.

Perfetti, C.A. (1983). Reading, vocabulary, and writing: Implementations for computer-based instruction. In A.C. Wilkinson, (Ed.), *Classroom computers and cognitive science*. London: Academic Press.

Quilici, A.E., Dyer, M.G. & Flowers, M. (1986). AQUA: An intelligent Unix advisor. In L.Steels (Ed.), *Proceedings of the 7th ECAI*, Brighton.

Rich, E. (1983) Users are individuals: Individualizing user models. *International Journal of Man-Machine Studies, 18*, 199-214.

Rohr, G., & Tauber, M.J. (1984). Representational frameworks and models for human-computer interfaces. In G.C. van der Veer, T.R.G. Green, M.J. Tauber, & P. Gorny (Eds.), *Readings on cognitive ergonomics - Mind and computers*. Heidelberg: Springer-Verlag.

Rothkopf, E.Z. (1986). Machine adaptation to psychological differences among users in instructive information exchanges with computers. In F. Klix & H. Wandke (Eds.), *Man-computer interaction research, Macinter I*. Amsterdam: North-Holland.

Rumelhart, D.E., & Norman, D.A. (1983). Analogical processes in learning. In J.R. Anderson (Ed.), *Cognitive skills and their acquisition*. Cambridge, MA: Harvard University Press.

Sharratt, B.D. (1987). Top-down interactive systems design: Some lessons learnt from using command language grammar. In H.-J. Bullinger, B. Shackel, & K. Kornwachs (Eds.), *Human-computer interaction - Interact 87*. Amsterdam: North-Holland.

Shneiderman, B. (1980). *Software psychology*. Cambridge, MA: Winthrop.

Simons, P.R.J. (1980). *Vergelijkenderwijs: Onderzoek naar de invloed van metaforen op het leren*. Tilburg: Van Spaendonck drukkerij.

Singley, M.K., & Anderson, J.R. (1985). The transfer of text-editing skill. *International Journal of Man-Machine Studies, 22*, 403-423.

Streitz, N.A. (1986). Cognitive ergonomics: An approach for the design of user-oriented interactive systems. In F. Klix, & H. Wandke (Eds.), *Man-computer interaction research, Macinter 1*. Amsterdam: North-Holland.

Suppes, P. (1979). Current trends in Computer-Assisted Instruction. In M. Rubinoff, & M.C. Yovits (Eds.), Advances in Computers. New York: Academic Press.

Tauber, M.J. (1988). On mental models and the user interface. In G.C. van der Veer, T.R.G. Green, J.-M. Hoc., & D. Murray (Eds.), *Working with computers - theory versus outcome*. London: Academic Press.

Ulich E. (1987). Individual differences in human-computer interaction: Concepts and research findings. In G. Salvendy (Ed.), *Cognitive Engineering in the design of human-computer interaction and expert systems*. Amsterdam: Elsevier, 10B, 29-36.

van der Veer G.C. (1983). Individual differences in cognitive style and educational background and their effect upon the learning of a programming language. In H. Schauer, & M.J. Tauber (Eds.), *Psychologie des Programmierens*. Wien: Oldenbourg.

van der Veer, G.C., Tauber, M.J., Waern, Y., & van Muylwijk, B. (1985). On the interaction between system and user characteristics. *Behaviour & Information Technology, 4*, 284-308.

van der Veer G.C., & Beishuizen J.J. (1986). Learning styles in conversation: A practical application of Pask's learning theory to human-computer interaction. In F. Klix, & H. Wandke (Eds.), *Man-computer interaction research, Macinter I*. Amsterdam: North-Holland.

van der Veer, G.C., van Beek, J., & Cruts, G.A.N. (1987). Learning structured diagrams - Effect of mathematical background, instruction, and problem semantics. In P. Gorny, & M. Tauber (Eds.), *Visualization in Programming*, Berlin: Springer-Verlag.

van der Veer, G.C. (1989). Users' representation of systems - Variety as function of user interface, culture, and individual style. In F. Klix, N.A. Streitz, Y. Waern, & H. Wandke (Eds.), *Man-computer interaction research, Macinter II*. Amsterdam: Elsevier.

Waern, Y. (1983). *Prior knowledge as obstacle and help in computer aided tasks*. Working papers from the cognitive seminar, (17). Department of psychology, University of Stockholm.

Waern, Y. (1987). *Limits to human performance: Hard-ware, know-ware and will-ware*. Position paper to the SIGCHI workshop on User Models, CHI 87, Toronto.

Watt, D. (1979). *Final report of the Brookline LOGO project, part III: Profiles of individual student's work*. Cambridge, MA: MIT Press.

Wilson, M., Barnard, P., & Maclean, A. (1985). Analysing the learning of command sequences in a menu system. In P. Johnson, & S. Cook (Eds.), *People and computers: Designing the interface*. Cambridge: Cambridge University Press, 63-75.

Winston P.H. (1984). *Artificial intelligence (2nd ed.)*. Reading, MA: Addison Wesley.

CHAPTER FOUR

Analysis and Models of Operators' Activities in Complex Natural Life Environments

Maurice de Montmollin
Université Paris-Nord and MAST Group

1. ACTIVITIES, OPERATORS, ENVIRONMENTS

1. Delimitation of the Domain

The domain of ergonomic studies explored in this paper is intentionally limited in accordance with the three following assumptions: (1) Operators actual activities have to be distinguished from the tasks they are requested or supposed to perform; (2) operators working in natural life environments have to be distinguished from anonymous and universal human beings; (3) complex natural life environments have to be distinguished from the interfaces, as the whole has to be distinguished from one of its parts.

As an inference from (1), this paper will not review the numerous and interesting papers concerning the analysis and modelling of tasks (a recent review on task analysis is presented by J. Algera, 1988). As an inference from (2), this paper will not review the innumerable papers, mainly in cognitive psychology, and more generally in cognitive sciences, concerning the "basic mechanisms" of human beings. As an inference from (3), this paper will not review the large quantity of papers concerning the domain of "Human-Computer Interaction", where the "human" is often some "naive user" confronting an "interface".

Concerning this delimited and limited domain of activity analysis, this paper is led to quote more European references than American ones, and among the European, more French-speaking (French and Belgian) ones. The geographical and historical specificity of this French-speaking orientation is commented on by De Keyser et al. (1988), and in French by De Keyser (1988b). Concerning more or less directly the same domain, one can quote also the following books or general articles, in English: Goodstein et al. (1988); Hollnagel et al. (1986); Montmollin and De Keyser (1986); Rasmussen (1986); Rasmussen et al. (1987); Wisner et al. (1988); and in French: Daniellou (1986); De Keyser (1988); Hoc (1987a); Leplat (1985b); Montmollin (1986b; 1990); Spérandio (1987; 1988); De Keyser & Van Daele (1990); Amalberti et al. (1991). The journal, *Le Travail Human* (largely in French, edited by J.-M. Hoc) is regularly publishing articles and special issues concerning this topic (e.g. De Keyser, 1988a; Hoc & Visser, 1988). The other references in this paper do not pretend to constitute an exhaustive review of the published studies; they are given as typical examples.

The three distinctions mentioned earlier will now be briefly developed.

1.1. Operators Exist

In ergonomics, cognitive engineering, and related areas, the very large majority of published studies are not empirical but apodictic and normative. When studying a work situation (the operator in the control room of NPP or a refinery, the clerk in a bank, the pilot of a fighter plane ...), the model of the operator in this situation is, indeed, built following the requirements of the task the latter is asked to perform. These requirements are generally derived from technical documents concerning the machines, the processes, the organisation; from statistical data concerning performances when accessible; and from interviews with the operators and the hierarchy. The result is a model of the ideal operator, "designed", or rather imagined by the analyst, as a part of the work situation designed by the engineer. This model could be implemented (and sometimes actually is) in some automation, or expert system, when the same objectives can be reached by replacing the operator in the system by some non-biological component. Occasionally, and in any case after its design, this normative model is validated by comparison with the actual behaviour of the operator. But in reality it often appears that it is the human behaviour itself which is "validated", and assessed as "normal" if in conformity with the prescribed behaviour.

The overwhelming conclusion of all the ergonomic studies of work analysis studies which, in contrast to the normative ones, try to model the natural activities of the operator, is that these activities never conform to the prescribed tasks. This is also true, and perhaps particularly so, for the successful operators. The rationalistic and optimistic conception of F.W. Taylor, and of his modern followers, splitting the work into preparation (by the engineer) and execution (by the operator) actually succeeds only if the operator is intelligent, and not only obedient; that is, if by heuristics, technical cunning and personal adaptive competency, the operator controls the natural situations, which never seem to occur exactly as they were supposed to.

Nevertheless, Taylor and his modern followers are not completely wrong. The chemico-physical processes, and the administrative ones as well, are rational, and no industry survives without strong normative constraints concerning the tasks. Operators are not just free artists. Indeed, they always have to adapt their activity to at least some of the characteristics of the prescribed tasks, as they were designed by the hierarchy, but (fortunately) they also exist by themselves - they do not just blindly follow the prescribed procedures. Prescribed tasks cannot be considered as dogmas, but they can serve as guides. In fact, the objectives of the tasks (production, quality, security, etc) cannot be reached without some organisational constraints, nor without the personal contribution of operators. In short, real work is a dialectical interaction between normative tasks and intelligent activities. Thus, in this perspective, there is no relevant work analysis without analysis and modelling of the operator's activity.

Such an interaction also works at the methodological level: models for analysing operators' activities can sometimes be "borrowed", as tentative models, from the normative task domain. Work analysis is empirical.

On the distinction between task and activity in ergonomics, see Leplat and Hoc (1983); on performance models, see Roth and Woods (1988); a good example is given by Visser (1988), of the actual opportunistic organisation of the activity as deviation from the theoretical plan.

1.2. Operators are Operators

Operators are not to be considered as universal human beings, whose universal characteristics and limits could be discovered and measured from any *homo sapiens* (for instance an undergraduate student), allowing the construction of general "laws". This assumption is derived from the great difficulty in practice of reducing always very specific and complex work situations to a limited number of components, which could be universal enough as to explain, by re-combination, all the possible diverse situations. It is derived also, and particularly, from the symmetrical empirical impossibility of reducing the always specific complex activities, that is the local "stories", to a limited number of universal broad characteristics, which could be relevant for the description of all the possible diverse working "stories". In short: activity analysis is more oriented towards time than typology. Thus, ergonomic activity analysis here is less ambitious - and less easy. It is not like the "Lego basic box", which allows a child to build an unlimited number of objects with a limited number of basic building blocks.

This mistrust about the universal models is primarily concerned with the old-fashioned typologies of aptitudes and capacities, as established by differential psychology. But this mistrust also concerns the cognitive models now in fashion, issued from the cognitive psychologists' flirtation with cognitive scientists in the area of Artificial Intelligence (AI), particularly Expert Systems. These models - for instance describing "the structure of knowledge" - are attractive, but for the analysis of local particular operators' activities, they are just hypothetical suggestions.

The methodological conclusion of this assumption is that ergonomic analysis and modelling of activities cannot be anything but natural field analysis, in an ecological perspective. Laboratory experiments are considered here as analysis of the experimental situation itself, and nothing else. Experimental situation is almost never real work situation. Therefore, data from laboratory experiments are useful, but in the same way that data concerning the behaviour of monkeys in cages are useful for the explanation of the behaviour of wild monkeys in the wild. There is no industrial environment where workers have to solve the Tower of Hanoi problem eight hours a day, every day, and get paid for it. Time is considered differently as well: minutes and hours are considered in laboratory experiments, whereas weeks, months and even years are relevant in natural situations. In the laboratory, complexity has to be avoided to allow for the control of very few independent and dependent variables; in contrast, complexity has to be respected in field work.[1]

That is never easy. Thus, whenever possible, full-scale simulation is an acceptable compromise, because the objective is to insert into the simulated system as many independent variables as possible, which nevertheless can be partially controlled (an opportunity seldom possible in a natural situation). Meanwhile some "field experiments" are sometimes possible, but mostly in the domains where costs are less relevant (e.g. NPP, aviation).

In this context, there is no such discipline as "applied ergonomics".[2] Models and theories are required to cope with experienced operators working in natural complex situations. But what about the requirement of "scientificness", if the analysed situations, and the corresponding activities, are so complex, specific, and local that any generalisation of the results is practically impossible? Unfortunately, generalisation in this domain is only possible at a relatively high level of abstraction, resulting in a proportionally low level of effectiveness. That is the reason why ergonomists dealing with activity are at a loss when they have to speak about the results. Any discourse is generalisation, and, in any case, the problems they have to cope with are, more and more, problems of (re)design and the transfer of technology, which requires at least some generalisation. The provisional answer to this contradiction is that the format of the models and methods can be partially generalised, but the content and data themselves cannot - except very cautiously.

Concerning simulation, laboratory experiments, and field studies, see Bisseret (1988); Funke (1988); Leplat (1982); Lewkowitch (1988); Montmollin (1986a); and Moray (1986).

1.3. Operators do not Work with Interfaces Alone

The best-known example of ergonomic/human factors realisation - at least in advertising - is still the chair. It is of course essential for any operator, from the office clerk to the fighter pilot, not to be hampered by a badly designed chair. But what about the operator's work, or more precisely, activity? That person's task is not to be seated, but to write, for example, an administrative report, or to fight hostile aircraft. The chair is only one part of the whole "work situation" which includes, hardware such as the displays, or software such as the meaning of an alarm, or even the "programs" operators are constructing for personal use.

Interfaces presenting information (e.g. VDU), are certainly more important today than chairs. A large quantity of studies devoted to their design concern the physical dimensions (e.g. contrasts on the screen), and the psychological ones as well (e.g. format of information on the screen). But, as in the case of a chair, the question here is: Interfaces for what? Experienced operators are not naive users who have to be convinced to buy or to use a friendly microcomputer; they are people who have to solve problems not directly concerning the interface, but rather, a complex environment, for instance an unusual incident in a chemical process, or a conflict between the planes above an exceptionally overcrowded airport. Natural life environments cannot be reduced to interfaces, even when interfaces are the only windows between the operator and the environment (which is seldom the case). The more complex the environment, the more this ecological approach is relevant.

Concerning what they call the "natural problem solving habitat", E.M. Roth and D.D. Woods (1988 p.41), identify "the three mutually constrained factors: (1) the problem-solving (or cognitive) demands imposed by the world to be acted on; (2) the capacities and architecture of the agent or agents who act on the world; (3) the external representation through which the agent experiences that world". This "external representation" is, in this instance, clearly a representation of something for someone for the purpose of something.

This conception of interfaces as interfaces *only* is particularly relevant when analysing the work of operators in process control. In these settings (e.g. NPP, chemical plants, refineries, steel factories, etc), the process itself cannot be directly observed by the operators. The information they need for their activity is artificially coded, and displayed on walls and, recently, on additional screens. The display of information is generally more or less analogical with the physical process itself, that is, the "machine" in the man-machine system. If "sophisticated" engineers try to "facilitate" (in their opinion) the work, by transfer to the screen(s) of the totality of information, which moreover is modified and interpreted by some intermediate software, it could happen that for the operator the task is no longer the control of the process, but more the interpretation and control of the interface, which becomes the "object" of the operator's work. This is not always the best solution!

On this "irony of automation", see Bainbridge (1983); Guy and Lejon (1988); Hellman (1988) "abandoning the plain surface"; Kasbi (1988); and the section "Ergonomics in informatics: Contribution from work analysis" in Patesson (1986). A critical analysis of the HCI paradigm is presented by Carroll (1989).

2. ANALYSIS AND MODELLING OF OPERATORS' ACTIVITIES

As a consequence of this severe limitation of the domain (specific local activities of operators working in specific local complex environments), the empirical studies we can now rapidly review cannot be structured as if some metamodel could allow elegant generalisations. The state of the art is at present, better described as a catalogue of roughly gathered "cases" than as a coherent theory about some general cognitive laws. Nevertheless, broad categorization of models of operators' activities can be suggested. These models are not alternative; they can often be used simultaneously.

The main distinction proposed here is between: (i) models of individual or collective cognitive processing activities, overt or covert, which convey the operators along temporal paths, from one state to another in the "stories", or "scenarios", which are constructed by their interaction with their working environment, and (ii) models of the acquired cognitive structures, or competencies (knowledge, know-how, meta-knowledge, etc) hypothesised by the ergonomist in order to explain the processing of information, both individual and collective.

As human error is nowadays a crucial topic in ergonomical analysis, it will be treated separately, by way of conclusion.

2.1. Cognitive Processing Activities

Operators reason, that is, they control their actions. They make inferences, starting with a "sign", or some meaningful information, and ending with a conclusion, or "decision". What are these "signs"? What significance is given by the operator to the many bits of information flowing from the environment to the mind? Any particular significance is always given in relation to a task, that is, to the constraints the operator will have to cope with. How, if any, can we identify these "starting signs" and the final "conclusions"? Is the operator's reasoning split by goals and sub-goals? In other words, what are the models of the "course of action", for the very minute analysis of this "semiotics of working activities", or succession of events and actions, with a sophisticated accent on the meaning (for the operator) of these events and actions? (On this topic, see Boël & Daniellou, 1984; Pinsky & Theureau, 1987a, b; Theureau, 1991; Valot & Amalberti, 1989.)

Among the diverse models of, or approaches to, operators' cognitive activities, correlated with the diverse objects of work analysis, the following seem the most frequently used:

(i) Models centred on diagnosis and problem-solving: (Alengry, 1986; Bainbridge, 1984; Fichet-Clairfontaine, 1985; Hoc, 1987c,; Housiaux, 1988; Navarro, 1987; Samurçay & Hoc, 1989). In industrial and administrative natural situations the interesting thing is actually not the "problem solving", but the "problem setting" activity (if the problem is clearly defined, there is some predetermined procedure for solving it). In other words, the very challenge is the construction of the problem, not the finding of the solution. That is one of the reasons not to reduce the natural world problem-solving paradigm to the classical experimental one.

(ii) Models centred on analogies and representations (Bainbridge, 1988; Leplat, 1985a; Montmollin & de Keyser, 1986). Analogy seems a rather common modality of reasoning for experienced (as opposed to novice) operators. This powerful heuristics allows the operator to "ident-ify" rapidly a "situation", dispensing with the whole algorithmic process of diagnosis, but sometimes it also allows stubbornly false identifications. Such "identifications", or "comprehensions", are commonly called "representations" by psychologists, a very polysemic concept indeed, with a variety of different meanings such as: psychological phenomena (e.g. "patterns", or "images"); permanent functional knowledge; and collective social ideologies. Here "representations" are considered as part of cognitive activities.

(iii) Models centred on temporal aspects of work (Böel & Daniellou, 1984; Decortis, 1988; Fichet-Clairfontaine, 1985; Hoc, 1987a, b; van Daele, 1988). Numerous micro-analyses are exploring the place of time in the process of reasoning, particularly in process control, where time is the great actor, and often the great enemy. Time means anticipation for the operators. As an example of the importance given by operators to time constraints, it has been observed that reasoning is oriented more on consequences than on causes.

(iv) Models centred on strategies, regulations, changing of level, planning. It often seems relevant for the description of cognitive activities to identify some "meta-reasoning", which allows the operator not to be limited with a too proximate temporal horizon, or a too limited set of cognitive tools. The models concerning strategies (De Keyser, 1988b; Montmollin, 1990; Rasmussen & Jensen, 1974) describe here the set of behaviours exhibited as an operator gradually reaches a decision and takes action to deal with a poorly defined problem, or a problematic situation. Common examples of strategy are the general "data driven" reasoning, or in contrast, the construction of a hierarchy of goals and sub-goals (see also "conduite"). Regulation (Faverge, 1972; Faverge et al. 1966) is a concept originated by J.-M. Faverge, whose studies concerning this topic were influenced by the cybernetical models (the search for a stable state). This concept now seems often synonymous with strategy (see for instance Cellier, 1987; Dorel & Queinnec, 1980; Terssac, 1980; for the East European aspects of the concept of regulation, see Hacker, 1980). Spérandio (1972), analysing the activity of air flight controllers, demonstrated that their procedures were modified, according to the number of planes (i.e. the "workload"), following a model of discontinuous changing of levels of activity. A similar behaviour is described by Stassen et al. (1988 p.252), as "a combination of human performance and mental load during human supervisory tasks". Vermersch (1976; 1978) transposed the Piagetian "stages" into the work domain, showing the modifications ("accommodation") of modalities of reasoning following the possibilities of "assimilation" of the difficulties of the task. The three well-known stages (skill, rule, knowledge) of Rasmussen's model (e.g. Rasmussen, 1986) can also be considered as a model of levels giving operators the opportunity to adapt their behaviour following the characteristics of the occurring events (e.g. an unusual incident in process control). Planning and the making of plans and schemas was studied by J.-M. Hoc in various situations (mainly the activity of programmers in informatics), both from theoretical and empirical points of view (Hoc, 1987a; Samurçay & Hoc, 1989).

Until recently, models of collective activities were a rather neglected area in ergonomic research. The workplace, and the operator isolated in this workplace, were the dominant paradigms. When oriented to the collective aspects, a majority of studies were devoted to the normative allocation of tasks, and to the corresponding design of prescribed communication, which is a different topic. Social psychologists for their part have seldom observed interactions in real professional groups, coping with real work situations.

Communications and interactions in the workplace are no longer a sort of "post-scriptum" to the work analyses of individual operators, but are becoming more and more the central and direct object of analyses. Activities are analysed through the communications (mainly verbal) they bring about. Particularly interesting is when communication is mediated, e.g. by radio or phone.

Concerning the explored areas of collective activities, and communications, see Falzon (1989); Falzon et al. (1988); Hollnagel and Weir (1988); Kasbi (1988); Lacoste (1983; 1991); Navarro (1987); Savoyant and Leplat (1983); Swaanenburg et al. (1988); and Theureau and Pinsky (1983). In this domain there are also some interesting contributions from American ethno-methodologists (see for instance Hutchins, 1983; 1987; and Scribner, 1985).

As the object of work analysis here is the activity of information processing (as opposed to the task which has to be performed), the methodologies are directly linked with the models of activity. The aforementioned enumeration lists some of the models or approaches proposed by the ergonomists, but as every new work situation has to be analysed as specific, the analyst has to be cautious not to adopt too rapidly, by analogy, a model adapted to some familiar situation previously analysed. One of the more sensible decisions concerns the determination of the units pertinent for each analysis (that is, pertinent for the aims of each analysis). It is not an easy task. If too "micro", the analysis may never end or the results will be too sophisticated. If too "macro" some crucial element could be missed. There is yet in this domain a lot of work for methodological (i.e. theoretical) ergonomics. For instance, what is a "decision"? Following the scale of the analysis, a "decision" could be the only final conclusion of a very long sequence of reasoning. Some interesting examples are given by D. Dörner in the managerial area (Dörner, 1987; see also Fischoff, 1986, and the collective book edited by Rasmussen et al., 1991). But every micro action, like looking at a display, could also sometimes be named a "decision". Stop rules in work analysis are always a challenge.

Concerning the sensible topic of verbalisation analysis, there is, fortunately, a fairly large quantity of field studies, including the contribution of such exotic (for ergonomists) scientists as linguists, sociolinguists, or specialists in "natural logics". See for instance Bainbridge (1979); Caverni (1988); Cleeremans (1988); Falzon et al. (1988); Grize (1981); Lacoste (1981; 1983); Navarro (1987); Pollack (1985); Praetorius and Duncan (1988); and Theureau and Pinsky (1983).

2.2. Competencies

In the ergonomic perspective described here, competencies is the conventional term for acquired relatively stable cognitive memorised structures, enabling the operator to act or to perform a specific task, or a family of similar tasks.

A trivial example of the distinction between activity and competency is the contrast between remembering (a behaviour, which can be recorded, and is part of a "story"), and memory (which does not exist, except as an imaginary construction by the psychologist to explain the remembering). A less trivial and more ergonomical example could be the temporal succession of inferences overly made by an operator in the control room to cope with a dysfunctioning of the process, on one hand, and, on the other hand, the knowledge about this process which is supposed, by the ergonomist, to be necessary for such inferences and which may not be stated explicitly by the operator alone.

Part of competencies are different modalities of knowledge (declarative, procedural, of functioning, of use...), know-how, memorised rules and acquired routines, meta-knowledge, i.e. thinking about one's own knowledge, and also "representations" (here as structures, as opposed to representations, as part of the cognitive process).

Meta-knowledge is a recent and promising topic. Operators are often neither behaving nor reasoning in conformity with how they "know" they should behave and reason. They "discuss" their own knowledge (e.g. of procedures), and adapt it to the present circumstances. They can be conscious of such a "discussion". It seems that in complex systems, efficient operators have such a flexible, adaptive, i.e. intelligent, competency.

There are many theoretical and practical problems concerning competencies. What is their genesis, and particularly what is the nature and function of experience? Experience is indeed a strange and challenging, although common concept. Everyone apparently knows what it is, but nobody is really able to describe and explain it. Even in highly proceduralised systems, the experience of operators is a necessity, although often recognised only tacitly by the hierarchy. Other linked problems concern levels of abstraction, hierarchies, inclusions, and commonalities of cognitive structures. Possibilities of transformation, transfer, and more generally generalisation of competencies are very practical questions in technically evolving industries. Workers have to adapt themselves to some new, but often similar tasks. What do "new" and "similar" mean for the operator? To what extent are the professional local competency dependent on prerequisites? What sort of (re)training is necessary? Is an "on the job training" possible? More generally, what is a relevant technical education?

Competency differs from skill, if skill means a more general capacity (e.g. "manual skill"), not restricted to a precisely identified task, or family of tasks. Competency differs also from expertise (as in the Expert System vocabulary). Expertise here is meant only as "excellent" competency, thus referring more to the abstract activity involved in performing a task imposed by the expert system technology, rather than to real daily activity of the living expert. In this perspective, extraction of knowledge is regularly derived from interviews, not from observation or recording of activities.

The diverse psychological models concerning "schemata", "frames", "mental models" etc. can certainly help the ergonomist to model the cognitive structures necessary to explain the operators' activities, but these models have always to be implemented and adapted, if possible, to the local stories. An incident situation is not "schematised" by the operator in a nuclear power plant the way it is "schematised" as incident situation by a programmer debugging perverse software.

Competencies also differ from aptitudes and abilities, which are much too abstract and general traits, unable to explain the actual local professional activities. They also differ from their social counterparts, qualifications; but this difference is now a stimulating common field of research between ergonomists and sociologists (for instance through the concept of tacit skill).

Analysis of competencies is indeed difficult. The operators themselves, when interviewed, tend to describe their prescribed tasks, and the corresponding knowledge, not the actual processes and knowledge. A fairly good technical opportunity for the analysis of natural competencies is given when they are in a dynamic state: their genesis (from novice to expert); their transformation (from one task to another one, for instance when a process is automatised); their transfer (from one operator to another, for instance during "on the job" training by a senior worker); more generally their communication, for instance in a working team.

On competencies and knowledge in ergonomics, see Caverni (1989); De Keyser (1987); Hoc (1987a, b); Leplat (1986; 1990); Montmollin (1986b); Montmollin and De Keyser (1986); Norros and Sammatti (1986); Ochanine (1981); Roth and Woods (1988); Stassen (1986); Stassen et al. (1988).[3]

3. BY WAY OF CONCLUSION: "HUMAN ERROR" OR "HUMAN FAILURE"?

An unexpected issue of the ergonomic studies of operators' activities is the critical discussion of the popular concept of "human error", supposed to explain incidents and accidents. There is, for instance, in case of railways or road accidents, a traditional orientation to pinpoint the human error made by the driver. Actually, there is some very suggestive and useful psychological and ergonomical taxonomies on human errors (particularly by Reason, 1987; 1990; see also Goodstein et al., 1988; Leplat, 1985b; Rasmussen et al., 1987).

Nevertheless, the ergonomic orientation sketched in the preceding pages is different, concerning the role of operators in incidents and accidents.

Considering the dynamic activities (the local operators' "stories"), analyses lead to the conclusion that—with the very rare exception of drunkenness or sudden madness—the so-called erroneous decisions, or unsafe acts, were the final result of often long and sophisticated reasoning, with deep roots in the operators' whole professional experience (or inexperience). Rather than to focus on the "error", it seems more efficient to speak of human "failure", resulting from large sequences of reasoning and acting, often in a very rational way. In this perspective, there are no longer isolated local errors, but cognitive activities issuing in situations which are assessed as "incidents" or "accidents" by the social environment. The common conception that accidents derived resulting from human error(s) is often directly derived from the normative models of work. Human error is defined as deviation from the prescribed task, which is considered as "normal" (i.e. the "norm"). There is no consideration of the fact that these deviations are also, and largely more often, the only way to avoid an accident...

As activities cannot be explained without the sustaining competencies, the conclusion concerning human failure is that the final word is on the side of these professional competencies. The better, that is the deeper, the more flexible, the higher the probability that the operator will become an efficient "manager of the unexpected". More constraining rules and procedures, more disciplinary regulations do not appear to be the only solution to the problems of safety.

Complex natural life environments require complex natural life activities and competencies.

On this conception of human failure, see the aforementioned references, and Amalberti (1989); Daniellou (1986); Leplat and Rasmussen (1987); Norros and Sammatti (1986).

NOTES

1. For technological and economical reasons, the fields studied by today's ergonomics are unevenly distributed: Process control (from Nuclear Power Plants to bus traffic), office automation, or computer programming are on the whole better represented than rural, artistic or managerial occupations...
2. That does not mean that the journal Applied Ergonomics is not an excellent one!
3. In France, half a dozen of theses in ergonomics are at the present time prepared on these topics, in hospitals, control rooms, workshops in mechanics, and administrative settings.

REFERENCES

Alengry, P. (1986). Recherche des inadéquations du système mme-machine dans le cadre de l'évaluation d'un dispositif assistance à l'opérateur intégré sur des chaîes de fabrication automatisées. In R. Patesson (Ed.), *L'homme et l'écran. Actes du colloque de Nivelles, 1985*. Bruxelles: Presses de l'Université Libre de Bruxelles.

Algera, J.A. (1988). Task analysis and new technologies. In V. De Keyser, Th. Qvale, B. Wilpert, & S.A. Ruiz Quintillana (Eds.), *The meaning of work and technological options*. Chichester: John Wiley.

Amalberti, R. (1989). Vigilance, attention, automatisation et conduite de processus. In *Entretiens "Science et Défense", Paris, May*, Bellicize Publishers, 123-131.

Amalberti, R., Montmollin, M. de, & Theureau, J. (Eds.). (1991). *Modèles de l'analyse du travail*. Liège: Mardaga.

Bainbridge, L. (1979). Verbal reports as evidence of the process operator's knowledge. *International Journal of Man-Machine Studies, 11*, 411-496.

Bainbridge, L. (1983). Ironies of automation. *Automatica, 19* (6), 775-779.

Bainbridge, L. (1984). Diagnostic skill in process operation. In M.L. Matthews, & R. D. G. Webb (Eds.), Reviews. *Proceedings of the 1984 International Conference on Occupational Ergonomics, 2*. Toronto, Canada.

Bainbridge, L. (1988). Types of representations. In L. P. Goodstein, H. B. Andersen, & D. E. Olson (Eds.), *Tasks, Errors and Mental Models. A Festschrift to celebrate the 60th birthday of Professor Jens Rasmussen*. London: Taylor and Francis.

Bisseret, A. (1988). Modeles pour comprendre et réussir. In J. P. Caverni, C. Bastien, P. Mendelsohn, & G. Tiberghien (Eds.), *Psychologie cognitive: Modèles et méthodes*. Grenoble: Presses Universitaires de Grenoble.

Böel, M., & Daniellou, F. (1984). Elements of process control operator's reasoning: Activity planning and system and process response-time. In *Ergonomics Problems in Process Operations*. European Federation of Chemical Engineering Publications, (Series N38): The Institute of Chemical Engineering and Pergamon Press.

Carroll, J. M. (1989). Evaluation, description and invention: Paradigms of human-computer interaction. In M. C. Yovits (Ed.), *Advances in Computers: Vol. 28*. New York: Academic Press.

Caverni, J. P. (1988). La verbalisation comme source d'observables pour l'étude du fonctionnement cognitif. In J. P. Caverni, C. Bastien, P. Mendelshon, & G. Tiberghien (Eds.), *Psychologie cognitive: Modèles et méthodes*. Grenoble: Presses Universitaires de Grenoble.

Caverni, P. (Ed.). (1989). Psychologie de l'expertise [Special issue]. *Psychologie Française, 33* (3).

Cellier, J.-M. (1987). Processus cognitifs et activités de régulation. *Bulletin de Psychologie, 40*, 379, 331-332.

Cleeremans, A. (1988). Relations entre performance et connaissances verbalisables dans le contrôle de processus. *Le Travail Humain, 51* (2), 97-111.

Daniellou, F. (1986). *L'opérateur, la vanne, l'écran. L'ergonomie dans la transformation des industries de processus*. Montrouge: ANACT.

Decortis, F. (1988). Dimensions temporelles de l'activité cognitive lors des démarrages de systèmes complexes. *Le Travail Humain, 51* (2) 125-138.

De Keyser, V. (1987). Structuring of knowledge of operators in continuous processes: Case study of a continuous casting plant start up. In J. Rasmussen, K. Duncan, & J. Leplat (Eds.), *New technology and human error*. Chichester: John Wiley.

De Keyser, V. (Ed.). (1988a). L'ergonomie des processus continus [Special issues]. *Le travail Humain, 51*, (1 & 2).

De Keyser, V. (Ed.). (1988b). De la contingence à la complexité: L'évolution des idées dans l'étude des processus continus. *Le Travail Humain, 51*. (1), 1-18.

De Keyser, V., Decortis, F., & Van Daele, A. (1988). The approach of Francophone ergonomy: Studying new technologies. In V. De Keyser, Th. Qvale, B. Wilpert, & S. A. Ruiz Quintanilla (Eds.), *The meaning of work and technological options*. Chichester: John Wiley.

De Keyser, V., & Van Daele (Eds.). (1990). *L'ergonomie de conception*. Brussels: De Boek Université.

Dorel, M., & Queinnec, Y. (1980). Régulations individuelles et interindividuelles en situation d'horaire alternant. *Bulletin de Psychologie, 33*, 465-471.

Dörner, D. (1987). On the difficulties people have in dealing with complexity. In J. Rasmussen, K. Duncan, & J. Leplat (Eds.), *New technology and human error*. Chichester: John Wiley.

Ellman, R. (1988, June 14-16). Human factors and personal computing: From surface to structure. In *Man-machine systems, analysis, design and evaluation*. Preprints of the IFAC/IFIP/IEA/IFORS conference, Oulu, Finland, II, 313-319.

Falzon, P. (1989). *Ergonomie cognitive du dialogue*. Grenoble: Presses Universitaires de Grenoble.

Falzon, P., Amalberti, R., & Carbonnel, N. (1988, June 14-16). Man-machine dialogue: The role of interlocutor models. In *Man-machine systems, analysis, design and evaluation*, Preprints of the IFAC/IFIP/IEA/IFORS conference, Oulu, Finland, II, 511-516.

Faverge, J.-M. (Ed.). (1966). *L'ergonomie des processus industriels*. Bruxelles: Institut de Sociologie de l'Université Libre de Bruxelles.

Faverge, J.-M. (1972). L'analyse du travail. In M. Reuchlin (Ed.), *Traité de psychologie appliquée: Vol. 3*. Paris: Presses Universitaires de France.

Fichet-Clairfontaine, P. Y. (1985). *Etude ergonomique de l'influence de la conception de la salle de commande, de la stabilité du processus, et de la diversification de la production sur l'activité des opérateurs dans 4 unités de processus continu*. Unpublished thesis, Université Paris-Nord.

Fischoff, B. (1986). Decision making in complex systems. In E. Hollnagel, G. Mancini, & D. D. Woods (Eds.), *Intelligent decision support in process environments*. Berlin: Springer-Verlag.

Funke, J. (1988). Using simulation to study complex problem solving: A review of studies in the FRG. *Simulation & Games, 19* (3), 277-303.

Goodstein, L. P., Andersen, H. B., & Olsen, S. E. (Eds.). (1988). *Tasks, errors and mental models. A Festschrift to celebrate the 60th birthday of Professor Jens Rasmussen*. London: Taylor and Francis.

Grize, J.-B. (1981). Discours et connaissances. *Communication & Cognition, 14*, 343-357.

Guy, M., & Lejon, J. (1988, Oct 19-20). Ergonomic analysis of operator activities in conventional control rooms for implementation of centralized CRT-key board equipment. *Proceedings of the 7th European annual conference "On human decision making and manual control"*. Paris: Electricité de France.

Hacker, W. (1980). *Allgemeine Arbeits-und-Ingenieurpsychologie. Psychische Struktur und Regulation von Arbeitstätigkeiten*. Berlin: VEB Deutscher Verlag der Wissenschaften.

Hoc, J.-M. (1987a). *Psychologie cognitive de la planification*. Grenoble: Presses Universitaires de Grenoble.

Hoc, J.-M. (1987b). Prise de conscience et planification. *Psychologie Française, 32* (4), 247-252.

Hoc, J.-M. (1987c). Analysis of cognitive activities in process control for the design of computer aids. An example: the control of blast furnaces. In H. J. Bullinger, & B. Shakel (Eds.), *Human computer interaction - INTERACT 87*. Amsterdam: Elsevier.

Hoc, J.-M., & Visser, W. (Eds.). (1988). Psychologie ergonomique de la programmation informatique [Special issue]. *Psychologie Française, 51* (4).

Hollnagel, E., Mancini, G., & Woods, D. D. (Eds.). (1986). *Intelligent decision support in process environments*. Berlin: Springer-Verlag.

Hollnagel, E., & Weir, G. (1988, June 14-16). Principles for dialogue design in man-machine systems. In *Man-machine systems, analysis, design and evaluation*. Preprints of the IFAC/IFIP/IEA/IFORS conference, Oulu, Finland, I, 269-273.

Housiaux, A. (1988). Supports d'information centralisés et diagnostic en situation d'urgence dans un centre néonatal. Le Travail Humain, 51 (1), 173-184.

Hutchins, E. (1983). Understanding Micronesian navigation. In D. Gentner, & A. L. Stevens (Eds.), *Mental models*. Hillsdale, NJ: Lawrence Erlbaum Associates.

Hutchins, E. (1987, June 23-26). *The ontogenesis of a Quatermaster*. Paper presented at the First International Workshop "Activity, Work and Learning", Karjaa, Finland.

Kasbi, C. (1988, Oct 19-20). Les aspects organisationnels de la conduite dans la validation du simulateur S3C. *Proceedings of the 7th European annual conference "On human decision making and manual control"*. Paris: Electricité de France.

Lacoste, M. (1983). Des situations de parole aux activités interpretatives. *Psychologie Française, 28*, 231-238.

Lacoste, M. (1991). Les communications dans le travail comme interactions. In R. Amalberti, M. de Montmollin, & J. Theureau (Eds.), *Modèles de l'analyse du travail*. Liège: Mardaga.

Leplat, J. (1982). Le terrain, stimulant (ou obstacle) au développement de la psychologie cognitive. *Cahiers de Psychologie Cognitive, 2*, 115-130.

Leplat, J. (1985a). Les représentations fonctionnelles dans le travail. In S. Ehrlich (Ed.), Les représentations [Special issue]. *Psychologie Française, 30* (3-4).

Leplat, J. (1985b). *Erreur humaine, fiabilité humaine dans le travail*. Paris: Armand-Colin.

Leplat, J. (1986). The elicitation of expert knowledge. In E. Hollnagel, G. Mancini, & D. D. Woods (Eds.), *Intelligent decision support in process environments*. Berlin: Springer-Verlag.

Leplat, J. (1990). Skills and tacit skills: A psychological perspective. *Applied Psychology: An International Review, 39*, 143-154.

Leplat, J., & Hoc, J.-M. (1983). Tâche et activité dans l'analyse psychologique des situations. *Cahiers de Psychologie Cognitive, 3*, 49-63.

Leplat, J., & Rasmussen, J. (1987). Analysis of human errors in industrial incidents and accidents for improvement of work safety. In J. Rasmussen, K. Duncan, & J. Leplat (Eds.), *New technology and human error*. Chichester: John Wiley.

Lewkowitch, A. (1988, Oct 19-20). Les simulateurs: Des outils de recherche privilégiés pour l'ergonomie. *Proceedings of the 7th European annual conference "On human decision making and manual control"*. Paris: Electricité de France.

Montmollin, M. de (1986a). Analysis of the competence of operators confronting new technologies: Some methodological problems and some results. In F. Klix, & H. Wandke (Eds.), *Man-computer interaction research, Macinter*. Amsterdam: Elsevier.

Montmollin, M. de (1986b). *L'intelligence de la tâche: Elements d'ergonomie cognitive*, (2nd ed). Berne: Peter Lang.

Montmollin, M. de (1990). *L'ergonomie* (rev. ed.). Paris: La Découverte.

Montmollin, M. de, & De Keyser, V. (1986, Sept 10-12). Expert logic versus operator logic. In G. Mancini, G. Johannsen, & L. Martensen (Eds.), Analysis, design and evaluation of man-machine systems, *Proceedings of the 2nd IFAC/IFIP/IEA/IFORS conference*, Varese, Italy, 1985. Oxford: Pergamon Press.

Moray, N. (1986). Modelling cognitive activities: Human limitations in relation to computers aids. In E. Hollnagel, G. Mancini, & D. D. Woods (Eds.), *Intelligent decision support in process environments*. Berlin: Springer-Verlag.

Navarro, C. (1987). Communications fonctionnelles et complexité des tâches dans le pilotage d'un avion de ligne. Le Travail Humain, 50 (4), 289-304.

Norros, L., & Sammatti, P. (1986). *Nuclear power plant operator errors during simulator training*. (Research Rep. No. 446). Espoo: Technical Research Centre of Finland.

Ochanine, D. (1981). (Transl.) In L'image opérative. Paris: Université Paris I.

Patesson, R. (Ed.), (1986). *L'homme et l'écran: Actes du colloque de Nivelles, 1985*. Bruxelles: Editions de l'Université Libre de Bruxelles.

Pinsky, L., & Theureau, J. (1987a). *L'étude du cours d'action. Analyse du travail et conception ergonomique*. Paris: Collection d'ergonomie et de neurophysiologie du travail du CNAM, 88.

Pinsky, L., & Theureau, J. (1987b). Description of visual "action" in "natural" situations. In J. K. O'Reagan, & A. Lévy- Schoen (Eds.), *Eye movements: From physiology to cognition*. Amsterdam: Elsevier.

Pollack, M. E. (1985). Information sought and information provided: An empirical study of user/expert dialogues. In L. Borman, & B. Curtis (Eds.), Human factors in computing systems, II. Amsterdam: North-Holland.

Praetorius, N., & Duncan, K. D. (1988). Verbal reports: A problem in research design. In L. P. Goodstein, H. B. Andersen, & S. E. Olsen (Eds.), *Tasks, errors and mental models. A Festschrift to celebrate the 60th birthday of Professor Jens Rasmussen*. London: Taylor and Francis.

Rasmussen, J. (1986). *Information processing and human-machine interaction: An approach to cognitive engineering*. New York: North-Holland.

Rasmussen, J., Brehmer, B., & Leplat, J. (Eds.). (1991) *Distributed decision-making: Cognitive models for cooperative work*. Chichester: John Wiley.

Rasmussen, J., Duncan, K., & Leplat, J. (Eds.). (1987). *New technology and human error*. Chichester: John Wiley.

Rasmussen, J., & Jensen, A. (1974). Mental procedures in real-life tasks: A case of electronic trouble-shooting. *Ergonomics, 17*, 293-307.

Reason, J. (1987). (Chap. 1, 2, 5, 7, 11). In J. Rasmussen, K. Duncan, & J. Leplat (Eds.), *New technology and human error*. Chichester: John Wiley.

Reason, J. (1990). *Human error*. Cambridge: Cambridge University Press.

Roth, E. M., & Woods, D. D. (1988). Aiding human performance. I: Cognitive analysis. *Le Travail Humain, 51* (1), 139-172.

Samurçay, R., & Hoc, J.-M. (1989). De l'analyse du travail à la spécification d'aides à la décision dans des environnements dynamiques. *Psychologie Française, 33* (3), 187-196.

Savoyant, A., & Leplat, J. (1983). Statut et fonction des communications dans l'activité des équipes de travail. *Psychologie Française, 28*, 243-253.

Scribner, S. (1985). Vigotsky's uses of history. In J. W. Wertsch (Ed.), *Culture, communication and cognition: Vigotskian perspectives*. Cambridge, MA: Harvard University Press.

Spérandio, J.-C; (1972). Charge de travail et régulation des modes opératoires. *Le Travail Humain, 46* (2), 229-238.

Spérandio, J.-C. (1987). L'ergonomie du travail informatisé. In C. Lévy-Leboyer, & J.-C. Spérandio (Eds.), *Traité de psychologie du travail*. Paris: Presses Universitaires de France.

Spérandio, J.-C. (1988). L'ergonomie du travail mental (2nd ed.). Paris: Masson.

Stassen, H. G. (1986). Decision demands and task requirements in work environments: What can be learnt from human operator modelling. In E. Hollnagel, G. Mancini, & D. D. Woods (Eds.), *Intelligent decision support in process environments*. Berlin: Springer-Verlag.

Stassen, H. G., Johanssen, G., & Moray, N. (1988, June 14-16). Internal representation, internal model, human performance model and mental workload. In *Man-machine systems, analysis, design and evaluation*. Preprints of the IFAC/IFIP/IEA/IFORS conference, Oulu, Finland. I, 252-261.

Swaanenburg, H. A. C., Zwaga, H. J., & Duijnhouver, F. (1988, June 14-16). The evaluation of VDU-based man-machine interfaces in process industry. In *Man-machine systems, analysis, design and evaluation*. Preprints of the IFAC/IFIP/IEA/IFORS conference. Oulu, Finland. I, 129-134.

Terssac, G. de (1980). Activité mentale et régulation des conduites: Etude de quelques postes dans l'industrie chimique. In C. Benayoun, G. de Terssac, Y. Lucas, M. Membrado, & E. Soula (Eds.), *Les composantes mentales du travail ouvrier*. Montrouge: ANACT.

Theureau, J. (1991). Les raisonnements dans le travail. In R. Amalberti, M. de Montmollin, & J. Theureau (Eds.), *Modèles de l'analyse du travail*. Liège: Mardaga.

Theureau, J., & Pinsky, L. (1983). Action et parole dans le travail. *Psychologie Française, 28*, 225-264.

Valot, C., & Amalberti, R. (1989). Les redondances dans le traitement des données. *Le Travail Humain, 52*, (2) 155-174.

Van Daele, A. (1988). Ecran de visualisation ou comunication verbale? Analyses comparatives de leur utilisation par des opérateurs de coulée continue en sidérurgie. *Le Travail Humain, 51* (1), 65-79.

Vermersch, P. (1976). *Une approche de la régulation de l'action chez l'adulte. Registres de fonctionnement, déséquilibre transitoire et microgénèse.* Unpublished thesis. Paris: Université René-Descartes.

Vermersch, P. (1978). Une problématique théorique en psychologie du travail. *Le Travail Humain, 41* (2), 263-278.

Visser, W. (1988, June 14-16). Towards modelling the activity of design: An observational study on a specification stage. In *Man-machine systems, analysis, design and evaluation*. Preprints of the IFAC/IFIP/IEA/IFORS conference. Oulu, Finland. I, 51-56.

Wisner, A., Daniellou, F., Pinsky, L., & Theureau, J. (1988, June 14-16). Process supervision and control: Design of technical systems and organization. Training of operators. In *Man-machine systems, analysis, design and evaluation*. Preprints of the IFAC/IFIP/IEA/IFORS conference. Oulu, Finland. II, 511-516.

CHAPTER FIVE

The Support of Cognitive Capacity in Future Organisations: Towards Enhanced Communicative Competence and Cooperative Problem-structuring Capability

Niels Bjørn-Andersen and Lars Ginnerup
*Copenhagen Business School, Howitzvej 60,
DK-2000 Frederiksberg, Denmark*

INTRODUCTION

Cognitive science has contributed substantially to the improvement of human-computer interaction (HCI). However, in order to achieve further improvements it is necessary to extend the traditional, narrow concept of an individual working with a machine to include the social environment of these individuals. An argumentation for this notion is presented based on a survey of studies of the social and organisational aspects of computerisation. It is argued that it is useful to study group decision support systems or computer supported cooperative work under the two related categories "support for enhanced communicative competence" and "support for enhanced cooperative problem-structuring capability". The paper concludes with a listing of research areas of particular interest.

1. EXTENDING HCI FROM "SCREEN AND KEYBOARD LAYOUT" TO "SUPPORT OF COOPERATIVE WORK"

Cognitive science has provided an important basis for developing a more user-friendly interface. PCs especially are giving individuals much better support today for what they want to do. However, no individual is an island. We are all part of groups/organisations where the effectiveness of the larger unit is infinitely more important than the efficiency of the individual. Furthermore, reality is becoming increasingly complex, and we use other role players to help us shape our own values and handle contextualisation processes as we go along. Accordingly, even though we still have a long way to go in improving the human-computer interface for individuals, there is growing recognition that major advancements in the human-computer interface could be achieved, if the social environment of the individual were taken into account more explicitly in the design of new systems. In other words, computer support of cooperative work. (See e.g. "Conference on Computer Support of Cooperative Work", Austin, MCC Software Technology, 1986.)

Historically, there is a clear trend. In the beginning of the 80's we saw a significant increase in the number of distributed systems in the form of terminals, personal computers, and wordprocessors introduced into offices, shops, homes etc. The characteristic features of this first wave of technology included a fairly user-unfriendly interface differing only marginally from that provided for computer specialists.

The second major wave in distributed systems is currently taking place with a worldwide recognition of the advantages of introducing user interfaces based on principles similar to those first introduced on the Xerox Star system and the Macintosh. This type of interface utilises the desk-top metaphor, icons, pull-down/pop-up menus, the mouse, etc., to provide a substantially improved interface between individual users and the machine. With this development, interface design has become qualitatively improved, and substantial achievements are likely in the future with the advent of inexpensive high resolution screens, improved display technology, increased possibility of image processing, voice input/output, multi-function work stations etc. However, these technical achievements are used almost exclusively to support individuals and their machines. The possibility of supporting several individuals in their different joint activities has hardly been addressed in hardware and software design or telecommunication, and only sparsely addressed in the literature on systems analysis/design/implementation.

We believe that the third wave of distributed systems will be characterised by substantial advancements in the direction of the support of cooperative work. It will be necessary to study the environment of the individual or the situated context in which that person operates (Suchman, 1987). The study of groups and larger entities of organisations will be the cornerstone in: (1) improving an understanding of the role technology should play in supporting a multitude of individuals; and (2) deciding how to design future systems to meet this challenge. The difference between these trends in the developments of the 80's and the 90's could be described in the following way. (For a more detailed discussion see the report from the first workshop on the topic of modelling the nature of the office for cooperative work—Bjørn-Andersen et al., 1986):

1. We have to study human actors instead of human factors. This means that we have to view individuals as more than a collection of less than optimally designed hands, neurons, eyes etc., the deficiencies of which have to be accommodated in the design of systems. Individuals must be viewed in the context of what they try to achieve, etc.

2. We should focus on effectiveness issues instead of efficiency issues. Speed of data entry becomes less important than what is entered.

3. We should focus on goals and functions of a work group as a supplement to behaviourally defined office activities and very detailed task analysis. Study the "what" rather than the "how", the "content" rather than the "form".

4. We should recognize the unstructured nature of office work. Whereas some office work might be very formally described using principles of scientific management (Taylor, 1967) a substantial part of office work demands a contextualisation process on the part of the employees, through which an individual in the work group defines the problem and the proper "standard operating procedure". Most work in offices is not a large set of rules with few exceptions - it is the exception that is the rule. Some studies have shown that employees can spend up to 80% of the time on handling non-preprogrammed and non-proceduralised tasks (Strassmann 1985).

5. Recognize the importance of the discourse systems that people use in the different social settings. These are based on shared meaning and shared knowledge to support a particular organisational structure, a particular line of business, or a special professional group.

6. Recognize the importance of informal networks and social support in carrying out most tasks.

7. Recognize that many decisions are not made according to rational decision models, but can best be described in terms of non-rational, political models.

To some extent support of cooperative work has already started with a number of smaller experiments and small-scale implementations. Many individuals share common databases of different types, and cooperate in order to write documents by exchanging files. Electronic mail has also found a place in many organisations, and is used to facilitate "asynchronous" communication between individuals separated in space and time. Furthermore, different types of support for problem structuring and decision-making in groups have also been implemented in a number of organisations. These two main types of support will be discussed in more detail in sections 3 and 4 in this paper.

In 1986 in Austin, Texas, the First Conference on Computer-Supported Cooperative Work was organised. In the foreword to the proceedings at that conference, the programme chair specified the issues in computer support for cooperative work as follows:

1. The nature of cooperative work groups - including group aspects (e.g. mission, identity, leadership, cohesive makeup, embedded organisation and interaction time/space), as well as individual aspects (e.g. contribution, commitment, need satisfaction, and role playing). An ideal situation would have all members knowing and sharing common goals, suggesting ways to reach those goals and taking responsibility in carrying out the associated work. Questions raised attempt to bound and define cooperative work and identify those things which enable it to occur effectively, e.g.:
- in what situations is shared information space (model) necessary?
- what are interesting models for cooperation (e.g. design)?
- how important are negotiations and conflict resolution?
2. The nature of the technology - including current (e.g. networking) as well as the potential for improvements with future technology from a number of technical arenas (e.g. AI, Human-Computer Interfaces). Questions raised attempt to clarify technology developments, e.g.:
- what are the hard problems holding back technology developments?
- what are the multi-user interface issues?
- how can AI help?
3. The nature of the relationship between groups and technology. Questions raised include:
- what is the proper balance between humans and machines?
- what are the effects of current technology on group structures?
- (given that we see a) trend in society towards highly specialized and dispersed experts, what (is the) need to cooperate via the computer ... to

solve the complex problems of the future?

- how will technological innovation affect the way large-group activity is organized in the future?

- what methods do we have to understand/study these phenomena?

This fairly lengthy citation from the conference proceedings is presented in order to give an impression of the variety of issues and solutions within the rather broad area of computer support for cooperative work. However, this does not constitute a research programme and even less a research project. Instead we shall suggest some ideas for research in sections 5 and 6.

The article is structured in such a way that we proceed with a general discussion of the importance of social and organisational issues in relation to the understanding and design of computer systems. This is then followed by two sections taking two different but complementary perspectives: a communication perspective (support for enhanced communicative competence) and a decision-making perspective (support for group decision-making).

2. SOCIAL AND ORGANISATIONAL ASPECTS OF COMPUTING

Social and organisational aspects of computerisation have long been recognized as important. In the early days of computerisation this realization came about primarily as a result of studies on the impact of computers (outstanding examples still worth referring to are: Hoos 1960; Mumford & Banks, 1967). Early case studies in confined environments, superficial surveys and weakly founded predictive forecasts of the first generation computer systems were later followed by more authoritative studies with larger empirical bases and better theoretical foundations (see Bjørn-Andersen et al., 1979; and Bjørn-Andersen et al., 1986b).

However, the general picture that emerges from these and a long row of similar empirical studies is that the introduction of computerisation has been a long sequence of unintended organisational and human consequences. Both disasters and success stories are plentiful and the picture is very kaleidoscopic. It is, however, hard to draw a definite conclusion concerning the impact that computer systems will have on, for example, job content, work qualifications, alienation, organisational culture etc.

Reviews and surveys of this literature (e.g. Bjørn-Andersen & Rasmussen 1980; Hirschheim 1985; Kling 1980; and Mowshowitz 1986) summarise many of the most important empirical studies and conclude almost unanimously that:

- the technology is not deterministic, i.e. that a good fit between the human/organisational system and the computer system is a design issue
- the impact observed is strongly contingency based, i.e. depending on the context, a particular system will result in different consequences. It is therefore important to develop taxonomies for identifying the proper type of system and the proper development/implementation procedure.

Several models are proposed in the literature in an attempt to categorise the different types of impact with the primary aim of providing a basis for a technology assessment before implementation.

A useful attempt at defining the so-called steps of "benefit analysis" is shown in Figure 5.1 (Schäfer et al., 1988). The horizontal axis illustrates how technology assessment might be extended from a narrow isolated view focussing on the technical level to a comprehensive view looking at functional and organisational levels.

As regards a definition of the dimensions which might be applied in the comprehensive evaluation, an example of an assessment model is shown in Figure 5.2. This model provides an overview of those

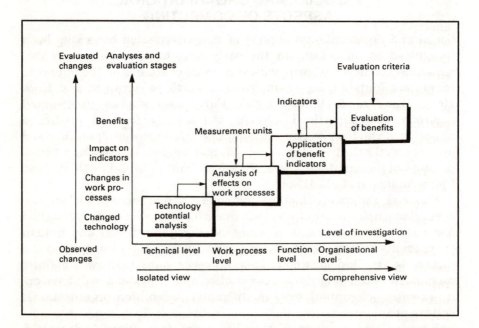

FIG. 5.1. Fundamental steps of technology assessment.

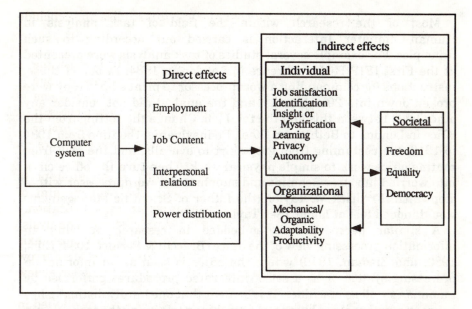

FIG. 5.2. Model of computer impact (Adapted from Bjørn-Andersen & Kjaergærd, 1987).

dimensions in the organisation and society which are potentially influenced when a new computer system is introduced. However, this also means that these dimensions give a strong indication about which dimensions in the environment might potentially form the basis for design.

Many attempts have been made to understand and model the nature of cooperative work, and several taxonomies exist. We find it particularly useful to classify the work according to its scientific background. i.e. whether the organisation (or the group) is seen as a:

- rational system
- human activity system
- socio-emotional system
- socio-political system

Seeing the organisation as an exclusively rational system or at least assuming that it is useful to understand and model its function using a rational model was the dominating perspective in organisational theory until the late 40s, when Simon (1949) dismantled it by introducing the notion of satisficing. It is built on an engineering paradigm where the objectives of an organisation are analysed top down all the way into their primitive or smallest sub-functions and routines.

Most of the research within the field of task analysis in Human-Computer Interaction is carried out according to such principles. For example several studies of task analysis were presented at the First IFIP HCI conference in London in 1984. In one of these, instructions for commanding a wordprocessor to print a hard copy were broken down into 20 sub-tasks, and the analyst did not consider any other level between this and the total job. Change the setting from the office in London to Bethlehem Steel, Pennsylvania, the time from 1984 to 1910, the costuming from grey skirt to overalls, and the task from routine office work to simple physical work. Then turn the office clerk into worried labourer Schmidt and supplant the wordprocessor with a stopwatch. Fredrick W. Taylor (the father of Scientific Management) would indeed feel at home. (See Taylor, 1967).

A similar perspective is embedded in research applying an information processing view of the office (Bracchi & Pernici, 1984; Ellis, 1980; and Zisman, 1979) where the office is seen as an information processing system or as a set of integrated procedures performed by humans as well as machines. It is evident that one hardly distinguishes between whether it is a human or a machine performing the task. Within the area of Decision Support Systems, Sutherland (1983) argues for a similar approach.

A competing perspective is found in the notion of the office as a human activity system. This concept was coined by Checkland in his seminal work on soft systems methodology (Checkland, 1981). The work is a strong attack on "hard systems thinking" represented by the perspective mentioned earlier. Checkland argues on the basis that it is not enough to see the office as a rational system. He sees the organisation as a set of interlinked, purposeful human activities which are embedded in a social system. This has to be taken into account when analysing and modelling future information systems. In this way he recognizes the social relationship even though he does not offer very specific guidelines on how to take these into account and how to model them.

Secondly, Checkland argues that organisations are largely confronted with very complex, unstructured problems in a poorly defined environment that defy conventional structured methodologies. This means that it is necessary to develop "rich pictures" (pictorial informal representation of objectives, actors, information flows, conflicts, etc.) and "root definitions" (verbal specification of customers, actors, transactions, *weltanschauung*, problem owner and environment of the system defined on the basis of the rich picture), together with the problem owners in the organisation, in order to better understand the problem setting.

Several important research activities within the area of Human-Computer Interaction could in our opinion be classified as applying the perspective of the organisation as a human activity system. The work on the informal nature of office activities by Suchman (1987) and Wynn (1979) and the work on improving the interface between systems designers and users by Blomberg (1986) are examples which are useful in improving the HCI within the broader interpretation we are promoting.

Similarly the language-action perspective applied so convincingly by Winograd and Flores (1986) would fit into this category. Only language for purposeful action is planned. As Winograd (1988) phrases it:

> By starting with a language/action perspective, we have found it possible to create systems that are more effective in getting work done, whenever that work involves communication and coordinated action among a group of people.

However, as pointed out in the same article, this perspective does not deal with implementation, roles, authority, group interests, conflicts etc. Others (e.g. Kaasbøll, 1986; and Sørgaard, 1987) also apply the language/action perspective, even though to some extent they incorporate some of the issues that Winograd deliberately omits. This perspective will be dealt with more extensively in the next section.

The social-emotional perspective is better in identifying "social richness" (Ruhleder, 1987) through a focussing on human/social/organisational issues. A prominent representative of this perspective is Mumford who has been actively promoting it for more than two decades (See Mumford & Ward, 1968; Mumford & Weir, 1979; and Mumford, 1983). This perspective has its roots in the "socio-technical work design" tradition which goes back to research at The Tavistock Institute in London performed after the Second World War.

More recently, systems design activities along social-emotional dimensions are taking place in Finland within the "Human Scale Information Systems" project (See Nurminen, 1982) and the multi-disciplinary work on systems design in Oulu (See Kerola, 1986) based on the work by Kolb (1984) on experiential learning. Here the concept of tacit knowledge plays a major role.

Finally, a substantial amount of work is being done in what we call the socio-political perspective. Gerson and Star (1986) point out that "the products of office work are the result of decentralized negotiations, where changing patterns of task organisation and alliance inevitably give rise to inconsistent negotiations", which leads them to argue for the need to study "due process" in the work place.

Work within the area of organisational culture will contribute to a sharpening of this perspective. It is evident that the area relies to a large extent on sciences like group sociology, organisation theory, anthropology, phenomenology, etc.

In "Understanding the Office: A Social Action Perspective", Hirschheim et al. (1986) apply this perspective by specifying the difference between what they call "Human Activity Aspects" and "Social Community Aspects":

Human Activity Aspects	*Social Community Aspects*
Organisation as structure	Organisation as culture
Formal	Informal
Purposeful	Non-purposeful
Instrumentally directed	Non-directive
Conscious	Unconscious
Designed	Emergent
Empirical, analytical knowledge	Tacit, intuitive knowledge

Although some of the concepts might be debated, it is obvious that these represent two alternative views of the office. With this we hope to have shown that each of the different perspectives has something to offer in the attempt to support cooperative work through the enhancement of communicative competence. We shall then move to the second area of this article, that of group decision support systems.

3. SUPPORT FOR ENHANCED COMMUNICATIVE COMPETENCE

Conversation as dance.   It is interesting to note that Flores (former member of Allende's Chilean government) and Winograd (American pioneer of the AI movement) should be among the first ones to apply the rich European tradition of theories of intentionality (Husserl, Heidegger, Merleau-Ponty, Gadamer) to systems design, thereby creating a system for the coordination of commitment in organisations.

This system called: The Coordinator System can be regarded as a kind of time manager which takes care of mutual intentionality and commitment. The system tracks each user's conversations, reminds them of their pending commitments, and keeps a record of the status of a group project.

Based on Searle's taxonomy of speech acts, Winograd and Flores (W. & F.) have so to speak choreographed the pattern of recurrent conversations for action in organisations and thereby revealed the fundamental steps.

According to W. & F. (1986), "there are a surprisingly few basic conversational building-blocks (such as request/promise, offer/ acceptance, and report/acknowledgement) that frequently recur in conversations for action...It is like a dance, giving some initiative to each partner in a specific sequence." (p. 159). "These networks of recurrent conversations are the core of organization. They are embodied as intercommunicating offices, each specialized in fulfilling certain kinds of commitments." (p. 158).

W. & F.'s theory of language is based on a combination of hermeneutics and phenomenology (concentrating on the work of Heidegger and Gadamer) with the theory of speech acts (Austin, Searle, and to a lesser degree Habermas' Social Action Theory).

But what have these different and difficult philosophical approaches to do with each other, and how is it that they are considered relevant for designing computer-based tools?

Here is a preliminary minimal characterisation of this alternative proposal for the foundation for design of computer-based tools with respect to management:

In "A Taxonomy of Illocutionary Acts", Searle argues that there are five and only five basic categories of illocutionary acts: assertives, in which we tell our hearers (truly or falsely) how things are; directives, in which we try to get them to do things; commissives, in which we commit ourselves to doing things; declaratives, in which we bring about changes in the world with our utterances; and expressives, in which we express our feelings and attitudes. (Bernsen, 1984).

As alluded to earlier, W. & F. concentrate their work on the notions of directives and commissives. Let us therefore expose these notions. According to W. & F. these are the essential building-blocks of conversations for action in organisations:

Directives.   These attempt (in varying degrees) to get the hearer to do something. These include both questions (which can direct the hearer to make an assertive speech act in response) and commands (which attempt to get the hearer to carry out some linguistic or non-linguistic act).

Commissives.   These commit the speaker (again in varying degrees) to some future course of action (cf. p. 58).

What is interesting about W. & F.'s approach though, is that the concept of The Coordinator for use in organisations (with special regard to the coordination of commitment) does not rely on truth conditions. Instead of referring to some kind of index with respect to the sincerity of intentionality (for instance individually and precisely specifying the "sincerity conditions" that are necessary for an act of promising) and thereby leaving it all up to the mental states of the individual speakers and hearers of the organisation, the Coordinator explicitly keeps track of the social and psychological contracts entered into by participants in the networks of recurrent conversations. This is done by offering context cues for communication and thereby making the interactions transparent; that is, providing a ready-to-hand tool that operates in the domain of conversations for action. Then it is no longer enough just to send a message, but instead you are prompted to classify your utterance and in this manner enter a diagram of conversation like "make request" and the corresponding "make promise".

But what is the rationale for this view of organisational coordination?

Organizations exist as networks of directives and commissives. Directives include orders, requests, consultations, and offers; commissives include promises, acceptances, and rejections...

People in an organization (including, but not limited to managers) issue utterances, by speaking or writing, to develop the conversations required in the organizational network. They participate in the creation and maintenance of a process of communication. At the core of this process is the performance of linguistic acts that bring forth different kinds of commitments. (p. 157)

And finally:

Computer-based tools can be used in requesting, creating, and monitoring commitments. (p. 158)

Key implementation issues

In extending the aforementioned discussion, two key implementation issues for human-computer-human network interaction can be pointed out:

1. On the positive side there is commitment: (screening of speech acts according to illocutionary points, force (i.e. manner and degree), and propositional content; a time manager taking care of mutual intentionality and commitment).

2. A more negative issue is flaming: (network as organisational talebearer; in the extreme: gossip entered anonymously giving rise to counterproductive infiltration).

In the latter case we also urgently need some tools or devices to filter out the information float of junk mail and unsolicited material in general. In this sense the Information Lens project carried out at MIT, which deals with the problem of getting the right messages through, is most interesting.

Information Lens "draws on an artificial intelligence programming tool that allows each user to tailor the system to his personal needs. The computer can be instructed to discriminate among electronic messages - recognising the difference, say, between a routine announcement of a new pencil procurement policy and an urgent reminder that your boss wants your group's report before the end of the day. And it can cull information from other computers' databases that relate to the projects a group is working on, routing it speedily to each group member's terminal and automatically updating his files." (Richman 1987).

Distributed model-power and the holographic metaphor
Although the capture of quantifying corporate models by nature is limited, we do think that new organisational metaphors for the benefit of cognitive representation are needed, due primarily to the implications of IT regarding organisation theory. Morgan, (1986, p.95), shows what the fuss is all about:

> Brains and organisations as holographic systems: To compare the brain with a hologram may seem to be stretching reason beyond reasonable limits. However, the way a holographic plate enfolds all the information necessary to produce a complete image in each of its parts has much in common with the functioning of a brain. And it is possible to extend this image to create a vision of an organization where capacities required in the whole are enfolded in the parts, allowing the system to learn and self-organize, and to maintain a complete system of functioning even when specific parts malfunction or are removed. Some highly innovative organizations have already begun organizing in this way.

What is interesting about the holographic metaphor is that especially advanced information technology may be strongly conducive to the realisation of potentialities by delivering powerful facilities for corporate modelling, distribution of model-power and competence, thereby providing prerequisites of multi-level insight and decentralised decision-making authority. The advent of distributed and knowledge-based Group DSS may very well lead into holographic principles of reasoning within the information frame of the business concerned.

Furthermore, Glazer has suggested a holographic theory of decision-making. The theory claims that humans make decisions by evaluating all qualities about the available alternatives holographically (i.e. by way of Fourier-analysis). Such holistic evaluations are experienced as intuition, not as rational considerations. (Glazer, 1989).

4. SUPPORT FOR GROUP DECISION MAKING

Decision Support Systems (DSS)

The management philosophy behind the design of Decision Support Systems directly addresses the mental models of the decision-makers in terms of providing facilities for making explicit what is implicit in the reasoning processes. Often a DSS is referred to as a learning system in the sense that it provides facilities for experimental selection of solution strategies. The main target is to facilitate problem-structuring in ill-defined or initially unstructured decision situations by directing attention to the substantial critical decision set and ruling out distractors. The starting point is to provide support for the (useful) mental models referred to by the decision-makers; but the goal is to devote more efforts to the handling of complexity and uncertainty by providing effective and user-friendly tools customised for the decision task at hand. Consider the case of portfolio composition systems. Investigations have revealed that a portfolio manager usually monitors single issues although the essential idea of portfolio management is to address the whole set of securities in order to spread the risks involved. A DSS for portfolio management would therefore be designed with the deliberate purpose of facilitating more holistic comparisons and judgements while still supporting the monitoring of single issues (cf. Stabell, 1984 for a more detailed discussion concerning how to embed learning processes in the design of DSS).

Japan is not at the leading edge in the development of decision aiding technology, partly because of the tradition-bound way of approaching decision-making in organisations. The Japanese ritual of "ringi", a collective decision-making process in which a policy document passes from manager to manager for approval, is one explanation.

This conservative corporate culture may have contributed to Japanese managers missing the first decision support wave. Spreadsheets and other software for traditional decision support applications, such as financial modelling, have sold only a few hundred thousand copies in Japan. Considering the installed base of more than 3 million microcomputers, Japanese users appear uninterested in standard Western approaches to decision support. But now technology is catching up with the need for group interaction in the decision-making process and Japan is slowly coming to grips with imported DSS products as well as cultivating some home-grown varieties. (DATAMATION, October 1, 1986, pp. 68-11).

However, in Europe (as in the U.S.) research and development concerning Decision Support Systems have been going on for more than a decade and the results obtained are quite promising.

When considering the leverage of supporting DSS research and development in Europe, one should be aware that Group DSS seems to be the new frontier. Especially with respect to well-balanced trade-offs between parties with conflicting preferences, the strong European tradition of democratic institutions and democracy in the workplace might serve as a platform for development and implementation of context-sensitive Group DSS. This reference viewpoint would also be conducive to the realisation of the real potentiality of GDSS as organisational feedback sensitive systems.

Group Decision Support Systems (GDSS)

The aim of group decision-aiding technology is not just to support specific task-oriented work groups. Rather, the subject matter is a question of supporting group work and coordination throughout the entire organisation.

Group Decision Support Systems is one of the most inter- or even trans-disciplinary fields within information systems research. Jarke (1986b, p. 148), succinctly depicts the historical background by way of the following triangle and notes that:

By the mid-1970s, artificial intelligence (AI), databases (DB), operations research (OR), and communications (CO) were well established areas of research. Ten years later, new areas such as office systems (OS), knowledge base systems (KBMS), and model management systems (MM) have been studied that merge several of these areas. For full-fledged distributed GDSS, however, an even deeper integration of all four basic areas will be needed.

But why is it that Group DSS can be viewed as representative of the general approach, which we prefer to call "the DISCURSIVE systems approach" inspired by Habermas, Hirschheim and Klein—(not to use an older but fully comparable expression such as "inquiry systems", coined by Singer, Churchman, Mitroff)?

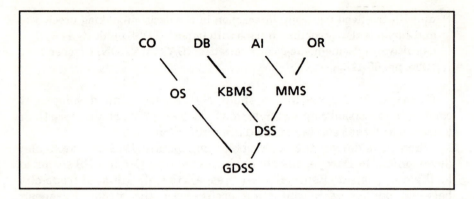

FIG. 5.3. Group DSS: An historical background (Jarke, 1986b).

The answer to this question is that we cannot conceive of distributed and knowledge-based GDSS without implying the existence and use of local/wide area network, electronic mail, data base management systems, individual DSS and application generators in general, not to mention network- and communications protocols, and even AI. Hence the GDSS concept is sufficiently entangled not to fall short of the posed organisational complexity when considering communicative competence and distributed model-power.

It may be argued that the explicit emphasis on decision-making is exaggerated given what we do know about organisational functioning as often resembling some kind of loosely coupled system (cf. Weick, 1969; or March & Olsen, 1979: the garbage can metaphor).

The loosely coupled perspective suggests (as a descriptive, and certainly not as a normative theory of organisations), that streams of actors, problems, solutions and opportunities for decision-making intersect rather casually in various fields of the organisation, thereby leading to only temporary commitments among the people involved, who, would nevertheless expect some kind of pay-off for the time and energy they have invested in the matter of concern.

But this statement might indeed serve as an argument for the concept of GDSS, notably if the emphasis is on group support, rather than decision-making in the narrow sense (i.e. as a discrete event versus a recurrent activity). In addition, as a point of criticism the "loosely coupled" objection is not decisive when taking into careful consideration the very possibility of maintaining an organisational discussion by using the facilities of a networked GDSS. Viewed in this manner the GDSS concept is interesting because it provides facilities for structuring discursive processes while still offering the opportunity for informal communication.

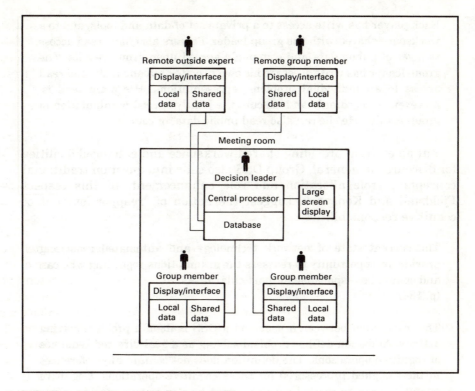

FIG. 5.4. Virtual meetings (Robey, 1986).

The elementary technical components (building blocks) of a Group Decision Support System are: data manager, dialogue manager (static, dynamic or adaptive dialogues), model manager, communications manager. In various combinations and configurations these technical components comprise the architecture of GDSS.

Whereas a DSS typically consists of three main technical components, namely: a data manager, a dialogue manager and a model manager, the most important additional feature of a Group DSS is the communications manager, which (more or less automatically) takes care of the network- and communications protocol according to specifications initially agreed by participants in the group decision process. This feature yields new opportunities as we shall see.

Jarke suggests (1986b, p.147) a conceptual architecture for Group DSS called MEDIATOR, in which there are two types of users: a group leader or mediator and any (reasonably small) number of group members or "players".

Each player has write access to a private set of data and tools, and to a workspace shared with the group leader. Players also have read access to a set of public data and commonly agreed upon group results. The group leader has write access to his own private data and tools, and read access to all individual problem representations. His main task is, however, to coordinate and execute the jointly agreed manipulation of group results. He/she can also read public data, of course.

But apart from providing shared workspace and enhanced facilities for discourse in general, Group DSS also calls into question traditional concepts of role allocation and role enhancement. In this respect Fjeldstad and Konsynski suggest the notion of "reapportionment of cognitive responsibilities":

The current state of network technology and automated reasoning provide an opportunity to reassess the assumptions regarding who can and should be responsible for particular tasks.
(p. 184)

The interaction between a user and a DSS is itself a problem solving activity. Anderson defines problem solving as a goal-directed sequence of cognitive operations. The definition does not contain any references to the assigned processor(s) for these cognitive operations. Cognitive operations can be carried out either by a human or by a machine. In a DSS environment, the problem solving task is characterized by a sharing of cognitive tasks between the user and the DSS.
(p. 190)

In conclusion, it is appropriate to recognize the distributed processing concept emerging in both the hardware/software environment as well as in task management in DSS environments. The partnership role of the DSS in the decision making activity will not be realized until we are able to accommodate a full assessment of the proper apportionment of cognitive tasks among all participating intelligent processors both human and system.
(p. 200)

(Quotations from Fjeldstad & Konsynski's contribution in IFIP/DSS, 1986).

To be a little more precise, let us consider some of the facilities provided by the GDSS called Co-oP (cf. Bui & Jarke, 1986). First of all it is worthwhile to note that Co-oP provides its users with two model bases:

i) a Content-Oriented Model Bank (COMB) offers a large set of explicative (e.g., linear programming, financial models) and time series models (regression models, smoothing techniques)

ii) a Multiple-Criteria Decision Model Bank (MCDMB) offers a set of interactive MCDMs for the most common types of decision problems. As yet, only two MCDMs are stored:

The ELECTRE method for selecting one, and only one, best alternative among many, and Saaty's Analytical Hierarchy Process for ranking all alternatives according to the decision-maker's needs.

The basic steps of the Co-oP group decision process are similar to the typical procedure of a multiple-criteria group problem-solving process that is governed by norms imposed by the group:

1. Problem definition.
2. Group constitution, i.e., group norm definition.
3. Prioritisation of evaluation criteria.
4. Determination of individual preferences, i.e., individual selection of alternatives.
5. Aggregation of individual preferences, i.e., group selection of alternatives.
6. Evolution of individual and group preferences through consensus-seeking and compromise (negotiation).

Group communication situations can be classified along at least five dimensions:

1. Spatial distance among decision-makers distinguishes between decision-making in the same location (e.g. in an electronic boardroom) and remote decisions (via video-conferencing, electronic mail: i.e. local or wide area network, telephones, etc.).

2. Temporal distance determines whether decision-makers are convened in a (local or remote) synchronous mode, or whether they submit their input to the decision process asynchronously, that is, when convenient, e.g. by opening a time window (cf. Keen, 1986, or due to some group norm explicitly defining time management.

3. Centralisation of control distinguishes democratic decision processes from those in which there is a group leader possessing relatively more information and/or power and thereby trying to take control (cf. Daroca, 1984). This is a matter of establishing symmetrical versus asymmetrical conditions for multi-person dialogue.

4. Degree of cooperation distinguishes a setting of cooperative group work from one in which (possibly hostile) parties bargain concerning some issue of common interest (e.g. seller-buyer negotiations). From a

purely systemic point of view this may not be a key critical issue, but from the management point of view it certainly is as Jarke (1986b, p.146) points out:

> Interaction among decision makers is not necessarily cooperative; different goals and perceptions must be traded off in a multiperson decision process.

5. The diminishing/salience of social context cues. Context cues serve to alert listeners to the information load that bystanders in the domain are implicitly required to be aware of (cf. the notions of "listening in a background" and "consensus domains" revived by Winograd & Flores, 1986, and the notion of meta-contexts suggested by Bateson). Consequently this view of human information processing assumes that human actors are information constructors rather than information gatherers. The implications for knowledge propagation are intricate; but even more so it seems as if Group DSS provide some opportunities for turning up and down the social context cues. We know very little, if anything, about this issue, but a preliminary minimal characterisation is obtainable from a few controlled experiments in relation to group processes in computer-mediated communication (see Siegel et al., 1986; Daroca, 1984; Sproull & Kiesler, 1986). We suggest that field experiments be set up to gather information in order to help us understand the perceived advantages/disadvantages. It seems obvious to draw upon the well documented social-psychological experiments concerning phenomena like Groupthink and Group Polarisation. For instance: how can we counteract the adverse effects of concurrence-seeking in policy-planning groups through the use of GDSS?

Let us briefly consider the implications of the various combinations of the dimensions for office automation outlined earlier. We can already imagine a mobile automated office installed in a wagon as part of a train transporting people to the central place of work located far away. Instead of simply commuting, employees get paid for conducting transactions, like dialing up various nodes or hubs using integrated computer and communications technologies. This is not just science fiction, but something already taking place on trains commuting from Stockholm to ASEA's central plant in Vasterås, two hours away. Neither is this exclusively a matter of efficiency, but one of attracting the specialised workforce living in Stockholm who do not want to waste time commuting.

Also, we can imagine "intelligent buildings" comprised of various ecological control devices and a telecommunications network, as the backbone of the organisation offering numerous hooks for tool-oriented edp-facilities like distributed and knowledge-based GDSS or automatic "data staging managers" providing access to external databases etc.

Requisite variety, structured group management techniques and gaming

How to provide for requisite variety

According to Reason (1990) it is a plausible assumption that only two basic cognitive processes are needed to account for the bulk of memory processes occuring when solving problems.

What is it that calls things to mind?

In case of cognitive under-specification one would point to the following primitives often employed subconsciously in the human knowledge base:

—similarity-matching - match like to like
—frequency-gambling - select in favour of high-frequency items/ patterns

Among the general activators is the affective "charge", which goes to show that cognitive processes are not only triggered in a rational way.

Our point in introducing this model is that if it holds, then the implications for organisational learning must be considered. As the main implication might suggest, people in organisations when confronted with a problem often behave exactly as they normally do, nothing more, nothing less (cf. standard operating procedures). This would be consistent with the thesis of a number of modern theories of organisational learning which state that people do not necessarily learn from experience; they mostly do or learn from what they are told by organisational myths.

This is a devastating thesis with respect to requisite variety! Indeed it is another significant reason for deliberately distributing models and model-power and setting up experiments like gaming.

Structured Group Management Techniques

An array of information-sharing and decision techniques such as Nominal Group Technique, Delphi Technique, COPE, Cognoter & Argnoter (an argumentation generating spreadsheet) have been (re)designed and reinforced by virtue of advanced information technology. The first two techniques can be considered rational, but naive, though in the electronic versions more convenient to use and thus they represent a more inviting process tool. The last three techniques are examples of "group-ware" especially designed to facilitate teamwork through better decision-making aids and project and problem management.

Gaming

Corporate models also provide the opportunity to set up integrated business and role games thereby providing the opportunity for rehearsing, e.g. conflict management. The point is that gaming in itself seems to create and maintain motivation.

Also gaming provides the opportunity to set up experiments and initiate self-reflective cognitive mapping, which otherwise would be most unrealistic to conduct (because of what is at stake in real life).

Another reason for initiating gaming is that people, when required to make their preferences explicit, simultaneously reveal the values of their working functions. By making such frameworks visible the situation might be conducive to establish more mutual respect among preference-conflicting parties, e.g. marketing and R&D.

Among the software packages, which could be useful tools for this purpose, are various programmes more or less based on utility theory, like HIVIEW & EQUITY developed at the Decision Analysis Unit, London School of Economics and Political Science, and PREFCALC developed by researchers at LAMSADE, Paris (to mention a few commercially available products).

Strictly speaking, utility theory gives no basis for aggregation of the elicited preferences of individuals. However, the problem-structuring procedures of utility (-like) decision models help to focus thinking in ways which can promote clearer communication. Moreover, making conflicting preferences explicit helps to uncover misunderstanding and mistrust.

Group dynamics revisited

Group dynamics

The reason for bringing these phenomena into this discussion is that it makes sense to think of GDSS as a setting or a set-up which allows for effectively counteracting e.g. some of the antecedent conditions of Groupthink (defective decision-making) or for that matter: Group Polarization and double-bind.

Groupthink

How to counteract the adverse effects of concurrence-seeking in policy-planning groups?

Theory and research perspectives. Janis summarises his work concerning the Groupthink phenomenon by giving some advice to counteract the seven symptoms of defective decision-making labelled Groupthink (cf. Janis, 1982). One of his main proposals is to "always give it a second chance" and it seems probable that the likelihood of following this advice will increase with the use of networked GDSS as it is far more convenient to convene participants in a decision-making process performed electronically. Namely, because participants in such electronic meetings can join in asynchronously and the conditions for dialogue can even be set up symmetrically (ensuring equal participation).

Directive leadership is one of the antecedent conditions of Groupthink, but this condition might be counteracted by turning off the power indicators, or, in the extreme, by inviting anonymous viewpoints. Such communication strategies are made possible by use of distributed GDSS.

Group Polarization

Research with dilemmas indicates a tendency for group discussion to reinforce the initially dominant point of view. The group polarisation hypothesis says that the average post-discussion response will tend to be more extreme in the same direction as the average of the pre-group responses. The hypothesis is validated through numerous studies, and the phenomenon quite well understood in that the literature converges on an explanation in terms of:

a) Informational influence:
the exclusively rational side of the subject matter, i.e., the weight of the arguments one-by-one and aggregated.

b) Social comparison:
the socio-emotional sides of the case, for instance according to group pressure or the bandwagon effect.

As to GDSS it seems likely that the informational influence will outweigh the social comparison due to the turning down of social context cues.

THE FUTURE PERSPECTIVE: NEW POSSIBILITIES OF MANAGING THE COGNITIVE CAPACITY OF ORGANISATIONS? CONCEIVING OF DISTRIBUTED AND KNOWLEDGE-BASED GDSS AS A PROTOTYPICAL EXAMPLE!

Some technological platforms are already provided:

Data staging managers are gradually making it possible to extract data from various external as well as internal databases for use in personal workstations (here we address the emerging grey zone of infoware...)

Various Multi Criteria Decision Methods (MCDM) based tools for use in case of intrapersonal or interpersonal preference conflicts. GDSS provides a set of preference aggregation techniques and mediation tools that can be used in conjunction with certain combinations of individually used MCDM; this is what is often called the ranking, rating and voting approach.

A promising prospect concerning integration of expert systems (AI) with GDSS:

One of the main distinguishing features concerning the difference between expert systems and decision support systems has to do with the degree of automation. Whereas experts in the field of expert systems (ES) go for automation, even of conclusions, builders of decision support systems would typically aim at aiding the user(s) during various phases of the decision-making process — and leaving to the users themselves to draw the conclusions.

In other words: the expression "support" in decision support systems is to be taken quite literally as the final decision is only the outcome of a very interactive process between the "chauffeur" and the "intelligent terminal".

Consider the following example of estimating price elasticity. This is a perennial issue in marketing as it is a very complex task where the knowledge required is extremely uncertain. Any imaginative expert system given the task of estimating price elasticity would probably be built on the concept of replicating specific human expert(s) whose knowledge has often proved successful in connection with "decisions that really matter" in business life. The expert system will then provide an answer, i.e. the most qualified guess the system can provide given its capabilities and data. In contrast, a decision support system for estimating price elasticity would not provide a single "best" answer. A DSS would be designed to assist the decision-maker in formulating the right problem, in analysing the alternatives and in making the decision, e.g. it is possible to use a DSS for a "what-if" type solution strategy in order to explore the imaginative alternatives and then decide on the preferred strategy (see Stabell, 1987 and Little, 1986, for a concise description of the philosophy of decision support in general).

The most recent advances in the design of GDSS offer possibilities of distributed problem-solving and decision-making, not just among human agents communicating electronically, but also among the agents and their machines. It is exactly this systematic distribution of cognitive capacity among human agents and machines that are interacting in a complex network, that makes it sensible to launch the notion of "the managing of cognitive capacity in organisations".

But apart from this fundamental difference between ES and DSS, one very promising perspective emerges: to merge the horizons of ES and DSS using the ES as a networked automatic switchboard between distributed DSS-tools and the users of such decision-aiding technology.

If we take a longer view, the following prospect is promising: to integrate expert systems with GDSS, for instance in such a way that the expert system functions as an automatic switchboard within the framework of a distributed and knowledge-based GDSS with the special purpose of ensuring compatibility with respect to problem definitions, employed tools and procedures, the latter primarily being a question of taking care of network- and communications protocols.

What is most interesting in this perspective is that the focal expert system functions as a cognitively assisting intermediary between decision support tools and their users. Such intelligent interfaces would free the users of some intricate and cumbersome computation routines, and of monitoring the compatibility of the procedures employed.

A prototypical example of a semi-ES design:

Stabell's concept based on intelligent help menus combined with task-relevant directions of how to log into a network for further assistance, when and if the help menus fail to guide.

A critical socio-emotional viewpoint from any technological platform:

We consider the following cues as a rudimentary critical assumption set concerning the quality of working life:

* Associative participation (affective charge loaded).

* Dissociative participation (affective charge unloaded). The real danger: alienation, reification of intentional communication, abdication from responsibility (these symptoms are already apparent in connection with risk management!). The solution: IT must involve not only data discipline, but simulations discipline as well.

* Loss of job contact.

5. SUMMARY AND SUGGESTED RESEARCH TOPICS

The aim of this working paper was to generate some ideas and point to promising areas of research within the subject area: human-work interaction and influences from advanced information technology with special emphasis on social and organisational aspects.

Where is the Frontier?

It seems reasonable, then, to conclude that Japan is not a leader with respect to the development of concepts in connection with decision support systems.

Furthermore, Europe is not yet behind the U.S. with regards to development of systems concepts in connection with the notion of computer-supported work groups/group work:

The area of computer-supported cooperative work is beginning to gain momentum in the U.S. Several theoretical pieces which are relevant to this area of research have been around for some time, but the notion of this actually constituting a research field is still evolving.

In 1985, when the idea of having this area as one of the future ESPRIT projects was first proposed at an ESPRIT workshop on office systems held in Brussels, there was hardly any empirical research in the U.S. However, in the early 1990s, it is clearly possible to talk about a field of research in its own right. Four months after the first small ESPRIT workshop on "Modelling the Nature of the Office for Design of Third Wave Office Systems" in Copenhagen in August 1986, the first full-scale conference on the subject was organised in Austin, Texas in December 1986 (Conference on Computer-Supported Cooperative Work). The NYU symposium in May 1987 had the same focus (Technological Support for Work Group Collaboration) and the theme of IFIP's 1988 conference (in Italy in June) was "Organizational Decision Support". Since then there has been a wealth of conferences.

The state of the art in this field is not yet very advanced. Little has been published in books or journal articles, and most of what is available is of a speculative nature. But the conferences keep showing that substantial efforts are being devoted to this field. The theoretical contributions are growing in number, and many interesting inferences are being made. The empirical contributions, however, are very few and there are many opportunities for research.

Among the existing American projects, the most profound results are likely to be obtained from:

1. The research group at the University of Arizona, headed by J.F. Nunamaker.
2. Xerox Park work especially related to the "Colab", "Media Spaces" and "Portland-Oregon" projects.
3. Micro-electronics and Computer Technology Cooperation in Austin, Texas from their Design-Interface Group headed by Clarence Ellis.
4. MIT's Information Lens project and The Media Lab.
5. NYU Decision room experiments.

In these pieces of empirical work, it is characteristic that the technical problems have been extremely large, and have yet to be solved. It is therefore far from being too late to set up similar experiments in Europe in order to gain a profound knowledge about how cooperative work of different types might be supported. In Europe we are a few years behind technologically, but we have a leading edge in understanding organisational and social behaviour which we should exploit. It is of course necessary to act quickly.

Apart from the aforementioned quite favourable political positioning, it is preliminarily recommended that attention be given to the following notions:

1. The notion of using expert systems as a switchboard between users of decision-aiding technology and various computer-based methods, techniques and tools (for instance: MCDM-based tools for decision-making) apart from the idea of letting expert systems take care of network- and communications protocols. A case in point: The Co-oP System (cf. Bui & Jarke, 1986 and Bui, 1987).

2. The notion of "turning up and down the social context cues" through the use of various electronic media. Very little is known about the characteristics of the various types of electronic encounters. For instance, how close are they respectively? And exactly what are the (context-dependent) advantages of communicating in the face-to-face as opposed to the face-to-file mode and vice versa?

3. The notion of applying the rich European tradition of hermeneutics and phenomenology (that is, theories of intentionality and interpretation) to systems designs ranging from computer-based communications facilities in general to the idea of a system for the coordination of commitment in complex organisations. A case-in-point: The Coordinator System (cf. Winograd & Flores, 1986).

6. SUGGESTED RESEARCH TOPICS

The theme of our paper is computer-based systems for cooperative work and group decision-making. We pay special attention to the area of Office Automation, but also we address the more abstract levels of senior management concerned with strategy formulation. The main focus of the discussion is Group Decision Support Systems. Although our focus in the paper is on the broader issues of computer-supported cooperative work and group decision-making, we retain the acronym GDSS (Group Decision Support System) to describe the array of technologies of interest.

An Extended Version of Office Automation
(The One Cluster)

In recent years much effort has been put towards the modelling of the office, cf. the FAOR-project (Functional Analysis of Office Requirements) within the ESPRIT programme. One of the main problems as to modelling is that every office functions in a different way. Due to this differentiation, and acknowledging the socio-emotional processes at work in the office, the need for more subtle and networked tools than those offered by ordinary concepts of integrated office systems, is recognized. So far analysis and applications have been preoccupied with terms of efficiency, i.e. "more of the same, but at a higher rate". The new concepts also address terms of effectiveness, that is, "more and different" or, something is missing. This means that more basic questions are put forward, and that the foundation of design is more solidly bound in conceptual terms, and most often implying inter- and trans-disciplinary activities. Among the contributing disciplines (some of them newly arrived) are cognitive, social and organisational psychology, cultural sociology, theories of social cognition, social and philosophical anthropology, macro ergonomics and even ethnomethodology.

We suggest that cultural cohesiveness in organisations be considered a most important key issue for the design of future generations of integrated office systems.

With respect to these complex social and organisational issues, the concept of The Coordinator System developed by Flores (cf. Winograd & Flores, 1986) is emphasised. Drawing on hermeneutics and phenomenology (especially work by Heidegger) and speech act theory (Searle, Austin), Flores, together with Action Technologies, has devised and marketed a networked tool for managing the commitments within small, medium-sized or large organisations. This is a good example of how to combine basic research and development of applications. The concept can be seen as representative of a new generation of computer-based tools for co-operative work, and we call attention to hermeneutics (the study of interpretation) and phenomenology (the philosophical examination of the foundations of experience and action).

Business and Information Systems Strategy Formulation Methodology and in particular Decision Support Systems for Upper Management (The Other Cluster)

Here is an example of avenues to explore in GDSS:

Building on "stratified systems theory" (cf. Jaques, 1976; 1982), the Decision Analysis Unit, London School of Economics and Political Science, has shown that so far only a few decision support systems provide effective help in generating knowledge representation of problems encountered by senior managers. Above the levels of management concerned with direct output, it seems most difficult to embed the procedural knowledge required to develop structure and handle uncertainty as to how to go about building a model of the problem. See Table 5.1 (from Humphreys & Berkeley, 1985), enclosed as an appendix.

As for senior managers, there is no completely "objective" way of determining the relative importance of different objectives, e.g. for a decision about a major future investment in telecommunications. In other words the proportion of discretion to rule-based work is greater the higher up one climbs the organisational hierarchy. Although handling of uncertainty at the more abstract levels of management seems to be a very messy problem, this might indeed constitute a research area in itself. An approach which has already proved successful is decision conferencing. The idea here is that decision-makers and problem owners contribute experience, knowledge and intuition concerning the issues at stake. At these meetings group facilitators, who are not subject matter specialists, provide expertise in problem-structuring languages and problem-solving methods in general aided by advanced information technology.

It is to be noted that Europe seems to be quite strong in decision technology techniques (cf. Humphreys & Wisudha, 1987, in which they have surveyed a large number of methods and tools for structuring and analysing decision problems).

The Managing of Cognitive Capacity in Future Organisations

The combination of extended Office Automation to support communicative competence with Group Decision Support Systems offers new and even unthought of possibilities regarding organisation. The possibilities, however, need to be considered with the help of new metaphors and conceptual frameworks for the alternation of organisational structures and formations. For instance: Is the well-known loosely coupled perspective in organisation theory compatible with the notion of dissipative structures and systems (Prigogine, 1984)? We also suggest consideration of the holographic metaphor. What is interesting in this is that especially advanced information technology may be strongly conducive to the realisation of the potentialities by delivering powerful facilities for corporate modelling, distribution of model-power, and competence, and thereby providing prerequisites of multi-level insight and decision-making authority. The advent of distributed and knowledge-based Group DSS especially, may very well lead into holographic principles of reasoning within the information frame of the business concerned.

We address the aforementioned key critical issues in total by using the suggested concept: "The managing of cognitive capacity in (future) organisations".

Finally, we present a checklist suggesting some ideas for research: Please note that the "Thinking ahead" column should be understood as complementing, not substituting the "State-of-the-art" column:

STATE-OF-THE-ART:	THINKING AHEAD:
reductionism	holism
(cause-effect)	(interdependency)
focus on single decision/-maker:	collective
Personal Computer	decision making,
individual DSS	computing to consensus,
	esprit de corps,
	teamwork,
	intelligent group
	interfaces,
	GDSS
stand-alone workstations	networked
	communications facilities,
	group productivity
	software

vertical thinking, analytical hierarchies naive belief in objectivity	lateral thinking, creativity contextualisation of intentionality
AI conceived of as "the shock of the future"	AI conceived of as "tools to shock the future with"
dumb concrete shell	intelligent buildings
efficiency	effectiveness
denotation one-to-one representation	connotation, context-dependency

POSTSCRIPT

Several other frameworks for GDSS classification have been proposed - ranging from mere configurational principles or various time-sharing principles to a more subtle and theoretical view of "collaborative work".

Huber (1984) provides a simple classification based on obvious aspects of decision-making processes like single/multi-purpose, inside/outside, fixed/portable. Kraemer and King (1988) in much the same way as Bui and Jarke (1986) distinguish six types of GDSS based on configuration of underlying technology and concomitant human-computer interaction.

DeSanctis and Gallupe (1987) delineate a taxonomy based on the following features of the application: small/large group, task type (planning, creativity, intellective, preference, cognitive conflict, mixed motive), and proximity of participants.

By strictly dissociating e.g. creativity from planning, DeSanctis and Gallupe seem to propose a very reductionist way of viewing GDSS, hence disregarding the possible cross- or trans-disciplinary benefits of advanced applications.

Further, our point is that sheer reification of the GDSS concept has to be avoided. As Bullen and Johansen (1988) point out: "Groupware is not a thing. Rather it is a perspective on computing that emphasizes collaboration - rather than individual use."

The learning aspects are also critical, as Cash, McFarlan and McKenney (1988) with a view to information technology (IT) in general note: "What makes the introduction and evolution of IT so challenging is that, in many of its applications, success comes only when people have changed their thinking processes. Hence we will refer to it as an "intellectual technology". Without this concomitant change in thinking, we too frequently have a technical success but an administrative failure".

Generally, it seems as if more attention is drawn to technical explanations of how specific types of GDSS might work in refined contexts, than to explore if - and if so, understand why - GDSS in real-life situations adds value to organisational decision-making processes as a whole.

Large-scale business organisations like ICL, Xerox, General Motors, Digital, Eastman Kodak, IBM and AT&T are experimenting with "decision conferencing", i.e. integrated use of "preference technology" and group facilitation. "Teamwork, of course, is not a new way to coordinate interdependent activities among separate units in an organization. What is new is that electronic mail, computer conferencing, and videoconferencing now facilitate this process. Today it is feasible for team members to coordinate asynchronously (across time zones) and geographically (across remote locations) more easily than ever before". (Rockart & DeLong, 1988).

Also, the public sector has shown some interest in implementing decision support systems and "groupware". Among the most intriguing examples is the Egyptian Cabinet. From November 1985 to March 1988, the Cabinet Information and Decision Support Center has grown from a startup organisation to one of over 150 people. Twenty-eight information systems/DSS projects have been implemented providing an array of services specifically targeted to the strategic decision-making level.

We tend to believe that real-life implementation is a more interesting scene, than rigid laboratory studies. But, of course, it is the dialectics between theory and practice, which lead to any valuable GDSS-design.

In a recent review article with respect to the growing body of GDSS literature, Lyytinen (1988) points out the following qualities of typical use relations in a "Computer Supported Cooperative Work" application: collective nature, autonomous use, contextuality, the interpretive mode of use, evolutionary nature, openness, goal ambiguity.

In addition to these qualities Jarke and others have brought to attention the social-psychological phenomenon known as "cognitive dissonance". This is a matter of coping with conflicting preferences with regard to past (and passed) viewpoints and most wanted present and future outcomes. By eliciting and explicating such differences in preference structure both intra- and inter-personally, the users may become uneasy and overwhelmed by cognitive dissonance and therefore be reluctant to follow any advice drawn from models generated by decision support devices. We believe that this is a crucial aspect of GDSS and suggest further investigation of this particular area.

REFERENCES

Bernsen, N.O. (1984). Searle's theory of intentionality. *Philosophy Today.*

Bjørn-Andersen, N., Broch, M., Due-Thomsen, B., & Kudsk, O. (1986a). *Modelling the nature of the office for design of thirdwave office systems.* Copenhagen School of Economics and Business Administration.

Bjørn-Andersen, N., Eason, K., & Robey, D. (1986b). *Managing computer impact: An international study of management and organizations.* Norwood, NJ: Ablex.

Bjørn-Andersen, N., Hedberg, B., Mercer, D., Mumford, E., & Sole, A. (1979). *The impact of systems change in organizations, an international study.* Amsterdam: Sijthoff & Noordhoff.

Bjørn-Andersen, N., & Rasmussen, L.B. (1980). Sociological implications of computers. In H.T. Smith, & T. Green (Eds.), *Human interaction with computers.* London: Academic Press.

Blomberg, (1986). *The variable impact of computer technologies in the organization of word activities.* MCC Software Technology.

Bracchi, G., & Pernici, B.(1984). The design requirements of office systems. *ACM Transactions on Office Information Systems, 2* (2).

Bui, Tung X., & Jarke, M. (1986). Communications design for Co- oP: A group decision support system. *ACM Transactions on Office Information Systems, 4* (2), 81-103.

Bui, Tung X. (1987). Co-oP. A group decision support system for cooperative multiple criteria group decision making. *Lecture notes in computer science.* Berlin: Springer-Verlag.

Bullen, C.V., & Johansen, R.R. (1988). *Groupware: A key to managing business teams?* (Working paper No. 169) Cambridge, MA: MIT Sloan School of Management, Center for Information Systems Research.

Cash, J.I., Jr., McFarlan, W.F., & McKenney, J.L. (1988). *Corporate information systems management. The issues facing senior executives.* Illinois: Homewood.

Checkland, P. (1981). *Systems thinking. Systems practice.* Chichester: John Wiley.

Daroca, F.P. (1984). Informational influences on group decision making in a participative budgeting context. Accounting. *Organizations and Society, 9,* 12-32.

DeSanctis, G., & Gallupe, R.B. (1987). A foundation for the study of group decision support systems. *Management Science, 33* (5), 589-609.

Ellis, C.A. (1980). Office modeling, an introspection into the what and why of office models. In H. Nafah (Ed.), *Integrated Office Systems.* Amsterdam: North-Holland.

Fjeldstad, O.D., & Konsynski, B.R. (1986). Reapportionment of cognitive responsibilities in DSS dialogues. In E. McLean, & H.G. Sol (Eds.), *DSS: A decade in perspective.* Amsterdam: North- Holland.

Gerson, E.M., & Star, S. (1986). Analyzing due process in the workplace. *ACM Transactions on Office and Information Systems, 4* (3), 257-270.

Glazer, R. (1989). A holographic theory of decision-making. (Working paper, pp. 55). New York: Department of Marketing, Graduate School of Business, Columbia University.

Hirschheim, R.A. (1985). *A social and organizational perspective.* New York: John Wiley.

Hirschheim, R.A., Klein, H., & Lyytinen, K. (1986a). Understanding the office: A social action perspective. In N. Bjørn-Andersen, M. Broch, B. Due-Thomsen, & O. Kudsk (Eds.), *Modelling the nature of the office for design of third wave office systems.* Copenhagen School of Economics and Business Administration.

Hoos, I. (1960). Impact of automation in the office. *International Labour Review, 82,* 363-373.

Huber, G.P. (1984). Issues in the design of group decision support systems. *MIS Quarterly, 8* (3), 195-204.

Humphreys, P., & Berkeley, D. (1985). Handling uncertainty. In G. Wright (Ed.), *Behavioral decision making.* New York: Plenum Press.

Humphreys, P., & Wisudha, A. (1987). Methods and tools for structuring and analysing decision problems. A catalogue and review. (Tech. Rep. No. 87-1). London: London School of Economics and Political Science, Decision Analysis Unit.

Janis, I.L. (1982). Counteracting the adverse effects of concurrence-seeking in policy-planning groups: Theory and research perspectives. In D. Brandstatter, & Stocker-Kreichgauer (Eds.), Group decision making. London: Academic Press.

Jarke, M. (1986b, June 16-18). Group decision support through office systems. In Decision support systems: A decade in perspective. *Proceedings of the IFIP working group 8. 3, working conference, Nordwijkerhout. Amsterdam: Elsevier.*

Jaques, E. (1976). *A general theory of bureaucracy.* London: Heinemann.

Jaques, E. (1982). *Free enterprise, fair employment.* London: Heinemann.

Kaasbøll, J. (1986). Intentional development of professional language through computerization: A case study and some theoretical consideration. *Proceedings of IFIP WG conference on system design for human development and productivity through participation.* Amsterdam: North-Holland.

Keen, P.G.W. (1986). Highways and traffic: Building the telecommunications infrastructure. In M. Jarke (Ed.), *Managers, micros and mainframes.* Chichester: John Wiley.

Kerola, P. (1986, August 14-16). On the foundations of a human-centred theory for IS use development. *Proceedings of VIII Scandinavian research seminar on systemeering.* Computer Science Dept, Aarhus University.

Kling, R. (1980, March). Social analysis of computing: Theoretical perspectives in recent empirical research. *Computing Surveys, 12* (1), 61-110.

Kolb, D. (1984). *Experiential learning - experience as the source of learning and development.* Englewood Cliffs: Prentice-Hall.

Kraemer, K.L., & King, J.L. (1988). Computer-based systems for cooperative work and group decision making. *Computing Surveys, 20* (2), 115-146.

Little, J.D.C. (1986). Research opportunities in the decision and management sciences. *Management Science, 32* (1).

Lyytinen, K. (1988). *Computer supported cooperative work (CSCW) - issues and challenges.* Unpublished paper. University of Jyväskylä, Department of Computer Science, Finland.

March, J.G., & Olsen, J.P. (Eds.). (1979). *Ambiguity and choice in organizations*. Oslo: Universitetsforlaget.

MCC Software Technology (1986). *Conference on computer supported cooperative work*. Austin, Texas.

Morgan, G. (1986). *Images of organization*. Beverly Hills: Sage.

Mowshowitz, A. (1986). Social dimensions of office automation. *Advances in Computers, 2.*

Mumford, E. (1983). *Participative design of socio-technical systems*. Manchester Business School.

Mumford, E., & Banks, O. (1967). *The computer clerk*. London: Routledge.

Mumford, E., & Ward, T.B. (1968). *Computers: Planning for people*. London: Batsford.

Mumford, E., & Weir, M. (1979). The ethics method. London: Associated Business Press.

Murtha, T. (1986, October 1). Supporting the local culture. *Datamation, 68* (11-12).

Nurminen, M. (1982). *Human-scale information systems*. Lecture notes. Institute for Information Sciences, Bergen University.

Prigogine, I. (1984). *Order out of chaos*. New York: Random House.

Reason, J. (1990). *Human error*. Cambridge: Cambridge University Press.

Richman, L.S. (1987, 8 June). Software catches the team spirit. *Fortune*.

Robey, D. (1986). *Designing organizations*. Homewood, IL: Dow Jones-Irwin.

Rockart, J.F., & DeLong, D.W. (1988). *Executive support systems: The emergence of top management computer use*. Homewood, IL: Dow Jones-Irwin.

Ruhleder, K. (1987). The use of techniques from the social science in office systems design. Irvine: University of California, Dept. of Information and Computer Science.

Schäfer, G., Donke, M., Hansjee, R., Hirschheim, R., Harper, M., & Bjørn-Andersen, N. (in press). *Functional analysis of office requirements*. New York: John Wiley.

Sherif, H. El, & Sawy, O.A. El. (1988, December). Issue-based decision support systems for the Egyptian cabinet. *MIS Quarterly*.

Siegel, J., Dubrovsky, V., Kiesler, S., & McGuire, T.W. (1986). Group processes in computer-mediated communication. *Organizational behavior and human decision processes, 37* (2).

Simon, H. (1949). *Administrative Behavior*. New York: Free Press.

Sproull, L., & Kiesler, S. (1986). Reducing social context cues: Electronic mail in organizational communication. *Management Science, 32* (11).

Stabell, C.B. (1984). Strategisk ledelse som virkefelt for EDB-baserte beslutningsstøttesystem. In Jonny Holbek (Ed.), Foretaksstrategi. Oslo: Bedriftsøkonomen.

Stabell, C.B. (1987). Decision support systems: Alternative perspectives and schools. *Decision Support Systems, 3*, 243- 251.

Strassmann, P.A. (1985). *Information payoff. The transformation of work in the electronic age*. London: Free Press.

Suchman, L. (1987). *Plans and situated actions: The problem of human-machine communications*. Cambridge: Cambridge University Press.

Sutherland, J.W. (1983, May-June). Normative predicates of next-generation management support systems. *IEEE Transactions on Systems, Man and Cybernetics, SMC-13*.

Sørgaard P. (1987). A cooperative work perspective on use and development of information systems. *Proceedings from information systems research seminar*. Vaskivesi, Scandinavia.

Taylor, F.W. (1967). *The principles of scientific management*. New York: Norton.

Weick, K.E. (1969). *Social psychology of organizing*. Reading, MA: Addison-Wesley.

Winograd, T., & Flores, F. (1986). *Understanding computers and cognition. A new foundation for design*. Norwood, NJ: Ablex.

Winograd, T. (1988). A language/action perspective on the design of cooperative work. *Human Computer Interaction, 3* (1).

Wynn, E. (1979). *Office conversation as an information medium*. PhD thesis. Berkeley: University of California, Department of Anthropology.

Zisman, M.D. (1979). Integrated office systems. In *Infotech: State of the art report*. Also in *Convergence: Computers and office automation, 1* (2).

FURTHER READING

Argyris, C. (1986). Skilled incompetence. *Harvard Business Review, 65* (5), 74-81.

Bertelson, P., Imbert, M., Kempson, R., Osherson D.S.H., Streitz, N., Thomassen, A., Viviani, P., & Chastenet, D. (1986). *Cognitive science in Europe. Survey and analysis*. Berlin: Springer-Verlag.

Bjørn-Andersen, N. (1985). Are "human factors" human? In N. Bevan, & D. Murray (Eds.), *Man/machine integration, state of the art report*. New York: Macmillan.

Bjørn-Andersen, N., & Kjærgaard, D. (1987). Choices en route to the office of tomorrow. In R. Kraut (Ed.), *Technology and the transformation of white collar work*. Hillsdale, NJ: Lawrence Erlbaum Associates.

Carroll, J.M, & Thomas, J.C. (1982). Metaphor and the cognitive representation of computing systems. *IEEE Transactions on Systems, Man, and Cybernetics. SMC-12* (2).

DeSanctis, G., & Gallupe, R.B. (1985). Group decision support systems: A new frontier. *Database, 16* (2).

Gregory, K.L. (1984). "Signing up": The culture and careers of Silicon Valley computer people. PhD thesis, Northwestern University.

Hammer, M., & Mangurian, G.E. (1987). The changing value of communications technology. *Sloan Management Review, 28* (2), 65-72.

Harmon, P., & King, D. (1985). *Expert systems: Artificial intelligence in business*. New York: John Wiley.

Hedberg, B., & Jonsson, S. (1978). Designing semi-confusing information systems for organizations in changing environments. *Accounting Organizations and Society, 3* (1), 47-64.

Huber, G.P. (1984). The nature and design of post-industrial organizations. *Management Science, 30* (8), 928-951.

IFIP/D55-1986 (1986, June 16-18). Decision support systems: A decade in perspective. *Proceedings of the IFIP working group 8.3, working conference, Nordwijkerhout*. Amsterdam: North-Holland.

Janis, I.L., & Mann, L. (1977). *Decision-making: A psychological analysis of conflict choice and commitment*. New York: Free Press.

Jarke, M. (Ed.). (1986a). *Managers, micros and mainframes. Integrating systems for end-users*. Chichester: John Wiley.

Jarke, M., Jelassi, M.T., & Shakun, M.F. (1987). MEDIATOR: Towards a negotiation support system. *European Journal of Operational Research, 31* (5), 314-334.

Kiesler, S. (1986, January-February). The hidden messages in computer networks. *Harvard Business Review*.

Kilmann, R.H. (1985). *Beyond the quick fix. Managing five tracks to organizational success*. San Francisco: Jossey-Bass.

Kling, R., & Scacchi, W. (1982). The web of computing: Computer technology as social organization. In M. Yovits (Ed.), *Advances in computers*, 21. New York: Academic Press.

Kling, R. (in press). Defining the boundaries of computing across complex organizations. In R. Boland, & R. Hirschheim (Eds.), *Critical issues in information system research*. New York: John Wiley.

Lewis, J. (1986, December 15). Group productivity software. *Datamation*, 79-80.

Reich, R.B. (1989, May-June). Entrepreneurship reconsidered: The team as hero. (Originally published 1987). *Harvard Business Review, 77-83*.

Stefik, M., Foster, G., Bobrow, D.G., Khan, K. Lanning, S., & Suchman, L. (1987). Beyond the chalkboard: Computer support for collaboration and problem solving in meetings. *Communications of the ACM, 30* (1), 32-47.

Sørgaard, P. (1988). *A discussion of computer supported cooperative work*. PhD thesis. Aarhus University, Computer Science Department, Denmark.

Turoff, M., & Hiltz, S.R. (1982). Computer support for group versus individual decisions. *IEEE Transactions on Communications, COMQ30* (1).

Wanous, J., Reichers, A.E., & Malik, S.D. (1984). Organizational socialization and group development: Toward an integrative perspective. *Academy of Management Review, 9* (4), 670- 683.

Weick, K.E. (1982). Management change among loosely coupled elements. In *Change in organizations. New perspectives on theory, research and practice*. San Francisco: Jossey Bass.

Zeleny, M. (1982). Multiple criteria decision making. McGraw-Hill series on quantitative methods for management.

APPENDIX
TABLE 5.1

Comparison of demand characteristics of tasks facing personnel having responsibilities at a given organisational level with structuring capabilities required in representing decision problems at that level[a]

Level number	Organisational level in employment hierarchy	Time span inherent in problem representation at given level[b]	Demand characteristics of tasks facing personnel with responsibility at given level[b]	Structuring capabilities required in representing decision problems at given level (decision support must also include capabilities of all lower levels)	Number of existing DSS incorporating support formalised at given level
	Sociocultural decision-making: Goal-closed small worlds structured within cultures (in theory, up to level 10)				
7	Chairman/MD of corporate group; head of large government department	20-50 yr	Anticipation of changes in sociological, technological, demographic and political developments; leading corporate strategic development to meet them	Isomorphic with Level 2, except can conduct sensitivity analysis, simulating changes in Level 5 representations; assessing their impact within cultural structure	None
6	Corporate group/sector executive	10-20 yr	Coordination of social and theoretical systems; translation of corporate strategic development into business direction	Isomorphic with Level 1, except each mode is now Level 5 problem representation within fixed cultural structure	None
	Individual decision-making under uncertainty: Uncertainties and preferences structured within goal-closed small worlds				
5	Corporate subsidiary/ enterprise managing director	5-10 yr	Problem not dealt with in context set wholly from above can modify boundaries of business within policy	Articulation of principles for conditional (goal) closing of an open system, and/or reopening of a conditionally closed system (e.g. through scenario generation)	None

TABLE 5.1 Contd.

Level number	Organisational level in employment hierarchy[b]	Time span inherent in problem representation at given level[b]	Demand characteristics of tasks facing personnel with responsibility at given level[b]	Structuring capabilities required in representing decision problems at given level (decision support must also include capabilities of all lower levels)	Number of existing DSS incorporating support formalised at given level
4	General management (e.g. development production or sales, within work system)	2–5 yr	Detachment from specific cases, seeing them representative examples of issues calling for development of a system	Selecting/interfacing capability between structural types (requiring use of problem-structuring language)	Very few (prototypes)
3	Department managerial/principle specialist	1–2 yr	Control of trend of tasks and problems arising; extrapolation from trend to ways of formulating problems	Restructuring capability within single fixed structural types (e.g. attribute generation in multi-attribute model)	A few
2	Front line managerial/professional	3 mo to yr	Formal operational, can anticipate changes in tasks due to any one of: object, production resource, pathway, or pathway resource	Manipulation of data on one variable at a time within fixed structure (e.g. sensitivity analysis)	Many
1	Shop and office floor	Less than 3 mo	Concrete operational limited to tasks concretely and physically at hand	Estimation of values at nodes within fixed structure (e.g. information retrieval system)	Many

aCharacteristics of Levels 8 to 10 can, in theory, be ascertained by extrapolation from Levels 3 to 5, respectively.
bThis information is summarized from the accounts given by Jaques (1976, 1982).

CHAPTER SIX

The Influence of Artificial Intelligence on Human-Computer Interaction: Much Ado About Nothing?

Erik Hollnagel
Computer Resources International, Bregnerødvej 144,
DK-3460 Birkerød, Denmark.

ABSTRACT

In this paper I discuss the potential influence of AI on HCI. The discussion is based on a pragmatic view of both factors. The definitions are formulated in the beginning of the paper, and are contrasted with the more "scientific" definitions and the current developments. This is followed by an analysis of the nature of HCI, which provides a distinction between an embodiment relation, and a hermeneutical relation between the user and the computer. In the embodiment relation, the computer serves as a tool for the user, whereas in the hermeneutical relation the computer assumes the role of the "text". It is argued that the embodiment relation is central to HCI, and the potential influence of AI is discussed with regard to how well AI can amplify the user's cognitive functions. A special consideration is given to the role of user modelling and natural language. The conclusions are that whereas AI has a potential for influencing HCI, this has not yet been fully realised. Furthermore, the development of HCI should be guided by a more comprehensive theory, which considers the context and the task rather than human-computer interaction *per se*.

INTRODUCTION

The topic to be discussed in this chapter is the influence of Artificial Intelligence (AI) on Human-Computer Interaction (HCI).[1] This very statement makes the assumption that there has indeed been an influence of AI on HCI. From one point of view this must indisputably be true:

1. Computer functionality is influenced by developments in AI.
2. *HCI depends on computer functionality.*
3. Therefore HCI must also be influenced by the developments in AI.

If we only consider the technological interpretation of this argument then the conclusion is correct; the influence of AI on computer hardware and software is clear. The growing interest in AI, not least the growing commercial interest, has guided the technological development towards more powerful processors and machines (e.g. from dedicated LISP processors to LISP chips and micro-LISP machines), more effective programming languages or paradigms (e.g. Flavours, Prolog, and Smalltalk), and more potent development environments (such as LOOPS, KEE, ART) with facilities for debugging, tracing, browsing, graphics, etc. Several of these developments have also had an effect on the more mundane types of HCI, partly because the system developer's sophisticated high-tech environment has been coveted by the common user. Examples of this are (on the surface level), the use of windows, mice, browsers, icons, graphics (nets), and more recently CAD and CASE environments. On a deeper, functional level such things as object-oriented paradigms, message passing, inheritance, possible worlds techniques, truth maintenance, etc., have had an influence on the ordinary programming languages and environments, as well as on the possibilities for specifying HCI in an MMS.[2]

However, these developments have mostly had a technical rather than a functional purpose.[3] In other words, to the extent that they have considered HCI it has been related to the interaction between the system developer (the scientist) and the computer, rather than between the ordinary user and an application. If we consider a functional instead of a technological interpretation of the argument, it is not clear whether the conclusion remains correct. It does rather seem to be a case of a *potential* versus an *actual* influence of AI on HCI. There is clearly a substantial potential influence, but to assess it requires that we have a clear view of what HCI is and what the influence should have been, i.e.

what the real needs of HCI are. Only then can we answer whether there was an influence, whether it did go in the right direction, and whether it was as effective as it could have been, given the possibilities of AI. Consequently we must begin by taking a step back and specifying precisely what we mean by AI and HCI. This will be discussed in the following sections, after which I will consider the potential influence of AI on HCI.

ARTIFICIAL INTELLIGENCE

Artificial Intelligence can be defined in a number of ways. Indeed, it is said that if you ask three specialists in the field you will probably end up with four definitions.[4] However, it seems to be generally agreed that the ultimate purpose of AI is to improve the understanding of the principles that make intelligence possible and thereby enable the re-creation of human intelligence in machines, i.e., in an artifact. This has recently been formulated (Hill, 1989, p. 29) by defining the following three goals for AI:

1. To understand better the mind by specifying computational models.
2. To construct computer systems that perform actions traditionally regarded as mental.
3. To establish new computation-based representational media in which human intellect can come to express itself with different clarity and force.

These goals correspond well to the original aim of innovators like Alan Turing and to the century-old dream of reducing reasoning to an algebra of thoughts, e.g. Leibnitz and the *calculus ratiocinator*. There is, however, a subtle but important difference between a reasoning machine and one embodying intelligence, as the former is more restricted than the latter. Reasoning may be the hallmark of intelligence but intelligence is more than just reasoning. Although it is difficult to define intelligence it does certainly include an ability for abstraction, for learning, and for applying knowledge creatively in new situations. Intelligence is thus characterised by a certain measure of disorder which is absent from reasoning.

The ultimate goal of AI can be approached in three principally different ways: by emergence, by simulation, and by formalisation. A brief characterisation of each is given in the following.

AI Through Emergence

The idea of producing AI through emergence is based on the indisputable fact that intelligence is seated in the brain, and therefore has the neural architecture of the brain as a substratum or basis. Accordingly the approach taken is to try to use the same basic components and structures, although implemented in silicon rather than carbon, and on that basis try to reproduce the set of phenomena that are taken to signify intelligence. The reason why I call this an emergent approach is that the proponents seem to hope that intelligence will "magically" result or emerge from this.[5] While the approach is basically correct in assuming that there can be no human intelligence without its neural basis, there is a lack of ideas about how intelligence can be expressed at such a basic level. Certain phenomena can be reproduced, but only because it has been possible to describe them in sufficient operational detail - usually because some gifted scientists have had a profound insight (i.e. using their human intelligence). On the whole the emergence approach can, somewhat unkindly but perhaps correctly, best be likened to the British Museum Algorithm[6] - except that in this case the monkeys have been replaced by elementary functional units (neurons).

The emergence approach has enjoyed a surge of popularity in the late 1980s under the name of neural networks or connectionism, but it actually goes a long way back (Barrow, 1989). During the 1940s there were tremendous developments in neurophysiology, partly brought about by developments in electronics, and scientists like Warren McCullogh exerted a substantial influence on a number of fields such as psychology, cybernetics, and control theory. In psychology there was also a growing movement that looked at the close connection between neurophysiology and psychology (cf. Hebb, 1961, org. 1949). It was obviously very attractive to be able to explain psychological phenomena in terms of neurophysiology, because that was the undisputed basis for how the brain worked. In that respect a very important book called *The Computer and the Brain* was published (posthumously) by John von Neumann. This book compared the functioning of the brain on the neurophysiological level with the functioning of the digital computer. The conclusion was that there were great similarities, e.g. that the functioning of the nervous systems was *prima facie* digital - in its architecture and fundamental mode of operation. John von Neumann, however, pointed out that there were differences, and that one of them was in the functional architecture: "...large and efficient natural automata are likely to be highly parallel, while large and efficient artificial automata will tend to be less so, and rather to be serial" (von Neumann, 1958).[7.]

John von Neumann also pointed out that it is possible for any computing machine to imitate any other computing machine - referring to Turing's theorem (not to be confused with Turing's test[8]). Thus, since the brain is a computing machine, it can be imitated by another computing machine. But von Neumann was careful to talk about the functions of the brain only, and not to go into the realm of intelligence. At the most he ventured into the field of neurophysiology and peripheral perceptual phenomena. These differences were, however, not fully appreciated at the time. What remained was the striking fact that the on/off behaviour of the neuron could be described as a switching circuit by Boolean algebra and that this made it possible to describe events in the brain by means of propositional logic. The fundamental functions of the brain could therefore be described in the same terms as the fundamental functions of the newly invented digital computer. It was this (misunderstood and misapplied) analogy which later gave rise to both the emergence approach and the formalisation approach.

AI Through Simulation

The idea of producing AI through simulation is an approach where one first tries to produce a good description of the phenomena that constitute intelligence (i.e. as operational as possible, but with differences depending on the implementation technology) and then tries to implement or reproduce these descriptions in an artifact, regardless of whether it resembles the brain or whether the methods correspond to the way the brain works. This is most clearly demonstrated in the cases of computer simulations and cognitive simulations, which have been a main part of the "psychological" AI approach and of cognitive science.

This approach has been very successful for the phenomena or examples of intelligence where a mechanism was either known or could be proposed, e.g. based on introspection or a study of the phenomena in lower animals. Examples are: basic perceptual phenomena such as pattern recognition and primitive learning, problem-solving, deduction, induction, and logical reasoning (whether Boolean, predicate or propositional) - going as far back as the Pandemonium (Selfridge, 1959), the Elementary Perceiver And Memorizer (Feigenbaum, 1961), the General Problem Solver (Newell & Simon, 1961), the Logic Theorist (Newell, Shaw, & Simon, 1957), and Argus (Reitman, 1965).[9] The simulation approach thus has a very impressive past. It has also been applied with reasonable success in some areas of language and information retrieval, such as parsing or working on structural levels, but has been spectacularly unsuccessful in more meaningful areas such as natural language understanding. The Achilles heel of the simulation approach is that it usually depends on the subjective judgment of an expert observer rather than a more objective, operational criterion. The simulation approach is, however, basically sound because it starts from an operational and verifiable description of the phenomena to be reproduced, rather than from theories and assumptions about the nature of intelligence.

AI Through Formalisation

The idea of producing AI through formalisation concentrates on the formal and well-defined description of how knowledge can be represented and how some intellectual processes (mostly reasoning) can be performed. This approach thus studies the same phenomena as the two other approaches (although often being ambitious enough to extend the study to include common-sense phenomena), but puts all its faith in the formal language approach, i.e. in some variant of logic (e.g. Smets et al., 1988). This imposes restrictions on the way facts are represented (e.g. in predicate form) and on the way in which they are treated. AI through formalism cares little about the basic resemblance of the techniques, in contrast to the emergence approach. Also, it does, in a sense, narrow the simulation approach by insisting on the use of formal representations.

The advantage of the formal approach is, of course, that the results are provably correct and therefore reproducible in a highly reliable way. A similar result by (cognitive) simulation may or may not be reproducible, depending on how many "kluges" there were in the system. The formal approach will always, in principle, either work or not work, and this is a highly desirable quality. The drawback is that it narrows the scope of intelligence to the extent that it can be captured by the formal approach - although the hope, of course, is that this will eventually include everything. At present the formal approach is, nevertheless, mostly confined to reasoning processes of various types, as evidenced by the many kinds of logic that have been developed to cope with the naturally complex ways of human reasoning. The basic assumption is that human intelligence (i.e. human reasoning) is inherently based on logic and on nothing else. Interestingly enough, John von Neumann (1958) referred to that assumption when he pointed out that the true language of the brain might be completely different from the "natural" languages we use:

> Just as languages like Greek or Sanskrit are historical facts and not absolute logical necessities, it is only reasonable to assume that logics and mathematics are similarly historical, accidental forms of

expression... Indeed, the nature of the central nervous system and of the message systems that it transmits indicate positively that this is so.

Consequently, the fact that we can describe the functioning of the brain with mathematics and logic does not mean that the language of the brain is the language of mathematics and logic, nor that intelligence can be reduced to mathematics and logic. The assumption is, however, rarely brought into question by the formal approach, whereas both the simulation and the emergence approach have a more relaxed attitude to it.

An Analogy: The Synthesis of Sound

An interesting analogy to the efforts of AI can be found in the attempts to synthesise natural sounds. The purpose here is to reproduce (and synthesise) natural sounds such as those produced by a musical instrument or, even more difficult, by the human voice. Many attempts have been made over the years and recently, during the 1980s, a considerable measure of success has been achieved. I am not referring to the use of digital sampling to store and reproduce natural sounds, but rather to the way in which a replica of the natural sound, so to speak, can be built from scratch. Early attempts were found in, for example, the Moog synthesiser, but today computer-controlled sound construction can produce the sounds of most musical instruments to such a degree of likeness that even experts find it hard to tell the difference. Yet although it is possible to reproduce a natural human voice singing a vocal, it is still impossible to reproduce it singing a song or speaking.

The progress in sound synthesis has been possible because we know that sound is composed of sound waves and because it has become possible to decompose the sound waves and identify the individual elements. We know the structure of sound, the nature of the elements, and are therefore able to reverse the process. The analogy with AI is that it is believed that the same approach can be used for human intelligence. Thus, if we can find the elements of thought and the basic principles by which they are composed, then we can reproduce human thought, i.e. create intelligent machines (although this approach considers human intelligence as no more and no less than human thought). The elements of thought are believed to have been found, e.g. concepts, predicates, propositions, but the rules are still missing. In the case of predicates and propositions a class of rules is known (logic). However, human thought is more than predicates and propositions - even though its essence can be represented by them - and the way we think is not adequately captured by logic, not even the more exotic varieties.

Human thought differs from logic because it contains some "disturbing" elements, for example: tacit knowledge and non-monotonic reasoning. This simply means that we suppose that there are a large number of conditions which are not expressed in the formal languages of logic and the formal representations. Concepts are probably more realistic than predicates, but no-one really knows how to capture a concept (except as a verbal expression) and how to deal with it. The analogy between sound synthesis and AI can therefore be used to argue that this is not the way to approach human intelligence, i.e. it is not the solution to the goal of artificial intelligence. Human thinking is just as removed from logic as singing and talking is removed from synthetic human voices. The missing step is precisely intelligence.

A Pragmatic Definition of AI

The fundamental problem with all three approaches is that they fail to address the real problem, i.e. what intelligence is. They all start from the assumption that intelligence is something which can be described and reproduced, and they all define intelligence in terms of the phenomena that the approach is suited to tackle. Even in the case of emergent phenomena the hope is that some fundamental principle, e.g. for learning or introspection, can be found which will enable machines to become intelligent - and certainly easily become more intelligent than humans can ever be. So, all three approaches (or combinations of them) depend on the discovery of a fundamental principle. The analogy is the discovery of similar principles in the exact sciences, such as Newton's laws or the Theory of Relativity. It must, however, be seriously questioned whether this assumption is reasonable - although one can neither prove or disprove it. Despite the possibility of the impossibility of reaching the goals of AI, the attempts have resulted in many spectacular progresses and improvements, not least in the interplay between technology and application.

However, for the discussion of the relation between AI and HCI it is necessary to have a relevant definition of AI. According to the formal definition the purpose of AI was to understand the principles that make intelligence possible. In contrast, a more pragmatic definition simply says that the goal of AI is to make computers more useful. Note that this definition addresses what AI can be *used for* rather than what AI *is*. The pragmatic definition concentrates on some of the basic characteristics of AI systems: (1) that they can use general knowledge and principles to infer heuristic rules from data, and (2) that they can apply these rules to solve some of the problems they are given.

AI can consequently be used in at least two different ways. On the one hand it can be used to improve the processing of data and information beyond the reach of algorithmic solutions. AI makes it possible to use knowledge and to produce knowledge from data and information. AI can thus provide higher order elaborations of the available data and information and, in Bruner's words, make it possible deliberately to "go beyond the information given" (Angling, 1973), e.g. in diagnosis and system state identification. In addition, AI can enhance HCI by providing added functionality, such as a more flexible communication, adaptive interpretation of commands and messages, adaptive presentation of information, explanations, etc.

This pragmatic definition of AI is obviously much better suited to the present discussion. In fact, understanding the principles that make intelligence possible may do very little to improve HCI as such. As we shall see in the following, the design of systems with improved HCI, as well as HCI specifications in general, is very much a pragmatic affair in the sense that at the end of the day it is the practical results rather than the deep theoretical insights that matter.

HUMAN-COMPUTER INTERACTION
From MMI to HCI

From a historical point of view HCI is rooted in the field of MMS, in particular the sub-field called MMI, (either Man-Machine Interface or Man-Machine Interaction). It started as the study of the man-machine *interface*, as the interest of human factors engineering was in studying and designing the equipment to be used in various industrial and transport environments. This was clearly an interest that sprung from very practical concerns and needs. It was, rightly, believed that a lot of good could be done simply by improving the interface between man and machine. The meaning later changed to become man-machine *interaction* when it was realised that it was not sufficient to improve the human factors of the interface, but that one also had to consider the actions in the system, the exchange of information, and the collaboration in command and control tasks. The name could have remained as MMI, but for some reason - probably the surge of interest from computer science and AI - it slowly changed to HCI.[10] If one judges from the number of papers and the sessions at international conferences, MMS has gradually been overshadowed by HCI. The field of MMS, however, still exists in good shape and may actually benefit from not being in the spotlight - for instance by having less inflated expectations about what can be achieved.

The main reason for the appearance of HCI as a separate field is clearly the rapid growth in the possibilities for actual interaction between humans and computers, spurred by the development and introduction of the micro-computer in 1982. Before that computers had mostly been used as part of the overall equipment and had driven displays, etc. They had generally been used from remote (dumb) terminals where the interaction was very limited because there was very little a character-based terminal could do (or was allowed to do). The new developments meant that there was a need to study how people interacted directly with computers. It was now staff in banks and other commercial institutions (office workers), rather than operators in a control room, that had to deal with the computer. The computer changed from being a mystical machine in the distance to being something right on your desk. Finally, the computer became the only piece of equipment or interface. Unlike this, a control room would contain plenty of other types of instrumentation and the computer would rather be an addition which might or might not be used.

The increasing use of computers was mostly for tasks which only involved the computer, rather than a computer with an industrial process behind it. Thus, the substance of the tasks was in many cases so-called cognitive tasks (knowledge intensive symbol and information manipulation) rather than regulation and control. Examples are the use of spreadsheets, word and text processors leading to Desk Top Publishing (DTP), drawing programs leading to Computer Assisted Design (CAD), and software development as a whole, leading to Computer Assisted Software Engineering (CASE). Indeed, computers were introduced to take over many functions which hitherto had been exclusively mental, such as planning, scheduling, assessment, registration, information retrieval, etc. This created a new category of computer users and a new category of computer usage, which became the proper domain of HCI applications. It is, however, a depressing thought that most wordprocessors, spreadsheets, and databases, which probably account for the largest part of computer usage, still carry rather miserable interfaces - most of them having been designed and decided by the early developers of the systems and none of them having had any benefit of developments in AI.

There was thus a clear and legitimate interest in studying HCI and in finding ways of designing and optimising this new environment. Parallel to the introduction of whole new fields where computers were used, there was a rapid spread of computers into traditional fields where the improved technology capacity of computers meant that not only were they added to conventional instrumentation but gradually replaced large parts of it. Examples are from aircraft cockpits, industrial process control, emergency handling, load scheduling (grid control), etc. The ideal was actually to have a completely computerised control room, be it in a nuclear power plant or in a brewery.

Task Decomposition and Task Control

There are two quite different paradigms of HCI. In one the human is considered as a computer, and all analyses are based on a mechanistic analogy. This is clearly expressed by Suchman (1987, p. 9) who writes: "The agreement among all participants in cognitive science and its affiliated disciplines, however, is that cognition is not just potentially *like* computation, it literally *is* computational" (Sic!). In the other the human and the computer are considered in relation to the task, without bothering too much about whether or not cognition is computation (Hollnagel, 1983).

The difference can easily be seen in the models that are being developed in the two paradigms. In the computational paradigm the focus is on parameterisation of human information processing activity and on the decomposition of user tasks into elements that can be adequately described by the models. The best known representative for this is the GOMS modelling technique (Card, Moran, & Newell, 1983), which describes tasks in terms of a set of essential elements called Goals, Operators, Methods, and Selection rules. This approach works well for tasks on the level of routine cognitive skills, such as the keystroke level in text editing, where the model has had some success in predicting performance with different text editors. But the strong mechanistic assumptions behind the decomposition and parameterisation make GOMS and similar approaches unsuitable for the description of more complex cognitive tasks.

In the task-oriented paradigm the focus is less on how the tasks are composed and more on how they are controlled. In the various HCI approaches, such as Barnard (1987) and Rasmussen (1986), tasks are described on a higher level in terms of cognitive functions that co-exist in a system with limited cognitive resources. The emphasis is on how the various functions are combined and controlled to achieve the goal, and on how this is influenced by the task characteristics and demands. The models thus work more on the strategic and tactical levels of the task than on the operational levels. They are accordingly useless for making predictions of the time taken to execute a procedure but can be used, e.g: for task allocation, procedure specification, identification of decision-making traps, estimation of error possibilities, etc.

The two approaches clearly have different purposes and different advantages (and disadvantages). Neither can, or should, they be used for all levels or aspects of human-computer interaction - although this has not prevented such attempts being made. They represent different solutions to the trade-off between depth and breadth (represented, for example, by parameterisation and control).

Stages in the Development Of HCI

One approach to understanding the current state of HCI is to look at how it has developed. As mentioned earlier, HCI is a descendant and specialisation of the study of man-machine systems. The development so far has been described by the following three phases (cf. Carroll, 1989).

Phase I: Evaluation

In the first phase, beginning in the early 1970s, HCI was mainly concerned with empirical laboratory evaluation of human-computer interaction. It was seen as a needed supplement to the method of software technology, which could not address issues such as usability and productivity. One particular area of research was the psychology of computer programming, but there was also a growing need for a systematic evaluation of various approaches to design. (This, by the way, coincided with a similar trend in MMS design, e.g. for control rooms of complex industrial plants.)

The armoury of HCI as an evaluation technique was inherited from experimental psychology and the behavioural sciences. These methods were efficient but generally very costly in terms of time and resources. The growth in computerised applications of various types created strong needs for quicker and more efficient methods as well as a solid basis for design guidelines (cf. the following). The first need is still unanswered; the second need was partly accommodated through the following phase of HCI.

Phase 2: Description

In the second phase, beginning in the early 1980s, HCI started to establish a set of theories for human-computer interaction based on cognitive psychology and cognitive science. Such theories were badly needed by the practitioners of HCI, who were otherwise left to rely on their own experience and common sense.[11] There has been no shortage of attempts to provide theoretically founded descriptions of HCI, some of them being very ambitious such as Card, Moran, and Newell (1983) and Kieras and Polson (1985). None of them are, however, sufficiently powerful to be used deductively, i.e. to derive precise solutions to design problems. In this respect they are not different from psychological theories on the whole, and it would indeed be surprising (although delightful) if HCI could outdo academic psychology on that account. HCI is still struggling with the goal of providing good theories, but this effort is clearly hampered by the uncertainty of whether HCI is science or engineering, cf. the following.

Phase 3: Invention

In the third and current phase, HCI is struggling to provide a lead in the invention of new systems (called usability-innovated invention by Carroll, 1989). This is a logical extension of the step from evaluation to description, growing from a passive to an active role. One of the reasons behind this is the concern that the development is too often driven by what the technology provides and, perhaps, that the psychologists are being overshadowed by the engineers - even though the former sometimes take to calling themselves cognitive engineers. While there clearly is a technology gap, the consequences of that are not necessarily negative; this will be discussed in the following section. A more legitimate concern is that because artifacts necessarily embody implicit theories of how they work, in particular about human-computer interaction (Carroll & Campbell, 1988; Fodor, 1968; Hollnagel & Woods, 1983), then everyone would stand to gain if these theories could be made more explicit, in particular if the theories could be used to drive HCI development. This issue is discussed in the last part of the paper.

The Technology Gap

There seems to be a clear consensus that developments in HCI (and MMS) are often technology driven, thereby running the risk of becoming solutions looking for a problem rather than solutions to a problem. Examples are many:

- the introduction of VDUs in the control of industrial processes;
- the availability of graphics (going from character-based to bit maps);
- the arrival of colours, from four colours to literally millions;
- the possibility of animation (i.e. using dynamics in pictures);
- windows, icons, and mice;
- relational database technologies;
- expert systems;
- hypermedia, hypertext, etc.

There is no end to this list, but the problem is that there is no clear pattern in it either. One may certainly try to predict the next technological development, but this does not necessarily mean that it will also become the next step. Technology is a continuous (and accelerating) development, which roughly doubles the capacity of hardware every three years, measured in relation to, for example, processing speed, efficiency, power consumption, etc. Contrasted with that the conceptual background (philosophies) is a step-wise development, where the steps (their time and size) are unpredictable; the doubling period for social systems and organisations is suggested to be in the order of 15 years. The conceptual development therefore, in a sense, lags behind the technological development. Even worse, the methodological developments (i.e. the tools that analysts and theorists have at their disposal) is slower still and the steps are even smaller. We are therefore at a relative disadvantage, even if we do not consider the technological gap to be serious.

The curves shown in Figure 6.1 can be seen as an illustration of some typical cases. At point A, for instance, the concepts are well advanced relative to the technology. This was probably the case in the mid-1940s when developments in information theory and cybernetics were actually ahead of the technological development (similar cases may be found even earlier, e.g. Charles Babbage and the Analytical Engine). At point B, the situation has changed. The technological developments have continued steadily, but the conceptual developments are lagging behind. However, a new way of thinking has brought the concepts a step forward so that the technological development is matched - at least for a time. An example might be Human Factors Engineering or AI in the late 1950s. If we go to point C, the situation is again different. The technological development has continued, but even when there is progress in the conceptual development it is insufficient to match the technology. An example could be cognitive psychology in the 1970s or cognitive science in the 1980s. (I am sure that the reader can find favourite examples that may be far better than the ones I have suggested here.)

The existence of the technology gap, i.e. the discrepancy between technological and conceptual developments means that there is rarely a clear idea of what one should do with a new possibility when it comes along. The result is often a simple replacement of old equipment with new equipment, although it is clearly realised that a mere replacement is not enough. Having more and faster computers and terminals (and expert systems) does not necessarily solve any of the fundamental problems in HCI, i.e. that they do not necessarily match any real needs. In order to improve the working conditions at all one must first find out what the real needs are, and then use the technology to answer them.

From that perspective the technology gap may not be so bad after all. The gap is only bad if it is seen as something that must be overcome,

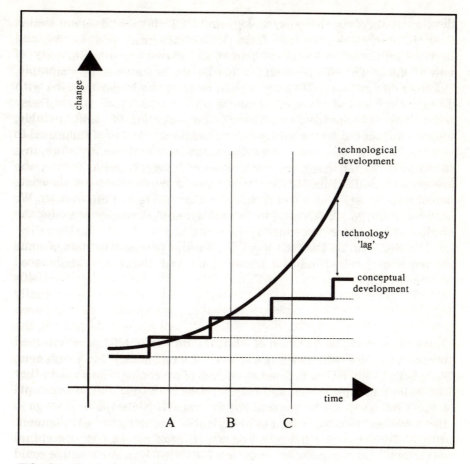

FIG. 6.1. The technology "lag".

e.g. something where one must develop new concepts or theories to live up to the possibilities of technology. But that addresses the wrong problem. Instead one could see the gap as representing an asset, i.e. a redundancy or richness in the technology which makes it easier to implement conceptual solutions, by offering a richer implementation environment and more possibilities for the designer. From this point of view the problem is actually far worse if the conceptual development is further advanced than the technological one (although that probably is a hypothetical case).

The notion of product-induced innovations is nevertheless very useful for characterising the present situation. Clearly, the technological developments run a lot faster than the conceptual or theoretical developments of cognitive psychology and HCI. But that does not mean that HCI must take the lead from the technological field, i.e. have a decisive influence on the development and invention (introduction) of new artifacts. The efforts should rather be concentrated on how one can shape or design the HCI functionality, or even the larger task design. The development of tasks, i.e. real-life problems, is much slower than technology development; so although the execution of tasks may be heavily influenced by technological innovations, the tasks themselves remain. For instance, producing a document does fundamentally remain the same task even though the technology of doing it has changed. There are greater similarities between writing on a typewriter (or even with pencil and paper) and a wordprocessor than there are differences: in both cases the goal is (ideally) to provide a manifest version of thoughts or ideas. The proper procedure is therefore to consider the task on this level rather than on the HCI level. This wider perspective reduces the influence of product-induced innovations and the worry about the technology gap.

The Nature of HCI

I have alluded to the question of what the nature of HCI is, where the two opposites are, whether it is a science or a technology. In Carroll and Campbell (1988), HCI is defined as an area of psychology concerned with "computers as experienced and manipulated by users." In the editorial of the first issue of the journal *Interacting With Computers*, Diaper (1989) defines the goals of HCI as being "to develop or improve the safety, utility, effectiveness, efficiency, and usability of systems that include computers." Diaper goes on to define HCI clearly as an engineering discipline and, although admitting that HCI might be a science as well, states that it is not so at present.[12]

The debate of whether HCI is a science or an engineering discipline demonstrates that HCI is no better off than AI when it comes to definitions. The discussions may in themselves be rather academic and may seem to be rather inappropriate in a field that is so young. It is more important to have a clear definition of what the purpose of HCI is. The vital question is therefore whether HCI considers the computer as the target or the mediator, i.e. whether it considers humans as interacting *with* computers or interacting *through* computers.

The important distinction is between learning to use the HCI artifact *per se*, and learning to use it to accomplish a task. In the first case the HCI artifact is the target as well as the means. In the latter case the HCI artifact is the means only, while the goal is something different. In the first case the HCI artifact therefore plays a double role and there is a tendency to focus on the functionality of HCI by itself. An example is the use of Hypercards, the use of a wordprocessor, or a programming language. It is, of course, always necessary to devote some effort to mastering a tool or an artifact, but the difference is whether one should remain with that or go on to consider how the HCI artifact is used to achieve a goal.

If HCI is seen as the study of how humans interact *with* computers, then human-computer interaction becomes a goal in itself and HCI may rightly be called a science. When human-computer interaction becomes a goal of its own, the context loses importance and the outcome becomes less important than the interaction *qua* interaction. It matters little whether the HCI in question occurs in using a text editor or in controlling a spacecraft. Consequently, the study of HCI may conveniently be pursued in environments that are academically "nice", such as text editors and electronic mail systems, thereby continuing the established tradition of experimental psychology.

If, on the other hand, HCI is seen as the study of how humans interact *through* computers, the computer is seen as a tool and the human-computer interaction is a means rather than a goal. The context suddenly becomes very important, and the HCI of text editors may conceivably be very different from the HCI of process control. The result of the interaction must be taken into consideration, and the HCI has failed if it does not contribute to a better result (whatever criteria are used). The study of HCI becomes more "messy" because it can no longer be carried out exclusively under laboratory conditions - but it also becomes more challenging and interesting. In addition, HCI may eventually be classified as an engineering discipline rather than a science, although the consequences of that change are doubtful.

Lest the reader should be in any doubt, I adhere to the view that HCI is the study of how humans interact *through* computers, i.e. that the computer is viewed as a tool (Hollnagel, Mancini, & Woods, 1986). The goal of HCI is consequently to study the interaction between humans and computers in the context of carrying out a given task, with the purpose of developing theories, methods and techniques that can be used to improve that interaction. This definition very much resembles the pragmatic definition of AI given earlier, and also clearly establishes the context in which the potential influence of AI and HCI should be investigated.

The Importance of the Task

It makes sense to emphasise the dependency of HCI on the task because one cannot expect to design HCI in isolation, just as one cannot evaluate HCI once separated from a task. In the discussion of HCI as evaluation there was a clear connection to the task; in discussing HCI as description, the task receded into the background partly because the tasks that were used for reference became contrived. In the discussion of HCI as invention, the task has disappeared completely. If these proposed phases in HCI development are correct, and the description seems eminently reasonable, the consequence must be that HCI should not serve as invention, but only as evaluation and description. We should realise that the current third phase, HCI as invention, is a move in the wrong direction and we should therefore abandon it before it develops too far. The necessary invention, in the sense of providing the basis for designing systems, should come from other fields of study which adopt a more system- or function-oriented approach and which consider the task or the goal as the point of departure; one obvious candidate is Cognitive Systems Engineering as proposed by Hollnagel and Woods (1983). In this context HCI is important both as evaluation and description, as the systematic experience with human-computer interaction may provide the guidelines for certain details of the HCI design. Or put differently, HCI can serve as a source of invention for HCI design, but HCI design is not the same as task design or total function design. Accordingly, one must either explicitly recognise the limited role of HCI, or reduce its scope.

Where does this leave AI and HCI? One question is whether AI can contribute to the task level design. The answer is that it probably cannot although certain disciplines, such as planning, may contribute with specific techniques. AI is thus confined to supporting HCI in its specific role as an engineering discipline dedicated to evaluating, describing, designing and developing HCI as a tool, as well as to support other aspects of the total task design where applicable (e.g. planning, scheduling, procedure activation, etc.). The simple fact is that neither AI nor HCI (nor psychology, for that matter) offer the solutions to the real problem, which is designing the task. But they can, alone or together, contribute to solving parts of the problem.

The Computer as a Tool

In the point of view taken here the computer is to be considered as a sort of tool, as a means to an end. The purpose of HCI is consequently to assist in the specification, design, and implementation of that tool, i.e. to produce computer systems which facilitate the user's tasks. In order to produce a good tool, it is necessary to know the following:

What the Purpose of the Tool Is.   This describes the needs for the desired tool as well as the fundamental requirements it must fulfil.

How the Requirements can be Specified as Tool Functions. The purpose specifies the goals, and the tool is the means to reach the goal; in order to do that it must be capable of providing certain functions.

How the Functions can be Implemented in a Tool. For some functions there may be several ways in which they can be implemented, for others there may not be any effective solutions.

How the the Tool can be Evaluated. Once the tool has been produced it is desirable (and sometimes even necessary) to assess the degree to which the product complies with the requirements.

These knowledge requirements are quite general and apply to areas other than HCI. Consider, for instance, a camera. The purpose of the camera is to make pictures by means of photography. The camera must therefore have (Blaker, 1980):

- a *lens* to form the image and put it on the film;
- a means of *focusing* this lens on subjects at various distances;
- a *view-finder* to allow image composition;
- a *shutter* to keep the image-forming light off the film until the desired moment and to control the time that the light is on the film;
- an *iris diaphragm* to control both the amount of light reaching the film (in conjunction with the shutter) and the depth of field in the image;
- a *light-tight container* to hold the film ready for exposure.

This description covers both the generic components and the functions they fulfil. For each of these functions there are several ways in which they can be implemented, going from the simple box camera to the modern "auto-everything" SLR. Finally, the different ways of implementing the functions can rather easily be evaluated and compared using various established references. Note, in particular, that the user-related aspects of the tool can also be evaluated and that there is, in this specific example, considerable emphasis on the human-tool interaction. (To the extent that modern SLRs are highly computerised there is also, in a sense, an element of HCI!)

Consider, as another example, an electronic spreadsheet. A spreadsheet normally has a number of purposes, such as planning, budgeting, tabulating data, calculation, information storage, and information presentation (so-called business graphics). The spreadsheet must therefore have:

- a number of *cells* that can hold data or formulae;
- a *tabulated grid* which organises the cells;
- a *window* which enables the user to see part of the grid;
- *formulae* which can connect different blocks, rows, columns or cells of the grid;
- *input* and *output facilities* (including graphic presentations);
- a (stylised) *command language* that provides the user with control over the spreadsheet and its facilities.

These, and other, functions can again be implemented in different ways (sometimes far too many), and there are ways in which the solutions can be evaluated and compared.

I believe that these two examples are sufficient to show the usefulness and the generality of the four types of tool requirements. The contribution of AI is clearly confined to the third of these requirements, i.e. how the desired HCI functions can be implemented, although knowledge of the possibilities of AI may have an influence on the other points as well. Before going on to consider the potential influence of AI on HCI I will, however, elaborate the role of HCI as a tool, and consider the various ways in which this can be understood.

A DEFINITION OF HUMAN-COMPUTER INTERACTION

With the risk of stating the obvious I would like to provide a working definition of what is to be understood by human-computer interaction. Taken at face value the term simply means the interaction between a user and a computer with the implied purpose of carrying out a certain task or achieving a certain goal. (See Figure 6.2a)

The computer is, however, rarely the target of the interaction but rather a tool or a mechanism, by which the goal can be reached. The user therefore interacts with an *application* (or the World) through the computer, and the latter serves as an intermediary in some sense.

The computer as an intermediary can have two completely different roles. In one case it can serve in an *embodiment relation*, defined by Idhe (1979), p. 8, as:

Relations in which the machine displays some kind of partial transparency in that it itself does not become objectified or thematic, but is taken into (my) experiencing of what is other in the World.

The embodiment relation can be established with all types of machines and not just computers. A classic example is the way in which

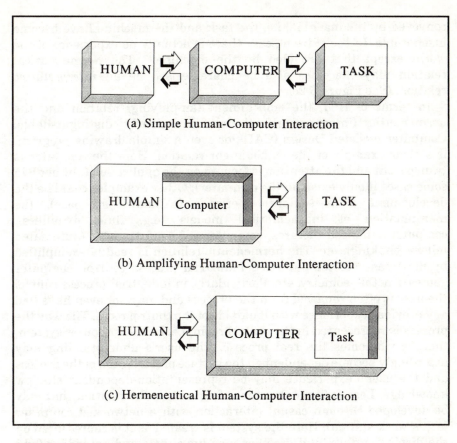

HUMAN   COMPUTER   TASK

(a) Simple Human-Computer Interaction

HUMAN   Computer   TASK

(b) Amplifying Human-Computer Interaction

HUMAN   COMPUTER   Task

(c) Hermeneutical Human-Computer Interaction

FIG. 6.2. Three types of human-computer interaction.

one can "feel" the surface of the road when driving a car. The machine somehow transforms the experience and mediates it to the user. More than that, it also amplifies the experience, e.g. by highlighting those aspects of it that are germane to the task while simultaneously reducing or excluding others. The embodiment relation may therefore also be characterised as an *amplificatory*[13] relation (see Figure 6.2b).

In the second role, the computer serves in a *hermeneutic* relation to the user. Ihde (1979 p. 11), notes that the user's "experiental terminus is with the machine. ... There is a partial opacity between the machine and the World and thus the machine is something like a text." Put differently, the user has moved from an *experience through* the machine to an *experience of* the machine. It is thus the state of the world as represented by the machine which in itself becomes important. The task is no longer experienced separately from the machine, but only as it is conveyed by the machine, i.e. the task and the machine have become inseparable. In the extreme case there is actually no experience of the world except that provided by the machine.[14] The hermeneutical relation may therefore also be characterised as an *interpretative* relation. (See Figure 6.2c).

In terms of HCI, the embodiment (amplifying) relation and the hermeneutic (interpreting) relation are clearly distinguishable. Computer Assisted Design (CAD), or even a simple drawing program, is a clear example of the embodiment relation. Here the computer is transparent and the attention is focused on the application (although in some cases it only exists in the computer). Other examples could be the development of a semantic network (a knowledge base), the manipulation of mathematical models (e.g. fluid dynamics), computer-enhanced pictures, computerised fund transfer (automated tellers, banking), etc. The hermeneutic relation is readily exemplified by most cases of computerised industrial process control, computer games, fractal geometry, etc. Particularly, in industrial process control the user is often removed from the process and may not even have had any previous experience with it outside of the control room. The way the process is represented in the control room, i.e. by the computer system, therefore becomes the real process. The user's understanding may accordingly become dependent on the surface presentation of the process and the user's experience may be representation-dependent shallow knowledge. Less extreme, but more frequent, is the relation that may be developed through casual interaction with a networked computer (e.g. a work station). Here the system is treated as it is represented on the display surface, and the user may have little understanding (and even less need to understand) what goes on underneath. This suggests the possibility that the more "advanced" the HCI is, the more likely we are to depend on it, and hence to be governed by an interpretive (hermeneutical) rather than an amplificatory (embodiment) relation.

The two relations are, of course, not mutually exclusive but rather represent two different ways of viewing the HCI. Consider, for instance, the case of ELIZA (described in Weizenbaum, 1976). For the computer scientists it was clearly a case of an embodiment relation because they were interested in the application, which was the program that simulated the non-directive therapeutic session. For the casual or unsuspecting user it was instead a case of a hermeneutical relation because for them ELIZA was real. What the computer represented to them was the application (literally, the text) itself. To take another example, a wordprocessor used to represent the embodiment relation when formatting was carried out by the use of format codes (e.g. early versions of WordStar) but is now more likely to represent the hermeneutical relation where the concept is What-You-See-Is-What-You-Get (e.g. the various forms of Desk Top Publishing).

The distinction between the two relations serves to clarify the nature of HCI. This is particularly interesting when assessing the influence of AI on HCI. AI clearly provides the possibility of amplifying the cognitive functions of the user, hence to permit new kinds of embodiment relations. But at the same time AI may be used to enhance the computer's functional repertoire and its interpretative powers, thereby strengthening its hermeneutical role. This may happen as a simple consequence of the increasing complexity of the applications and of the perceived need to increase the access to expert knowledge and expert skills. Thus the very development of expert systems may unknowingly favour the dominance of the interpretative role of computers, hence a *fragmented* rather than a *holistic* view of HCI (Weir & Alty, 1991). The development of user support systems and advanced HCI functions should, however, aim at amplifying the capacities of the user.

The embodiment relation of HCI means that the computer is used to amplify and extend what the user is able to do. Just as one can use a piece of chalk or a fountain pen to write, so one can use an HCI artifact to accomplish a given task e.g: filing, retrieving, deducing, printing, drawing, calculating—probably the best example is that I am producing this text through the use of an HCI artifact. The embodiment relation, however, demands that the effort and attention is on accomplishing the goal (in this case, expressing my ideas about HCI artifacts) rather than on using the HCI artifact. It is clear that there will always be an initial training period where one has to focus on the artifact in order to learn to use it, but this period should be of a limited duration.[15] Otherwise the HCI results in a hermeneutical relation where the computer becomes the text that the user is trying to interpret. This seems to be the view that dominates much of the cognitive science approach to HCI. The interpretation or understanding of the "text" can be made more or less easy by the way in which the HCI is designed.

Developing the Embodiment Relation

Consider, for instance, the case of Desk Top Publishing (DTP). One type of user may learn how to make a good-looking document, using the facilities of DTP without really understanding what is going on. Here "What-You-See-Is-What-You-Get" is quite literally true, and the user may become rather disappointed or confused if the final product on paper differs from what was shown on the screen. (This has been described as a case of WYGINWYT - What-You-Get-Is-Not-What-You-Think–by Helander, 1988.) Work on this level may increase the skills in using the DTP package without increasing the skills in making documents, and there is a hermeneutical relation between the user and the artifact. An extreme example is probably HAL in the film *2001*, as the astronauts here had to rely on him completely; (they did "kill" him in the end, but that was because HAL became unreliable). Another type of user may see the DTP as a convenient tool for making fancy-looking documents, but concentrate on the document rather than the package. The user knows that the same end result could be achieved in a different way. Here, there is an embodiment relation between the user and the artifact, in which the DTP software serves as an extension of the user's mind, so to speak. An even more extreme example would be the use of the so-called "outliners" or "idea generators".

It is tempting, although possibly misleading, to see a correspondence between the embodiment/hermeneutical relations and the two paradigms of human-computer interaction referred to earlier. In the mechanistic view the computer is put first, the focus is on how the computer works, and the bias is technological and mechanistic: man as an information processing system. The attention is on the use of the artifact *per se*, not on its use as a tool. This may gradually lead to a dependence on the computer so that the task can no longer be carried out without it: the computer and the task, in a sense, become one just as in the hermeneutic relation. In the cognitive view the human is put first, the focus is on how the human works, and the technological bias is reduced. The attention is fixed on the artifact as a tool, as one way out of many of accomplishing the task. The computer and the task are separate, just as in the embodiment relation. This leads to relative independence of the specific tool, although it may not be possible to perform the task without some kind of tool.

In the previous section I defined HCI as the interaction between humans and computers in the context of carrying out a task, i.e. an interaction *through* the computer rather than *with* the computer. It is a consequence of this definition that the relation between human and computer should be an embodiment relation. This means that the influence of AI on HCI must be in terms of amplifying the cognitive functions of the user. Consequently, some functions become more important than others. The HCI is, in the writing of a document for instance, only a candidate for AI improvements if one focuses on the production of a meaningful text rather than on the keystrokes. In producing the former a computer may assist, e.g. by keeping track (of contents, outlining), spelling control, counting (words, lines, pages), marking references, numbering sections, merging, replacing, finding. Another example would be the use of computers in a process control environment, such as a chemical plant or a hospital. Here the computer may assist the user in monitoring, detection, sequencing, compression, planning/scheduling, diagnosing, etc. All of these are functions that might be enhanced by the use of AI.

THE INFLUENCE OF AI ON HCI

Pseudo Needs and Real Needs

It is essential to make a careful distinction between AI influences that introduce new functionality, and influences that improve current HCI functions. Current HCI practice includes a number of technology driven improvements, but some of these cater to pseudo needs rather than real needs. A pseudo need does not (necessarily) address a real need from the HCI functionality and exists basically because the technology or possibility is there. Examples are the use of many colours in displays, multiple fonts in DTP, multiple (overlapping) windows, hierarchical menus, or the proliferation of fancy business graphics. In contrast a real need can either come from a recognised problem in (tool-related) human-computer interaction or appear because the technology changes the conditions under which the work is carried out and/or increases the possibilities. Examples are the telephone, the automobile, the satellite and the personal computer. More relevant examples are the introduction of large electronic networks (eMail), spreadsheets, etc. The distinction between pseudo needs and real needs may, however, be difficult to make and possibly even change over time. It is always easier to categorise things with the help of hindsight.

Starting from the assumption that HCI is dealing with the interaction between humans and computers to carry out a task and that the human-computer relationship should be one of embodiment rather than interpretation, we can look at the ways in which the computer may serve as an instrument for the user and the ways in which AI can be expected to enhance or improve these functions.

Functions in Human-Computer Interaction

In order to discuss the potential influence of AI on HCI it is necessary first to identify the aspects of HCI where improvements can take place. This can be done in a number of ways, but most of them begin by identifying a set of essential functions that are part of the human-computer interaction (or even more generally, the man-machine interaction). A representative number of these are shown in Table 6.1. Each column shows a set of functions that has been proposed for a specific application. In each column the functions have tentatively been distributed over the rows to indicate the range from perception (input) to action (output), partly corresponding to the groups of functions mentioned in the following. (This distribution is purely for illustrative purposes and should not be taken too literally.) It is not difficult to see that many of the functions proposed here can be translated into HCI function terms, and that they are candidates for improvement or amplification.

In addition to considering specific functions, a general improvement of the HCI can be achieved by enhancing the distribution and allocation of tasks between human and computer, i.e. by a better cognitive task analysis (cf. Woods & Hollnagel, 1988). It can also be achieved by better training, by a more specific selection of users, by improving the organisational context in which the HCI takes place, etc. Few of these are, however, at present susceptible to the influence of AI methods and techniques.

FUNCTION						
		amplification		activation	scanning	
	memory aids		structuring	evaluation	recognition	search
		attenuation		execution	recording	assimilation
	representation			identification	problem solving	analysis
			evaluation	interpretation	planning	inference
		reference		observation	coordination	explanation
	control mechanisms		comparison	procedure formulation	communication	specification
		navigation & control		task definition	steering	
	operations			action	execution	
Area	Decision Making	Cognition	Decision Making	Decision Making	Process Control	Information Processing
Ref.	Sprague & Carlson (1982)	Brookes (1985)	Hollnagel (1977)	Rasmussen (1974)	Rouse (1981)	Zmud (1983)

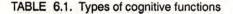

TABLE 6.1. Types of cognitive functions

HCI as a Tool

I will discuss the potential influence of AI on HCI by elaborating on the idea of the computer as a tool, as discussed earlier, and use that analogy to specify what the possible improvements of a tool can be. From a general point of view, and considering cognitive[16] rather than (bio)mechanical functions,[17] a tool makes it possible for the user to enhance the following groups of functions:

1. *Perception* and *discrimination* by detecting data which either are outside the normal range of sensitivity or discrimination, noticing differences or gradients, transforming representations to be within the range of sensitivity or discrimination, and detecting patterns (over time, space, modalities, ranges) that otherwise would go unnoticed.

2. *Interpretation* by better relating the current state to previous experiences, comparing the present situation to known cases, and assessing the match with established frames of reference and description (taxonomies, models, classifications).

3. *Planning* and *control* by simulating the consequences of hypothetical actions or decisions, maintaining consistency of assumptions, predicting probable developments, and showing greater precision in effectuating changes; this group also includes monitoring in the sense of following developments and maintaining focus (attention) over long periods and delays, checking for expected/anticipated events, etc.

In addition one might also consider functions such as communication, presentation of information, interpretation of commands, memory extensions (in range and duration), etc. In one sense, aspects of these functions are subsumed under those described earlier; in another sense, they constitute additional or supplementary functions which facilitate the embodiment relation of the artifact without directly being a part of it. In order to limit the present discussion I shall, therefore, refrain from going further into those.

AI can be applied to all of the aforementioned functions, but many of them can also be supported or improved by information technology in general. The limit between information technology and AI is, however, rather blurred because AI developments gradually become accepted and hence are no longer considered AI.

AI Enhancements of Perception and Discrimination

In most tasks where human-computer interaction plays a role, the detection and organisation of data, measurements, and information are important functions. The computer normally takes part in the pre-processing of data and information, i.e. after they have been collected from the source(s) but before they are presented to the user. This is necessary both because the amount of input data may be overwhelming (e.g. Schindler, 1989) and because there are some well-known limitations in the human capacity for information processing (Simon, 1972).

There are a number of ways in which human cognitive functioning can be amplified to improve perception and discrimination, which require more than simply applying computer science, statistics, and ergonomics[18]. One of the main AI fields that may have an influence here is computer vision. Although it still has far to go when compared with the capabilities of human beings, this field is a possible candidate for amplification of human vision. It is expected that computer vision, before the turn of the century, may make it possible to recognize complex images under a variety of lighting conditions, both when they are stationary and when they are moving (McRobbie & Siekmann, 1988). In addition, developments in pattern recognition and picture enhancements may improve the way in which objects are detected and traced. AI solutions serve, in a sense, as a set of "lenses" with different characteristics which facilitate the selection of one item out of a mass of items and the maintenance of focus.

In relation to perception and discrimination, attention is another good candidate for amplification. It is well-known that human attention varies and may deteriorate dramatically even after short periods of time (Kahneman, 1973). A computer's attention never varies and it has the capacity and tenacity to keep track of almost any number of events or lines of development. The problem is, however, not simply solved by replacing human attention with computer attention. The trick in having the computer amplify the user's attention is that the computer is able to interrupt the user in an appropriate way and at the right time. This has implications for the field of user modelling, cf. the following.

AI Enhancements of Interpretation

This group of functions includes analysis, comprehension, diagnosis, "going beyond the information given", prediction, reorganisation, rearrangement, etc. On the simplest level support can be given by non-AI facilities such as browsers, relational/associative databases, and various types of symbolic transformations. In the context of intelligent decision support systems I have made a distinction between three different types of inadequate information and three different roles for an artifact (Hollnagel, 1988):

Incomplete Information.   Where the information is under-specified (incomplete), ill-defined or imprecise. Here the computer should assist by providing supplementary information, e.g. by using default heuristics.

Insufficient Information.   Where the information is there although not available to the user without an additional effort. Here the computer should help as an intelligent assistant with the appropriate algorithmic or heuristic services.

Information Overflow.   Where there is more information than needed. Here the computer should serve as an intelligent filter, possibly based on pattern recognition and adaptation.

The reduction or filtering of information addresses the trade-off between demand and capacity. The classical (engineering) solution is to provide all the information in a semi-structured form and let the user do the filtering. The AI solution would be to have an artifact do the filtering and provide the user with only the necessary information. That, however, takes on a great responsibility and produces a host of problems for system designers. AI-based information reduction can, in principle, be based on two concerns:

System Centered.   Where an analysis of the system state-space and possible scenarios is used to define the information that is necessary from a technical point of view.

User Centered.   Where the filtering is determined by what the user can actually comprehend. This, unfortunately, is not a static measure but depends highly on the user and the current situation.

One could imagine a solution in terms of a two-stage process where the first stage uses a system centered (technical) filtering and the second uses a user centered (cognitive) filtering. The "slight" complication is that the user may actually need additional information, because the technical filtering is made under the assumption that the user knows what the designer expects. That is not always the case. This might be solved by endowing the filtering artifact with some kind of intelligence, for instance in the shape of a dialogue system (Alty & Weir, 1987), which could be used to provide the user with additional (the designer's tacit) knowledge that otherwise would not be available. That, again, puts a heavy burden on the ability to model correctly the user's state of knowledge.

Interpretation involves the combination of many pieces of information and inferring the consequences. Some of the relevant AI techniques are assumption-based truth maintenance (ATMS), consistency checking, consequence propagation, possible worlds techniques, etc. Another influence could come from the developments in automatic deduction systems. Although the main emphasis here is on deduction in formal environments (mathematics, logic) this has clear implications for verification issues in formally described systems, such as software systems and knowledge bases. In the long term it is possible that automatic deduction may assume the role of calculations, i.e. something that we routinely entrust to a computer as a natural part of the task. Other relevant AI fields are qualitative modelling (discussed later) and reasoning with imprecise or ill-defined knowledge, and reasoning with a combination of symbols (soft data) and numbers (hard data), e.g. Dubois and Prade (1989).

Expert Systems
Although Expert Systems as an AI technology can be applied on many different levels of human-computer interaction, it is appropriate to discuss them together with interpretation. Expert systems are one of the main results of applied AI and employ a number of techniques developed in AI, but looked at closely represent a rather incoherent field. The vices and virtues of expert systems have been extolled in many books and journals (e.g. Alty & Coombs, 1984; Guida & Tasso, 1988) and shall therefore not be repeated here. Instead I will take a look at how expert systems may be applied to enhance HCI.

Expert systems generally embody a set of expert knowledge together with the rules to apply it across a range of situations. Expert systems emulate what an expert can do, and may in the context of HCI be seen as an application specialist in the service of the user: a mediator and amplifier which translates user intentions into commands, as well as data and information from the system into knowledge that can be presented to the user.

Examples of expert systems in use are advice giving systems, diagnostic systems and planning and scheduling systems. The expert system technique is promising because it is quite easy to use. Some of the important functions which could serve to amplify the user's cognition would be making predictions (trend identification), checking consequences of actions (or potential hypothetical actions), maintaining consistency of knowledge (bases) or even outright truth maintenance as a basis for actions. All of these functions are part of the methodological armoury of expert systems, and may therefore be readily applied to enhance HCI.

Even though an expert systems may serve as a kind of translator it is nevertheless important to note that it should serve in an embodiment relation rather than in a hermeneutical relation. Despite all the impressive demonstrations of expert system capabilities, they are still unable to provide any genuine insights or interpretations on their own. Although their treatment of information is heuristic and rule-based rather than algorithmic, they still follow a deterministic path. The use of heuristics is primarily due to the lack of adequate algorithms, or the computational hindrances for algorithmic solutions (e.g. computational explosions).

AI Enhancements of Planning and Control

Planning is essential for action, in particular with regard to being ready to respond to changes in the system, allocating resources appropriately, and organising supplementary services and functions; control is needed to ensure a stable environment and to monitor the execution of actions. Planning and action become more difficult the more unpredictable the environment is, and control is used to reduce the variety either through feedback or feedforward. Planning and control together refer to a group of functions that include evaluation of options, prediction, decision-making, strategy formulation and execution.

The ability to develop and maintain an adequate representation or model of the system (application) and the context (environment) is of central importance for planning and control. This was realised early on by cybernetics, and expressed in the so-called "law of requisite variety" (Ashby, 1973). The law simply says that for a system with noisy input the only way to reduce the variety of the outcome is to increase the variety of the regulator, in other words: only variety can destroy variety (cf. Conant & Ashby, 1970). AI can exhibit a number of ways in which world modelling can take place, although most of them are dedicated to stand-alone planning systems and therefore not flexible enough to be used as a part of HCI. It is still conceivable that planning may be performed by a planning server, i.e. as a completely computerised part of the task that is called upon whenever necessary. This would be particularly important in the exploration of alternate paths or plans.

A special aspect of planning and control is consistency checking (of resources, of side-effects, of pre-conditions, etc.). These are things that people have a very hard time doing, but which may be carried out efficiently by an AI system. It does, however, presuppose that there already is available an adequate model of the system which can be used to support these functions.

Monitoring means keeping an eye on the way the system develops with the purpose of noting discrepancies. Monitoring differs from perception and discrimination because it is guided by a goal or a purpose; a clear expectation of what is going to happen. Monitoring can also refer to the user in person, i.e. assisting in navigating in the state space (knowing where I am, knowing where I came from, knowing where I am going).

Qualitative Modelling

Qualitative modelling is one of the "hot" areas of AI at present. The basic idea in qualitative modelling is to capture the essential characteristics of the system being studied without invoking any unnecessary detail. Qualitative modelling started by investigating how people thought of physical systems and phenomena (the so-called qualitative physics, cf. de Kleer & Brown, 1983), but is now widely used as an alternative way of describing physical systems. It is furthermore considered as a possible candidate for the modelling of mental functions, where there are no "conventional" quantitative models.

Qualitative modelling is claimed to have a number of advantages. First, it makes use of computational mechanisms that are simpler than those for quantitative models. Secondly, it can be used in cases where there are no reliable classical models. Finally, qualitative models are assumed to correspond better to peoples' commonsense understanding of how systems operate. This last aspect is particularly relevant in the case of planning and control. If AI can provide a modelling technique which closely resembles the user's natural way of understanding what goes on in the application, then this can be the basis for developing a tool to improve planning and control.

Qualitative Reasoning

Qualitative modelling is naturally contrasted with quantitative modelling, as it is known from e.g., engineering. Qualitative reasoning is interesting because there is nothing to contrast it with, i.e. there is nothing called quantitative reasoning. This is because all reasoning, in fact, is qualitative or discrete rather than quantitative or continuous. Reasoning is based on symbols. If the reasoning is with numbers, as expression of quantities, then it is rather called computation or calculation.

Qualitative reasoning in practical planning is to a very large extent default reasoning or reasoning with incomplete information. As such, it is a good candidate for a way of improving the HCI. The interaction between the user and the application can be enhanced if the computer is able to work on less than complete information, both in planning actions, in making decisions, and in effectuating them. Humans are capable of reasoning with incomplete knowledge, although it is generally discouraged in human-computer interaction because there are too many possibilities for faults (e.g. Reason, 1990). But if the main principles for default reasoning could be formulated and applied consistently (which seems to be the Achilles heel of humans), then the computer could effectively assist the user in carrying out a task. Default reasoning is therefore a good example of how an AI technique can improve HCI - in this case a technique coming from expert system developments as well as from the very foundations of AI. Yet, default reasoning is also a good example of a technique which not in itself indicates the direction in which HCI should develop.

Tool Needs of HCI

Even this short presentation has listed a number of areas where people, generally or under specific circumstances, are known to have problems and where some kind of assistance and amplification therefore may be of use. This list can easily be extended in the tradition of experimental cognitive psychology, although the value of doing so may be somewhat limited (cf. the discussion by Neisser, 1976). It is more constructive to point out that human cognition has some strong sides and some weak sides, and that a particular balance of these may be fostered by the conditions under which human-computer interaction is required to occur.

It follows that a conscientious design of the HCI may serve to amplify the strengths and compensate for the weaknesses - and also that an incorrectly designed environment may lead to the opposite result. It is important to realise that human-computer interaction can tend either towards an embodiment relation or a hermeneutical relation. AI can be used for both purposes, but I strongly believe that the best use of human cognition is made if HCI serves as a tool, i.e. where the improvements support the embodiment relation. Any improvement runs the danger of leading to a hermeneutical relation, i.e. the user trusting the computer and using it as a pillow or prosthesis. The best guard against that is always to produce more than one version of the tool, to have more than one function. Simply by having alternative ways of doing things and by being able to choose, the user will come to realise that the computer offers an opportunity rather than a restriction. The user may constantly choose to use the tool, but there is a crucial difference between trusting a tool and becoming dependent on a prosthesis.

In addition to the AI areas of relevance that have been mentioned earlier, there are two more which need to be commented on. One is the use of modelling, in particular user modelling, which has been referred to by all three groups of functions. And the other is the use of natural language, which has always had a special place in AI.

User Modelling

One way in which HCI can be improved, quantitatively and qualitatively, is by relieving the human user of the burden of adapting to the system by having the system adapt to the user. In other words, if the system has some degree of flexibility, some degree of adaptability, the user may be able to dedicate more effort to carrying out the task and less effort to mastering the computer.

In the view of HCI taken here, the human user can be seen as trying to control the computer to perform a task. The user will necessarily have an incomplete and, in some ways, incorrect understanding of what the computer is able to do, what it requires in terms of commands, what the effect of commands and combinations of commands are, etc. If the computer is able to take this into account, able to be forgiving vis-à-vis partly incorrect commands, and able - in Norbert Wiener's sense - to do what the user intended rather than what he ordered, then the HCI will be vastly improved. To do so the computer clearly needs what is commonly called a user model, i.e. a representation of the salient aspects of the user which are required to enhance the execution of the task.

What Is A User Model?

User modelling has often been promoted as the essential problem for HCI. The term "user modelling" itself is ambiguous and is used with a number of different meanings (Goodstein et al., 1988). Depending on the context and the author, a "user model" may be one of the following:

- The users' mental model of the system they are interacting with.
- The representation of the user as embodied in the system.
- The model of the user as applied by others, e.g. the system designer or the instructor.
- The users' knowledge (and beliefs) about themselves.

To make the confusion even greater, a number of different terms such as "mental model", "user model", "user image", and "conceptual model" are applied rather indiscriminately to refer to one or more of these four meanings. It is probably impossible to attain a uniform use of the terminology, cf. the earlier attempt made by Hollnagel & Woods (1983).

The whole idea of user models[19] is actually an artifact created by our linguistic conventions. Assume, for a moment, that the user knows something about a task or a domain. We do not know how this knowledge is structured, but as a good approximation we may assume that it is structurally homomorph to our own. We know from ourselves that some of the knowledge can be expressed in formal terms (as physical, mechanical models) but that it may depend on our education and our tendency, for example, to use mental images. When asked to explain what we know, we often use the language of logic and causality, i.e. corresponding to the physicalistic, mechanistic descriptions of the world. This is not necessarily because the knowledge is structured in this way but because it is the habitual manner of explaining or expressing ourselves to others. It is in that sense that the user's model is an artifact of the way it is communicated or formally described. Or, to put it differently, the mental models are "structures and processes imputed to a person's mind in order to account for that person's behavior and experience" (Carroll, 1984) - even by that person. It is therefore an unwarranted step from this description to assume that users have a mental model - or even multiple mental models - in their heads. We should rather concentrate on what the users do not know and on ways in which this can be employed to guide and control the amplification. I will call this a pragmatic approach to user modelling.

AI and User Modelling

User modelling is clearly one of the areas where AI should have a considerable influence. A central concern of AI is how to represent knowledge and how to formulate rules that can be used to reason about the knowledge "object". The adaptation that the computer should exhibit can be seen precisely as the result of reasoning about the user's expectations, capabilities, intentions, etc. AI has produced a number of different formalisms for knowledge representation, and has further spent considerable effort on defining various ways of reasoning and implementing them in computing artifacts.

The problem is often stated as "what is in a user's model?", but I believe this to be the wrong question. It should rather be "what does the user know about X?". Some of this knowledge may be expressed as a model, e.g. as a physical or mechanical analogy, but assuming that all the user knows is in that model is too restrictive. In a sense, the obvious answer to the question about what the user knows is that the user knows what we know, or a suitably large sub-set thereof. There may be specific items missing, but it is probably both easier and more useful to specify what is not known rather than what is known. The problem of user modelling could then be stated in terms of what the user does not know. It is, after all, more often in the interest of a specific task to know what the user does not know rather than what the user knows, because this may tell us where and how assistance is needed. The trick is simply to turn the whole thing on its head, and assume complete knowledge with some exceptions rather than the other way around. Following this "reversed" paradigm, the aim of user modelling is not to account for correct performance but to help in analysing incorrect performance and suggest improvements.

This approach to user modelling helps overcome one of the main problems, i.e. how one can ensure a reasonably complete knowledge. Since this is notoriously difficult, the preferred solution has been to remain in the domains where complete knowledge can be provided. That, however, means either that the domains remain very simple, (wordprocessors), or that the human performance in question remains simple (keystrokes, sensory-motor performance aspects) excluding cognitive embellishments such as erroneous actions, slips, switching between action levels and strategies, etc. This is precisely why user modelling has not come very far. Contrary to the assumptions underlying the prevalent models of cognitive science (Card et al., 1983; Kieras & Polson, 1985) human performance is neither error-free nor guided by rational choices (e.g. MacLean et al., 1985). The problems of user modelling are in many ways similar to the problems in natural language understanding, where it is known that one can produce artificial language understanding in a closed world but not in an open one. Human performance, however, does not take place under the closed world assumption, but can only artificially be restrained to do so.

Despite the great interest in user modelling and the many efforts, the influence of AI on HCI in this respect has been modest indeed. It is noteworthy that the success rate has been highest precisely in cases where the communication can best be expressed formally, e.g. in chess (although it is doubtful whether even Deep Thought contains a model of the opponent). These are also cases where the purpose is to adapt the response of the computer to compete with the user rather than to improve the HCI. Similarly, it has been possible to include a number of more or less sophisticated help functions (e.g. explanations) in commercial software packages, but none of them genuinely respond to the user by actively taking part in the dialogue. They rather react to the user's requests and queries by using sophisticated algorithms.

Natural Language Understanding and Natural Communication

Natural language understanding has remained a dream for AI since the very first days. And it is also a dream for HCI. The reasoning seems to be as follows:

1. Humans use natural language.
2. *Human communication is very effective.*
3. Effective communication must therefore be based on natural language.

Despite the obvious simplicity of this argument, it is widely acknowledged in the implicitly made assumption that human face-to-face interaction must be the paradigm for all HCI. This is, for example, the foundation for the arguments and analyses presented by Suchman (1987, p.70) in her analysis of human-machine communication. Consequently, human-machine communication is seen as "an extreme form of resource-limited interaction".

Most of the successes of natural language understanding have taken place in very restricted circumstances (the blocks' world, chess playing), but the hopes for natural language understanding are still high. It is predicted that by the end of the century systems will exist which can understand continuous text in specific domains such as office communication. This will, finally, lead to automatic translations and, more important for HCI, flexible dialogues with one's (personal) computer. The computer will be able to understand input expressed in natural language and also be able to provide the output as linguistic expressions. Quite apart from the uncertainty of such predictions it is worthwhile to examine the assumption that natural language understanding is necessary for effective human-computer interaction.

One of the many virtues of natural language is its flexibility, i.e. that it can be used to express literally everything: there is, by definition, nothing which cannot be described by language although it may not always be simple to do so. In particular, natural language allows a smooth transition from context to context, for instance during a conversation. While this may be a benefit in face-to-face communication, it is not necessarily a benefit for human-computer communication in the setting of carrying out a task. First of all, it is only the human who is able to switch contexts smoothly; the computer normally cannot do so, or at least only do it for a small number of pre-specified contexts. Furthermore, unless the switching of contexts is confined to a pre-defined set it will usually be disruptive to the execution of the task. The only way to prevent that and reduce the uncertainty in the situation, is to confine the communication by using a pre-defined code. Then, even if contexts are switched it will be easier to detect the intended context as one out of a finite number, rather than as one out of an infinite number. This will increase the efficiency and precision of human-computer communication, as well as reduce the computational overhead (because the number of possible meanings of the messages has been reduced).

It is noteworthy that although human beings in principle can use unrestricted natural language in communication, they rarely do so. On the contrary, in practically all situations of work the language is voluntarily restricted to increase the efficiency of communication. The basic solution is to use a well-defined lexicon (the vocabulary, the terminology) and a well-defined syntax. Examples are easily found in practical tasks in process industries and transportation, in sciences, in sports, and even in advertising - and examples of mishaps and accidents caused by not following the rules are abundant. All interaction with computers clearly take place in that way and although the individual user sometimes may feel it as a restriction, it is certainly more efficient than allowing users to use their own set of commands (Bench-Capon & McEnery, 1989).

The purpose of communication is to affect the conduct of the receiver as effectively as possible. This was pointed out already in 1949 when Claude Shannon and Warren Weaver formulated the mathematical theory of communication. They distinguished between the technical problem, the semantic problem, and the effectiveness problem and described the latter (1969, p. 5) as being concerned:

> With the success with which the meaning conveyed to the receiver leads to the desired conduct on his part. It may seem at first glance undesirably narrow to imply that the purpose of all communication is to influence the conduct of the receiver. But with any reasonably broad definition of conduct, it is clear that communication either affects conduct or is without any discernible and probable effect at all.

Communication therefore requires a language that is suited to its purpose. In human-computer interaction this means a language that suits the needs and capabilities of the user as well as the computer. The user's requirements are that the language must be easy to learn and easy to apply, i.e. it must make sense in the given context and for the given task. The computer's main requirement is that the language is easy to interpret, i.e. that the rules for using it are clear and unambiguous. In neither case is natural language the obvious candidate. The pursuit of natural language understanding is undoubtedly a worthy goal for AI in itself, and the results achieved in this may be very useful for HCI. But to assume that natural language is necessary for effective human-computer interaction and to set natural language communication as a goal for HCI is a misunderstanding of what HCI is all about.[20]

CONCLUSIONS

The discussions in this chapter have been based on pragmatic definitions of both AI and HCI. AI was defined as having the goal of making computers more useful by applying the basic characteristics of

AI systems: (1) that they can use general knowledge and principles to infer heuristic rules from data; and (2) that they can apply these rules to solve the problems they are given. This suggested two applications of AI: to improve the processing of data and information beyond the reach of algorithmic methods, and to enhance HCI by providing added functionality (more flexible communication, adaptive interpretation of commands and messages, adaptive presentation of information, explanations, etc.). HCI was defined as the study of the interaction between humans and computers in the context of carrying out a given task, with the purpose of developing theories, methods and techniques that can be used to improve that interaction. HCI was further characterised as being an engineering discipline rather than a science. It was finally pointed out how there could be either an embodiment relation or a hermeneutical relation between the human and it was concluded that the embodiment relation should be pursued. The influence of AI on HCI should consequently be in terms of amplifying the cognitive functions of the user.

A consequence of accepting HCI as an engineering discipline is that the real need is to make systems using HCI more efficient and reliable, rather than to develop HCI *per se*. This means that one must have a suitable broad framework for considering HCI. A candidate for that is shown in Figure 6.3. Here HCI is regarded as an essential aspect of how the MMS functions. That functioning is again influenced by a number of factors:

- The *task* requirements, derived from a task description.
- The *context* (or allowable performance envelope), derived from a description of the task environment.
- The *resources of the user*, derived from a user description.
- The *resources of the computer* (system), derived from a system description.

The particular theoretical basis for developing this framework may vary between application areas and schools of thought. But the fundamental message is that the development of HCI must be guided by something outside HCI itself. I will consider this in the following sections.

The Design-Theory Relation of HCI

In order to be useful, a design must be based on a theory or a conceptual structure.[21] Even engineering principles must have a conceptual foundation, although it may be implicit rather than explicit. Good engineering is the expression of established design principles. Bad

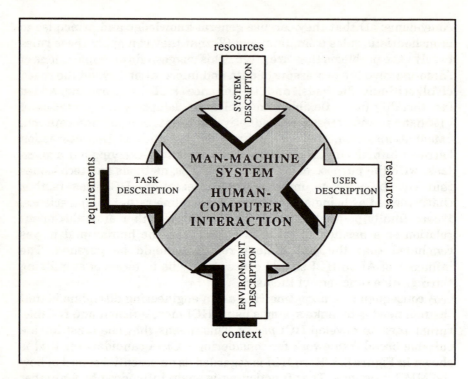

FIG. 6.3. A framework for MMS and HCI

engineering is a haphazard combination of available bits and pieces. Whether being the result of design or engineering, the HCI artifact will, in a sense, be the representation (or nexus) of a theory (cf. Carroll & Campbell, 1988; Hollnagel & Woods, 1983). The artifact is thereby, on the one hand, an expression of the capabilities of the theory (and therefore also a test of it) and, on the other hand, dependent on an appropriate theory (or theories).

In terms of HCI the situation is that there are many guiding and commonsense principles about human cognitive functioning, but no clear theories.[22] If HCI is required to be a source of invention, a source for design, then this is clearly a problem. But if HCI serves to facilitate the achievement of another purpose (e.g. problem-solving, diagnosis, decision-making, planning, control, tutoring, construction, design) rather than being a goal in itself - then the predicament is less embarrassing. Instead of being the representation of a theory of HCI, the artifact should be a representation of a theory for the particular task, e.g. tutoring, decision-making, planning, etc. There will normally be a number of theories for each task, and the goal is not to choose the correct one, but rather to choose one which is appropriate and to implement it consistently.

AI contains a number of examples of systems which have been built according to a theory. Most notable, in the field of HCI, is Weizenbaum's ELIZA (Weizenbaum, 1976). Other systems have been built according to specific theories about, for instance, decision-making (Fischhoff, 1986; Yntema & Torgerson, 1961) or coaching (Burton & Brown, 1979). Most of them have eventually failed, not because they were built according to a theory or embodied a theory, but because the theory turned out to be insufficient or inadequate. That is, however, not surprising as psychology and cognitive science are still rather immature.

The contribution of AI is to enable the HCI artifacts to be built, rather than to provide the theory on which they are built. We need to look elsewhere to find these. Since there is no single, unified theory there cannot be one generic type of HCI which is capable of solving all problems. One can, of course, specify certain characteristics of a general HCI structure which will avoid known difficulties associated with human cognition. This can be based on experience and good engineering practices rather than on a theory. But to be really efficient in solving a class of problems it is necessary to have a specific interface or an artifact that embodies a specific theory or set of theories about the task or the problem.

Interaction Design versus Task Design

Cognitive psychology, cognitive science, and cognitive engineering are all rooted in the same scientific paradigm which tries to produce a physical conception of objectivity and use that as the basis for explaining everything - including subjective mental processes (Nagel, 1986). The whole idea of man as an information processing system is probably the best example of that[23] - whether as a whole or as in specific models and theories - particularly in its latest guise as neural networks. So far the response to every failure of the reductionist approach has been a new attempt or a new set of theories, although this has not brought us very much further. This has led to an apparent impasse of HCI which is in stark contrast to the apparent success of its practical forerunner Human Factors Engineering.

According to this line of thinking the impasse is mainly due to its "ambition" of being a science (cf. the aforementioned description of the three phases) and its legacy of concepts from cognitive science. The success of Human Factors Engineering has been due to two facts:

1. The *task* was explicitly embodied in the machines, i.e. the machines could not be used for anything else.

2. The *interactions* were measurable, e.g. in anthropometric and psychophysical terms.

In interaction design, the purpose is basically to anticipate and constrain the user's actions (Suchman, 1987, p. 1987) to remain within the performance capabilities of the machine. In task design the purpose is rather to adapt the machine's functional repertoire to correspond to the user, so that together they can provide the functionality required by the task. The difference is therefore not only a "philosophical" one, but a very practical concern indeed.

In HCI the tasks are not explicitly embodied in the machines. On the contrary, the prevailing attitude is to design a general purpose "sandwich" layer between the application and the user, thus effectively hiding the task. Yet to be really effective the interface must reflect the task. That need not conflict with the goal of producing interfaces that are consistent between tasks and which avoid the most obvious traps and shortcomings of human cognition. With regard to the second point, the cognitive aspects of HCI are not easily made operational and measurable. To see that, one need only point to the laborious methodology both of the parametric approaches such as GOMS, and of the sociological approaches which consider tasks as situated actions.

The Need for Guiding Principles

One of the reasons why the actual influence of AI on HCI has been quite small, and certainly less than one would have expected, is that the goals of AI and HCI do not really coincide. As I argued earlier the ultimate goal of AI is to recreate human intelligence in an artifact. Despite the fact that the pragmatic goal was defined as making computers easier to use, it is the ultimate goal which has driven the main developments in AI.

The goal of HCI is, on the other hand, to facilitate the way in which computers are used as a tool in carrying out tasks. While this may seem similar to the pragmatic goal of AI, it is quite different from its ultimate goal - even though the recreation of intelligence in an artifact ought to have some purpose beyond the thing itself! The potentially useful contributions from AI are therefore the tools and techniques that have been developed over the years - for knowledge representation, rule interpretation, reasoning (logic), learning, system building and prototyping, modelling and simulation, etc. But it requires some very sound principles to use those tools and techniques appropriately. These principles cannot be expected from AI. Neither can they be expected to emerge from HCI, since HCI is the *application* of the theories to serve a well-defined purpose. The theories or the guiding principles must therefore come from somewhere else. My own favourite is the general systems approach, as exemplified by Cognitive Systems Engineering or by the goals-means analysis to system functioning. Other approaches may prove equally useful as long as they have very powerful analytical principles that can be used to match the needs with the means (e.g. Dowell & Long, 1989).

I believe that the success of HCI may depend on its ability to look outwards to the task, rather than look inwards to the cognitive mechanisms of the user. In other words, HCI should concern itself with the total task design, including human-computer interaction, rather than the design of the interaction *per se*. At the same time as HCI developed during the 1980s, there has also been a slow build-up of despair among cognitive psychologists who have gradually come to realise that their science offers no firm basis for HCI design. This frustration may eventually lead to a change in paradigm, as articulated by Kuhn (1970), but it is not easy to predict what the new paradigm is going to be. According to the line of reasoning in this paper, it should be a paradigm which is based on action, e.g. in the sense of servo-control, feedback, cybernetics, adaptation, rather than on technological metaphors for mental mechanisms. Psychology can show a number of attempts to emphasise the constructive rather than reactive nature of human cognition - going at least from Bartlett (1972; org. 1932) and Brunswik (1956) over Miller, Galanter, and Pribram (1960) and Neisser (1976) to contemporary efforts. Perhaps a return to this line of thinking can help to get HCI back on line.

NOTES

1.   HCI refers to the systematic study of the interaction between humans and computers rather than the interaction as such. It is thus used as a name for a scientific discipline or speciality, just as e.g. Human Factors Engineering, Ergonomics, and Man-Machine Interaction. HCI is the study of human-computer interaction; but HCI may also be the object of study in its own right, as this chapter demonstrates. For a further discussion of what HCI is, see Diaper (1989).

2.   A Man-Machine System (MMS) denotes a system composed of one or more persons and one or more machines which co-operate to achieve a specified goal. The term MMS thus covers a wide range of systems, from a cyclist or a driver of an automobile to a team of astronauts in a space-shuttle or dealers in an arbitrage center. The man (i.e. human being) in an MMS may be a casual user or an expert; the machine may be a piece of mechanical equipment or a network of computers. The study of MMS is covered by such disciplines as cybernetics, ergonomics and human factors engineering, control theory, systems theory, organisational theory, psychology, cognitive

systems engineering, etc. The field of MMS is thus a proper super-set of HCI.

3. The notable exceptions are Smalltalk, in its original idea, and LOGO (Papert, 1980).

4. One of the underlying reasons is the lack of a clear definition of intelligence, cf. the following sections. It is said about intelligence that there is more agreement on the behaviours referred to by the term than there is on how to interpret or categorise them (English & English, 1958). This is one of the reasons why Turing could discuss successfully whether a machine could think (Turing, 1950) without resolving the underlying issue of what intelligence is. The failure to recognise this distinction has been the cause of much misunderstanding and mischief in AI.

5. As an analogy, consider the search for a way of producing power by fusion. The approach that has been taken so far has been to replicate the conditions that are known to exist in the sun. This has proved to be extremely difficult and progress has been rather slow. Then, suddenly, two scientists, named Pons and Fleischmann, announced that they had created fusion in a completely different way, using a new (although not unknown) method. Unfortunately, it turned out to be a mistake (or so, at least, it seems at present). But the hope of finding an easy solution to the hard problems remains - in fusion physics as well as in AI.

6. The "British Museum Algorithm" denotes the non-selective generation of solutions which, if it is continued long enough, will eventually include the required solution. It refers to the story about a group of monkeys who, by randomly working with typewriters, eventually will reproduce all the volumes in the British Museum. The use of this term in AI seems to hav been started by Alan Newell and Herbert Simon (Simon, 1977, p. 331-332).

7. As early as 1948 Alan Turing commented that: "We could produce fairly accurate electrical models to copy the behaviour of nerves, but there seems very little point in doing so. It would be rather like putting a lot of work into cars which walked on legs instead of continuing to use wheels", (cf. Hodges 1983, p. 404).

8. Turing's theorem refers to the so-called "Entscheidungsproblem" where Turing showed that it was possible to specify an abstract universal computing machine on which any computation could be performed. This has come to be known as the Turing Machine (e.g. Arbib, 1964).
    Turing's test refers to the proposal in Turing (1950) of an Imitation Game as a way of finding out whether an interrogator could distinguish between a machine and a person.

9. It is interesting to note that many of these problems have been revived in the neural networks approach, although the methods obviously are different. There might nevertheless be some valuable lessons to learn from past successes and failures.

10. A contributing factor may have been the movement towards the abolishment of sexist language which grew in the 1970s.

11. The use of common sense as the basis for HCI design is certainly to be highly recommended. Common sense must, however, not be confused with common practice or convenience. Systems involving human-computer interaction are often built using existing tools and solutions without fully assessing the consequences of that. A common sense approach requires that one carefully and systematically analyses the problem and evaluates the solutions in their own right.

12. It is worth mentioning that the editor's preface to the *Handbook of Human-Computer Interaction* fails to provide a definition of HCI or even an attempt at characterising the field (Helander, 1988). Although the editor states that "this Handbook is concerned with the principles of Human Factors Engineering for the design of the Human-Computer Interface" (sic!), I seriously doubt that every author of the handbook will subscribe to that view.

13. A related use of the term was made at least as early as 1956, when Ross Ashby discussed the idea of "intelligence amplification" (Ashby, 1973).

14. This trend is reinforced by the growing power of graphical tools which make it all too easy to create so-called "artificial realities". Whereas this technique may serve a useful purpose in cases where alternative forms of representation are difficult to use, such as in Computational Fluid Dynamics, it is potentially quite dangerous because it only allows the hermeneutical or interpretative role of the computer. In other words, the user is *de facto* deprived of any other kind of reference to the task or the application.

15. One of the claims of the so-called user friendly systems, such as the WIMP environment on a Macintosh, is precisely that the learning period is very short and that even a novice can actually use the system in a very short time. The same claim is made, in various ways, for most of the software packages for the personal computers. While this is indeed a noble ambition, it is not always fulfilled in practice.

16. This does not subscribe to any specific theory or view of human thinking, problem solving or decision-making. There are, of course, obvious similarities to many known models and descriptions of human cognitive functioning and this is certainly no coincidence. We are, after all considering the same matter and share a common experience of it. I make no claims regarding the originality or even completeness of the functions listed here, although I am convinced that they all are necessary. The list is not intended to constitute a taxonomy or a model in any way, but simply serves as a vehicle for the present discussion. It thus follows the approach used by Mackay (1968).

17.   Tools are normally thought of in a very literal sense, e.g. a hammer, and most dictionaries define tools as instruments used in a physical activity. In that sense tools are amplifiers of (bio)mechanical functions, increasing reach, grasp, force, precision, etc. Other tools serve as amplifiers for the senses, e.g. telescopes, microscopes, high-speed cameras, etc. More advanced tools, such as cyclotrons, scanners, NMR spectroscopes, etc., depend on the use of computers and therefore represent a form of HCI, although they focus on perceptual rather than cognitive functions. The embodiment/hermeneutical distinction can, of course, be applied to tools of any kind.

18.   Perception refers to the awareness (or becoming aware) of something by a sensory process, while discrimination refers to the detection of differences in what is perceived.

19.   In most cases even the use of the term "model" is misleading. What we are talking about is, rather, a conglomerate of knowledge or set of representations of something, part of which may be in the form of a model. Consider, for instance, the user's knowledge of the system or application. This normally consists of a mixture of facts, assumptions, models, and various other things such as mental images, habitual reactions, associations, useful analogies, etc. The models can be of causal relationships, first principles, etc. The important point is that only a part o the user's knowledge about the system is expressed as a model in the conventional meaning of the term. The same goes, of course, for the user image, the agent model, and the self model. Instead of talking about user models we ought therefore to talk about mental representations, user representations, agent representations and self knowledge.

20.   To be fair, this point of view is not universally accepted, not even in Europe. The striving for natural language communication is probably more common, e.g. Suchman (1987) and Bunt (1988).

21.   In most cases where an MMS is built there is more need of solid engineering than of design and innovation. While there must be a continuous progress, most systems are needed for practical reasons and the application of known solutions is therefore preferred. Only where known solutions are inadequate will the need for innovative design be prominent.

22.   This is not to say that there have been a shortage of models and theories which have promised to be the final answer. One need only to peruse the recent *Handbook of Human-Computer Interaction* (Helander, 1988) to find a number of examples.

23.   The idea of man as an information processing system has its strong proponents but has also been criticised many times. Thomas Nagel (1986, p.16), for instance, writes:

Eventually, I believe, current attempts to understand the mind by analogy with man-made computers that can perform superbly some of the same external tasks as conscious beings will be recognized as a gigantic waste of time. The true principles underlying the mind will be discovered, if at all, only by a more direct approach."

Having myself been involved with cognitive psychology and AI for the last twenty years I can certainly agree with this, although one should not forget the many interesting by-products that have appeared on the way (e.g. expert systems).

REFERENCES

Alty, J. L., & Coombs, M. (1984). *Expert systems. Concepts and examples.* Manchester: NCC.

Alty, J. L., & Weir, G. R. (1987, September 28-29). Dialogue design for dynamic systems. *Proceedings of the 4th Annual ESPRIT Conference, Brussels.* Amsterdam: North-Holland.

Angling, J. M. (Ed.). (1973). *Beyond the information given. Studies in the psychology of knowing.* New York: W. W. Norton.

Arbib, M. A. (1964). *Brains, machines and mathematics.* New York: McGraw-Hill.

Ashby, W. R. (1973). *An introduction to cybernetics.* London: Methuen.

Barnard, P. J. (1987). Cognitive resources and the learning of human computer interaction. In J. M. Carroll (Ed.), *Interfacing thought: Cognitive aspects of human-computer interaction.* Cambridge, MA: MIT Press.

Barrow, H. G. (1989). AI, neural networks and early vision, *AISBQ, 69,* 6-25.

Bartlett, F. C. (1972). *Remembering. A study in experimental and social psychology.* Cambridge: Cambridge University Press.

Bench-Capon, T. J. M., & McEnery, A. M. (1989). People interact through computers not with them. *Interacting With Computers, 1*(1), 31-38.

Blaker, A. A. (1980). *Photography. Art and technique.* San Francisco: W. H. Freeman.

Brookes, C. H. P. (1985). A framework for DSS development. *Proceedings of Fifth International Conference on Decision Support Systems DSS-85,* San Francisco.

Brunswik, E. (1956). *Perception and the representative design of psychological experiments.* Berkeley: University of California Press.

Bunt, H. C. (1988). Natural language communication with computers: Some problems, perspectives, and new directions. In G. C. van der Veer, & G. Mulder (Eds.), *Human-computer interaction: Psychonomic aspects.* Heidelberg: Springer-Verlag.

Burton, R. R., & Brown, J. S. (1979). An investigation of computer coaching for informal learning activities. *International Journal of Man-Machine Studies, 11,* 5-24.

Card, S. K., Moran, T. P., & Newell, A. (1983). *The psychology of human-computer interaction.* Hillsdale, NJ: Lawrence Erlbaum Associates Inc.

Carroll, J. M. (1984). *Mental models and software human factors: An overview.* (Tech. Rep. No. RC 10616), Yorktown Heights, New York: IBM Watson Research Centre (No. 47016).

Carroll, J. M. (1989). Evaluation, description and invention: Paradigms for human-computer interaction. In M. C. Yovits (Ed.), *Advances in computers, 28*. New York: Academic Press.

Carroll, J. M., & Campbell, R. L. (1988). Artifacts as psychological theories: The case of human-computer interaction. Yorktown Heights, New York: User Interface Institute, IBM T. J. Watson Research Centre.

Conant, R. C., & Ashby, W. R. (1970). Every good regulator of a system must be a model of that system. *International Journal of Systems Science, 1*(2), 89-97.

de Kleer, J., & Brown, J. S. (1983). The origin, form and logic of qualitative physical laws. *Proceedings of the 8th International Joint Conference on AI, IJCAI 8.*

Diaper, D. (1989). The discipline of HCI. *Interacting With Computers, 1*(1), 3-5.

Dowell, J., & Long, J. (1989). Towards a conception for an engineering discipline of human factors. *Ergonomics, 32*(11), 1513-1535.

Dubois, D., & Prade, H. (1989). Handling uncertainty in expert systems. Pitfalls, difficulties, remedies. In E. Hollnagel (Ed.), *The reliability of expert systems*. Chichester: Ellis Horwood Ltd.

English, H. B., & English, A. C. (1958). *A comprehensive dictionary of psychological and psychoanalytical terms*. London: Longman.

Feigenbaum, E. (1961). The simulation of verbal learning behavior. *Proceedings of the Western Joint Computer Conference, 19*, 121-132.

Fischhoff, B. (1986). Decision making in complex systems. In E. Hollnagel, G. Mancini, & D. D. Woods (Eds.), *Intelligent decision support in process environments*. Heidelberg: Springer-Verlag.

Fodor, J. A. (1968). *Psychological explanation*. New York: Random House.

Goodstein, L. P., Andersen, H. B., & Olsen, S. E. (Eds). (1988). *Task, errors and mental models*. London: Taylor & Francis.

Guida, G., & Tasso, C. (Eds.). (1988). *Topics in expert system design*. Amsterdam: North-Holland.

Hebb, D. O. (1961). *The organization of behavior*. New York: Science Editions.

Helander, M. (Ed.). (1988). *Handbook of human-computer interaction*. Amsterdam: North-Holland.

Hill, W. C. (1989). The mind at AI: Horseless carriage to clock. *AI Magazine, 10*(2), 29-41.

Hodges, A. (1983). *The enigma of intelligence*. London: Unwin.

Hollnagel, E. (1977). Cognitive functions in decision making. In H. Jungermann, & G. de Zeeuw (Eds.), *Decision making and change in human affairs*. Dordrecht, Holland: D. Reidel.

Hollnagel, E. (1983). What we do not know about man-machine systems. *International Journal of Man-Machine Studies, 18*, 135-143.

Hollnagel, E. (1988). Information and reasoning in intelligent decision support systems. In E. Hollnagel, G. Mancini, & D. D. Woods (Eds.), *Cognitive engineering in complex dynamic worlds*. London: Academic Press.

Hollnagel, E., Mancini, G., & Woods, D. D. (1986). Afterthoughts. In E. Hollnagel, G. Mancini, & D. D. Woods (Eds.), *Intelligent decision support in process environments*. Heidelberg: Springer-Verlag.

Hollnagel, E., & Woods, D. D. (1983). Cognitive systems engineering: New wine in new bottles. *International Journal of Man-Machine Studies, 18*, 583-600.

Ihde, D. (1979). *Technics and praxis*. Dordrecht, Holland: D. Reidel.

Kahneman, D. (1973). *Attention and effort.* Englewood Cliffs, NJ.: Prentice-Hall.

Kieras, D., & Polson, P. G. (1985). An approach to the formal analysis of user complexity. *International Journal of Man-Machine Studies, 22,* 365-394.

Kuhn, T. S. (1970). The structure of scientific revolutions. *International Encyclopedia of Unified Science.* (2nd ed.).*(2).*

Mackay, D. M. (1968). Towards an information-flow model of human behaviour. In W. Buckley (Ed.), *Modern systems research for the behavioral scientist.* Chicago: Aldine.

MacLean, A., Barnard, P. J., & Wilson, M. D. (1985). Evaluating the human interface of a data entry system: User choice and performance measures yield different trade-off functions. In P. Johnson, & S. Cook (Eds.), *People and computers: Designing the interface.* Cambridge: Cambridge University Press.

McRobbie, M. A., & Siekmann, J. H. (1988). Artificial intelligence: Perspectives and predictions. *AICOM, 1*(4), 16-29.

Miller, G. A., Galanter, E., & Pribram, K. H. (1960). *Plans and the structure of behavior.* New York: Holt, Rinehart & Winston.

Nagel, T. (1986). *The view from nowhere.* New York: Oxford University Press.

Neisser, U. (1976). *Cognition and reality.* San Francisco: W. H. Freeman.

Newell, A., Shaw, J. C., & Simon, H. A. (1957). Empirical explorations with the Logic Theory Machine. *Proceedings of the Western Joint Computer Conference, 15,* 218-239.

Newell, A., & Simon, H. A. (1961, April 11-14). GPS - A program that simulates human problem-solving. *Proceedings of a Conference on Learning Automata,* Technische Hochschule, Karlsruhe.

Papert, S. (1980). *Mindstorms.* Brighton, Sussex, U.K.: Harvester Press.

Rasmussen, J. (1974). *The human data processor as a system component. Bits and pieces of a model.* Roskilde, Denmark: Risø Laboratory.

Rasmussen, J. (1986). *Information processing and human-machine interaction: An approach to cognitive engineering.* New York: North-Holland.

Reason, J. (1990). *Human error.* Cambridge: Cambridge University Press.

Reitman, W. R. (1965). *Cognition and thought.* New York: John Wiley.

Rouse, W. B. (1981). Human-computer interaction in the control of dynamic systems. *ACM Computing Survey, 13*(1), 71-99.

Schindler, M. (1989, December). Parallel systems demand complex visual debuggers. *Electronic Design International,* 49-56.

Selfridge, O. G. (1959). Pandemonium: A paradigm for learning. In D. V. Blake, & A. M. Uttley (Eds.), *Proceedings of the symposium on mechanisation of thought processes.* London: HMSO.

Shannon, C. E., & Weaver, W. (1969). *The mathematical theory of communication.* Chicago: University of Illinois Press.

Simon, H. A. (1972). *The sciences of the artificial.* Cambridge, MA: MIT Press.

Simon, H. A. (1977). *Models of discovery.* Dordrecht, Holland: D. Reidel.

Smets, P., Mamdani, H. E., Dubois, D., & Prade, H. (Eds.). (1988). *Non-standard logics for automated reasoning.* New York: Academic Press.

Sprague, R. H., & Carlson, E. D. (1982). *Building effective decision support systems.* Englewood Cliffs, NJ: Prentice-Hall.

Suchman, L. A. (1987). *Plans and situated actions. The problem of human-machine communication.* Cambridge: Cambridge University Press.

Turing, A. M. (1950, October).   Computing machinery and intelligence. *Mind, 59*, 433-460.

von Neumann, J. (1958).   *The computer and the brain.* Yale: Yale University Press.

Weir, G., & Alty, J. L. (Eds.). (1991).   *Human-computer interaction and complex systems*. London: Academic Press.

Weizenbaum, J. (1976).   *Computer power and human reason. From judgment to calculation.* San Francisco: W. H. Freeman.

Woods, D. D., & Hollnagel, E. (1988).   Mapping cognitive demands in complex problem-solving worlds. In B. R. Gaines, & J. H. Boose (Eds.), *Knowledge acquisition for knowledge-based systems*. London: Academic Press.

Yntema, D. B., & Torgerson, W. S. (1961).   Man-computer cooperation in decisions requiring common sense. *IRE Transactions on Human Factors in Electronics, HFE-2*, 20-26.

Zmud, R. W. (1983).   *Information systems in organizations*. Glenview, IL: Scott Foresman.

Author Index

Subject Index